The Transition

A Novel of Promise, Pitfalls, Perseverance, and Passion

Gene Hewett, Ph.D.

979-8-9853727-0-0 (hardcover)

979-8-9853727-1-7 (paperback)

979-8-9853727-2-4 (eBook)

About The Book

The Transition reads like a journey of a young man toward his academic and career goals. In many ways, the journey can be characterized as semiautobiographical. Several aspects of the childhood to adolescence to adulthood saga may be fictional. However, many aspects of the journey are factual and historical. Intertwined between the storylines is an evolving collage of early protest scenarios and romantic experiences framed in poetic style. In many ways, the collection represents an autobiographical sketch in romance. It begins by providing snapshots of the author's early relationships and evolves to romantic accounts experienced in adulthood.

The Transition features thirteen premium royalty-free images. The Transition has a traditional table of contents, a second one, titled "Musical Inspiration" (which includes QR Codes), and a third, titled "Photographic Images." The thirteen images are presented at the beginning and end of each of the six chapters. Including the cover, thirteen images were selected from Getty Images and iStock photographic resources on the www.istockphoto.com website.

In the short run, the author envisions that the collection will be made available in electronic, paperback, hardcover, and audiobook forms. In the long run, the author anticipates that it might be possible to package the saga into a Hollywood movie production.

Acknowledgements

A transition is a word or group of words that relates something that came before to what comes after. It is often said that when we transition, we have passed from one form or stage to the next. Examples include the transitioning of the seasons, the *rites of passage* from adolescence to manhood, changes in academic goals, and changes in career plans. In many ways, these changes can be illustrated by waterfalls. Many of us have witnessed images of a waterfall cascading over the side of a mountain. And we are often held in awe by the various shapes and forms the turbulent waters assume in their powerful descent.

I am particularly grateful to my late mother, Ms. Florence L. Hewett, my late sister Ms. Lynette I. Griffin, and my sister Ms. Elma Rowena Wilson- Vaughn. To each of them I wish to say thank you for instilling in me the confidence to know that it is possible to survive life's occasional setbacks. I thank them for helping me to realize that sometimes, when I least expect it, a chance encounter may unveil the promise and potential for new opportunities. I am especially grateful to the late Onnette J. Henry. The sound of her laughter truly illuminated my world. In addition, I have nothing but praise for Jaimela P. Foster, Ph.D. Dr. Foster's close friendship over the years helped to inspire me to press on.

I sincerely appreciate the steadfast efforts of the late J. Alfred Cannon, M.D., the late Henry S. Williams, M.D., and the late Leroy R. Weekes, M.D. As mentors and role models they encouraged, supported and inspired me along my academic and future career journey. These courageous men were *transformational* leaders by nature. They bestowed upon me knowledge and wisdom and shared the precious gift of time. It was the latter gift that helped to generate a surge when my quest towards the finish line occasionally faltered.

I owe a great deal of gratitude to those classmates who befriended me during the George Washington Carver Jr. High, Thomas Jefferson High, Claremont McKenna College, University of California at Los Angeles Medical School, University of California at Los Angeles Graduate School of Public Health, and University of Southern

California phases of my life. I am especially grateful to the faculty members who challenged and encouraged me in the latter settings.

I am also thankful for the friendship as well as words of wisdom Received from Hector F. Myers Ph.D. Dr. Myers serves as Professor of Medicine, Health and Society and Psychology at Vanderbilt University in Nashville, Tennessee. Dr. Myers, Attorney Clayburn H. Peters, Attorney John N. Doggett III, and I all graduated from Claremont McKenna College in 1969. The four of us bonded in Claremont as a result of the academic, social and political struggles of the times.

In addition, a special thank you is expressed to all the friends, co-workers, and students who helped me to stay focused during my academic and career journey. Finally, I would like to acknowledge the support and guidance received from the former members of my Los Angeles Lakers as well as Los Angeles Rams (of Inglewood), Season's Seats Group. For without the assistance of the eyes, ears, and suggestions of all of these parties, I might still be writing additional episodes to what could easily become an on-going collage of life experiences framed in literary and poetic style.

Musical Inspiration

Chapter 1

"What'd I Say" by Ray Charles

"Dancing in the Streets" by Martha and the Vandellas

"Baby, I Need Your Loving" by the Four Tops

"Walk On By" by Dionne Warwick

"Tequila" by the Champs,

"Take Five" by the Dave Brubeck Quartet,

"Watermelon Man" by Herbie Hancock

"Flight Time" by Donald Byrd

"Poinciana" by Ahmad Jamal

"The In Crowd" by the Ramsey Lewis Trio,

"Bumpin' on Sunset" by Wes Montgomery

"My Love Has Butterfly Wings" by John Klemmer.

"What It Is, Is What It Is" by Leslie Drayton

"Unfinished Business" by Leslie Drayton

"Until Further Notice" by Leslie Drayton

"Jazz House Party" by Leslie Drayton

"Urbanesque" by Leslie Drayton

"The Way You Do the Things You Do" by the Temptations.

"Stand" by Donnie McClurkin,

Chapter 2

"Cast Your Fate to the Wind" by the Vince Guaraldi Trio

"Sleepwalk" by Santo and Johnny

"Sherry" by the Four Seasons

"Twist and Shout" by the Isley Brothers

"Please, Please, Please" by James Brown and
  the Famous Flames

"Reflections"
"Reflections" by Diana Ross and the Supremes

"Ebony Lady"
"Are You Going My Way?" by The Whispers
"Mind Blowing" by The Whispers

Chapter 3

"When I Am Gone" by Brenda Holloway

"Going Out of My Head" by Little Anthony and the Imperials

"Hello, Young Lovers," by Nancy Wilson

"Guess Who I Saw Today," by Nancy Wilson

"You Can Have Him," by Nancy Wilson

"How Glad I Am," by Nancy Wilson

"Our Day Will Come," by Nancy Wilson

Chapter 3 – continued

"The Good Life," by Nancy Wilson

"Go Away Little Boy," by Nancy Wilson

"Don't Take Your Love From Me," by Nancy Wilson

"The Music That Makes Me Dance," by Nancy Wilson

"One-Note Samba." By Nancy Wilson

"I Can't Help Myself (Sugar Pie, Honey Bunch)"
   by the Four Tops,

"(I Can't Get No) Satisfaction" by the Rolling Stones,

"My Girl" by the Temptations,

"Shotgun" by Junior Walker and the All-Stars,

"Stop in the Name of Love" by the Supremes,

"Yes, I'm Ready" by Barbara Mason,

"Papa's Got a Brand-New Bag" by James Brown
   and the Famous Flames,

"Nowhere to Run" by Martha and the Vandellas,

"The Tracks of My Tears" by The Miracles,

"It's the Same Old Song" by the Four Tops,

"Ooo Baby" by the Miracles,

"How Sweet It Is (To Be Loved by You)" by Marvin Gaye.

"First Love"
"Endless Love" by Luther Vandross and Mariah Carey (1994),
"Endless Love" by Diana Ross and Lionel Richie (2014)

Chapter 4

"See You in September" by The Happenings.

"Somewhere in My Lifetime"
"Somewhere in My Lifetime" by Phyllis Hyman

"This Masquerade"
"This Masquerade" by George Benson

"For My Race Speaks the Spirit
    (Por Mi Raza Habla El Espiritu)"
"*Cuando Vuelva a Tu Lado*" (What a Difference
    a Day Makes)
Instrumental by Gato Barbieri
"*Europa* (Earth's Cry Heaven's Smile)" by Gato Barbieri

"Ain't No Way"
"Ain't No Way" by Aretha Franklin

Chapter 5

"It's Too Late," by Carole King

"It's Gonna Take a Miracle"
"It's Gonna Take a Miracle" by Denise Williams

"The Last Time I Saw Spring"
"This Is All I Ask" by George Benson

"Stoned Out of My Mind"
"Don't Let My Teardrops Bother You," by Dionne Warwick
"(I'm) Just Being Myself," by Dionne Warwick

Chapter 5 – continued

"Come Back," by Dionne Warwick

"Don't Burn the Bridge (That You Took Across)"
   by Dionne Warwick

"Stoned Out of My Mind" by the Chi-Lites

"You Make Me Feel Brand New"
"You Make Me Feel Brand New" by The Stylistics

"You're the Best Thing That Ever Happened to Me"
"Best Thing That Ever Happened to Me"
   by Gladys Knight and the Pips

"Traces of Love"
"Traces" by Gloria Estefan
"Mac Arthur Park" by The Four Tops

Chapter 6

"Firefly"
"Firefly" by The Temptations

"My Forbidden Lover"
"I Am So into You," by Peabo Bryson
"Feel the Fire" by Peabo Bryson

"Hold You"
"Hold Me" by Teddy Pendergrass and Whitney Houston

"Stardust"
"Stardust" by George Benson
"My Love Has Butterfly Wings" by John Klemmer

"Lead Me into Love"
"Lead Me into Love" by Anita Baker

"The Power of Love"
"The Power of Love" by Luther Vandross

"Vision of Love"
"Vision of Love" by Mariah Carey

"The Greatest Love of All"
"The Greatest Love of All" by Whitney Houston

"A House Is Not a Home"
"A House Is Not a Home" by Luther Vandross

"Finder of Lost Loves"
"Finder of Lost Loves" by Dionne Warwick

"I Will Always Love You"

"I Will Always Love You" by Whitney Houston
"I Have Nothing" by Whitney Houston

"If I Could"
"If I Could" by Regina Belle (1993)
"If I Could" by Nancy Wilson (1988)

Photographic Images

Book Cover - Yukikae4b, *Kirifuri waterfalls and Beautiful romantic maple leaf in autumn landscape at Senoo, Nikko, Tochigi Prefecture. autumn natural background*, Photography, iStock by Getty Images (ID: 673275822),
www.istockphoto.com/photo/kirifuri-waterfalls-and-autumn-beautiful-in-nikko-gm673275822-123344743

Figure 1 - Lady-Photo, *Forest Low Angle View*, Photography, iStock by Getty Images (ID: 508254404),
www.istockphoto.com/photo/forest-low-angle-view-gm508254404-85155675

Figure 2 - Bet_Noire, *Gavel and LawyerBooks Isolated on White. Justice, Law and Legal Concept. 3D Illustration*, Photography, iStock by Getty Images (ID: 674984256),
www.istockphoto.com/vector/gavel-and-lawyer-books-isolated-on-white-justice-law-concept-gm674984256-123758885.

Figure 3 - SeanPavonePhoto, *Point Vicente in Rancho Palos Verdes, Los Angeles, California, Photography, iStock by Getty Images (ID: 588588990),*
www.istockphoto.com/photo/point-vicente-light-house-gm588588990-101072447

Figure 4 - Pacaypalla, *Italy - Tuscany - Mediterranean - Tyrrenian sea - Argentario Sailing Week*, Photography, iStock by Getty Images (ID: 140408918,
www.istockphoto.com/photo/sailing-with-white-spinnaker-gm140408918-2808794

Figure 5 - LoveToShoot, *Coreopsis Flowers in Bloom on Point Dume*, Photography, iStock by Getty Images (ID: 153771600), www.istockphoto.com/photo/point-dume-malibu-gm153771600-15583390

Figure 6 - Toward76, *UK Riot Police run through flames*, Photography, iStock by Getty Images (ID: 153203806), www.istockphoto.com/photo/uk-riot-police-flames-gm153203806-20779519

Figure 7 - Iness_Ikebana, *Spring Harvest*, Photography, iStock by Getty Images (ID: 1312613921), www.istockphoto.com/photo/valencian-orange-and-orange-blossoms-spain-gm1312613921-401366388

Figure 8 - Richard Par, *A snapshot of the San Gabriel Mountains as seen from Los Angeles County, California*, Photography, iStock by Getty Images (ID: 675822914), www.istockphoto.com/photo/mount-baldy-as-seen-from-the-city-of-industry-gm675822914-124011733

Figure 9 - Fotoamator, *Footbridge in an Asian Style Garden with Trees and Bushes in Spring Bloom*. Photography, iStock by Getty Images (ID: 136904737), www.istockphoto.com/photo/japanese-gar-den-gm136904737-1519922

Figure 10 - Wolterk, *Los Angeles, United States - October 4, 2014: Royce Hall on the Campus of UCLA. Royce Hall is One of Four Original Buildings on UCLA's Westwood Campus.* Photography, iStock by Getty Images (ID: 517776847), www.istockphoto.com/photo/royce-hall-at-ucla-gm517776847-49342670

Figure 11 - Wolterk, *Los Angeles, United States - October 1, 2013: Unidentifed Students on the Campus of the University of Southern California. USC is a Private, Non-Profit Research University Founded in 1880 with its Main Campus in Los Angeles, California,* Photography, iStock by Getty Images (ID: 458584723), www.istockphoto.com/photo/university-of-southern-california-gm458584723-28223566

Figure 12 - Ron and Patty Thomas, *Molly Brook Cascades Through The Autumn Forest Near Groton Vermont*, Photography, iStock by Getty Images (ID: 108354929), https://www.istockphoto.com/photo/autumn-in-vermont-gm108354929-14277370

Contents

Chapter 1

I was born in November 1947 in Los Angeles, California. In retrospect, 1947 represented the beginning of my milestone years. Earlier that year Jackie Robinson became the first African-American in the twentieth century to play baseball in the major leagues. Achievement of this historical feat was a direct result of his outstanding athletic talents. Jackie Robinson's contribution to major league baseball signaled the breaking of an unwritten color line.

A flashback memory from age four combined elements that seemed to mirror an action movie genre. On that day I decided to take a solo trek up the steep hillside that bordered the northern perimeter of the Rose Hills Projects. I had to part dry, overgrown, four-foot-tall wild oats and sage scrubs during the ascent. My mission was to score tail feathers for a proposed Indian headband. Armed with a handmade bow, and arrows fashioned from reeds that grew along the hillside, I set off in quest of adventure. To assist the flight of the arrows, nails were placed in the tips of the reeds.

Just above a clearing, I spotted a posse of red-tailed hawks soaring high in the azure blue morning sky. The airborne birds of prey were probably circling the area in search of rodents and snakes. The hawks seemed to take turns rendering the characteristic two to three second hoarse, screaming *kee-eeeee- arr* sound. I took aim with the bow, and released an arrow in the direction of the predators. The unexpected projectile caused one hawk to make a mid-air adjustment in its glide path.

From a distance the birds of prey seemed to be relatively small in stature. I am not sure if the unwary predator viewed me as a nuisance, an aggressor, or an oversized rat. However, it appears that the hawk decided I was an accidental foe. Once that determination had been made, my fate was completely at its mercy. What followed was a seriously scary and intimidating assault. The provoked bird of prey began to swoop and strike, while slashing and grabbing with terrifying talons. During each attack, the hawk paused momentarily, hovering just a few feet from my face. I clearly had an up close and personal view of the massive 60-inch wing span.

Since I had already climbed about half-way up the steep hill side, Sprinting back down the rocky, pockmarked terrain was not an option. To do so probably would have resulted in a serious ankle sprain or a head over heels tumble. Even if the attack had taken place on a surface street, it was highly unlikely that I could have out distanced the hawk.

To the west, the hillside sliced off and became the jagged face of a cliff which plunged into the clearing below. Based on previous excursions with Hispanic running buddies I was keenly aware of the following; when sliding down the slopes on a dismantled large card board box, it was a good idea to choose a direction that was away from the *cut off low*.

Clearly the hawk was hell-bent on giving me a whipping. Therefore, my only option was to lay on my back against the incline, secure the bow into the earth, and brace for the onslaught. I probably thought *traérmelo*! The predator swooped once and hovered just out of reach of the rapidly moving semi-circle arc of the bow. The hawk then repeated the attack two more times. Each time I fought off the assault with a rapid back and forth motion of the bow. Realizing that I fully intended to whack the stuffing out of it, the bird of prey may have had second thoughts.

Perhaps encouraged by the *kee-eeeee-arr* sounds of fellow red-tails, the enraged hawk decided to join the posse and vacate the area. As I slowly made my way back down the rugged terrain I probably thought, *Well, I guess the shake a red tail feather party is over!*

In another flashback memory from age four I had a difference of opinion with my mother over some trivial matter. The back-and-forth dialogue escalated to the point where I told her I was leaving and was not coming back.

She replied, "Well, don't let the doorknob hit you where the dog should have bit you!"

That was probably the beginning of the story my sisters liked to tell. According to Lynette and Rowena, my mother and I used to argue like two old married people. At age four, I left the Rose Hills Projects with no immediate plans for returning anytime soon.

A young married couple who lived on the next level of the projects had a son who was about a year younger than me. When I arrived at their location, they were completing plans to take him on a picnic.

The couple asked if I would like to go with them.

I replied, "Yes."

Then they asked, "Don't you require permission from your mother?"

Recalling my mother's last words, I replied, "Oh, she don't care."

The parents appeared to be a little taken aback by my response and exchanged a brief glance. However, without putting much more thought into the matter, they decided to take me with them anyway. We were gone that entire morning and didn't return to the projects until early evening.

As I started walking back home, one of the neighborhood kids ran up to me and said, "Joey, you are supposed to be dead! Everybody in the projects thought you were dead!"

I replied, "Well, I am not dead!"

Apparently, owing to my lengthy absence, my mother had called the police, and a posse of people, including my two sisters, had been combing the Rose Hills Projects looking for me.

After moving from the two-bedroom, one-bath, upstairs-downstairs unit in the Rose Hills Project, my mother rented a three-bedroom, one-bath home with a den near Forty-Eighth Street and San Pedro. My sisters adopted an upstairs room adjacent to the attic as their bedroom. The almost cavernous household—at least compared to the Rose Hills dwelling—had two gas heater outlets. One heater was placed in a rather spacious living room, and the other in the guest bedroom. The combined thermal output from the heaters provided ample warmth from the brisk chill of the wintry months. However, out of an abundance of caution, my mother turned the units off while we slept. Since she did not require an alarm clock to wake in the mornings, she was always the first to rise and reignite the heaters.

Growing up on Forty-Eighth Street, I continually learned the advantages and disadvantages to having older sisters. When the latest dance craze such as the Twist hit the neighborhood, my sisters were reluctant to dance with me. I couldn't tell whether they considered it not a cool thing to do or something akin to incestuous behavior. However, when their rather attractive girlfriends wanted to dance, they would extend their hand to me and say, "C'mon, Joe. Let's dance!" I soon learned to appreciate that kind of assertive behavior on the part of women.

I fondly recall doing the Twist one afternoon with one of my sister Rowena's girlfriends. We were in the living room of the 48th Street dwelling. During the dance, on looking girlfriends shouted words of encouragement like "Ah, work it Joe baby!" I soon realized that I kind of liked being called baby by women. The two-part 7-inch single playing on the Hi Fi was the 1959 R & B hit "What'd I Say" by Ray Charles. Highlighted below are the rather catchy leading lines to the song.

See the girl with the red dress on

She can do the Birdland all night long

Yeah yeah, what'd I say, all right

It was during the 48th Street period that my Mother first referenced the Pittman family's 56-acres of undeveloped land in (name of city), Texas. I would later learn that the deed was dated August 2, 1898, from Sallie Simpson to Rosa (Rosie) Burse Edwards. Rosie was my great-great-grandmother. Rosie Burse Edwards passed away on December 24, 1919. The (name of city), Texas property was then passed on to all of her heirs. Rosie Edwards had eight children.

A major oil company had been slant-drilling oil from the property. As a result of the operation, royalty checks were being sent to my Mother. I recall her being quite upset when the checks stopped coming. Citing alleged declining oil reserve levels, the company determined it was no longer cost- effective to drill.

I also recall my Mother being quite upset by the actions of one of her cousins. Apparently, the family left the care and maintenance of the property to her. The cousin, in turn, elected to abandon the property. As the story goes, she ran off to New York with a man and didn't tell anyone.

As a result, in 1986, my family was prompted to sue an encroaching neighbor for trespassing. In his defense, the neighbor counter-claimed adverse possession. The neighbor provided the court with a deed. The signed, notarized deed stated that another cousin had sold the land to him.

The following family members were present during the 1986 court hearing; James Pittman (Uncle Jim), Maudell P. Williams (Aunt Maud), Anne P. Lilly (Aunt Anne), and Geraldine P. Wooten (Aunt Geri). Under the advice and guidance of their attorney, the family decided to dismiss the jury. As part of an out-of-court settlement, the encroaching neighbor received 25 acres. The neighbor resisted the family's request for a property division. So, as recently as 2022, the property was listed in the (name of county) records as 56-acres of undivided interest.

After a few years, the Forty-Eight Street landlord decided to purchase a new home for her retirement years. To achieve that goal, she needed to sell her rental properties. So, from the Forty-Eighth Street location, my family moved to a two-bedroom, one-bath rental with a den near Forty-Sixth Street and San Pedro. Once again, after a few years, the Forty-Sixth Street owner decided to sell the property and my family was forced to move.

I certainly have many fond memories of the Forty-Sixth Street location. Rowena, my eldest sister, had her wedding reception there in August 1963. My all-time favorite dog, Duchess, was a part of our family at that time. During the Forty-Eighth and Forty-Sixth Street period of my life, when I was thirteen and fourteen years old, I had a maturity-boosting part-time job at a local liquor store and pharmacy.

The liquor store was located at Forty-Eighth Street and Avalon. I was the unofficial stock boy and spent much of the time sweeping the concrete floors, pulling up weeds, and removing debris from the side of the building. I was also responsible for restocking the freezer and hauling out the trash. Restocking the freezer entailed hauling heavy boxes containing bottles or cans of, among other brands, Pabst Blue Ribbon, Rainier Ale, Lucky Lager, Old English 800, and Colt 45 malt liquor.

From a law enforcement perspective, my presence at such a young age in certain areas of the drugstore was ill-advised. The owner had no idea that I was showing up to perform these tasks after hours and on weekends. In addition to the seven dollars cash in my weekly pay envelope, I received a bonus now and then of a gallon of vanilla ice cream, a six-pack of 7-Up, and a family-sized bag of potato chips. I was thrilled to be generating my own income, but the treats were an added bonus.

One day, Jerome, the store clerk who hired me, informed me that he had been diagnosed with a heart ailment. Jerome also referred to his heart as his "ticker." As a result of the medical condition, Jerome decided to resign. Since he would no longer be working there, I would also have to leave.

Years later, I returned to the Forty-Eighth Street Pharmacy in search of part-time employment. I confessed to the Jewish pharmacist that I had worked there before and would be willing to resume my job of taking out the trash, sweeping the floors, clearing the broken glass and weeds from around the side of the building, and any other tasks he might wish. Well, the pharmacist became irate and informed me that Marie had tried to warn him there was a kid working in his pharmacy, but he hadn't believed her.

Growing up on Forty-Eighth Street, I was certainly familiar with Marie. She was an elderly lady who lived across the street from my house. And through the wild imagination of a child, her distinctively crooked nose closely resembled that of a witch. In many ways, she assumed the role of a self-appointed neighborhood watch person.

Among the children and teenagers, Marie had a reputation for being a snitch and an all-around busybody. However, from the parents' perspective, her penchant for spying on other people's business provided an invaluable service to the entire neighborhood. Between Marie and Mr. and Mrs. Catholic—the elderly couple who lived next door—all it took was one misstep for me to stand a good chance of getting a good old-fashioned talking to or butt-whipping or both.

Mr. and Mrs. Catholic spent much of their mornings and afternoons sitting in matching his-and-hers rocking chairs on their front porch. Since I had evolved into the "Cinderfella" stage of my life, I was quite often the recipient of words of encouragement from the couple. They rocked back and forth and watched as I performed my self-assigned duties: tended to the tall grass in the front lawn with a hand mower, edger and a rake; pulled up the weeds that sprouted around the perimeter of our home on Forty-Eighth; turned over the sod in the front garden area with a pitchfork and hoe; and used metal shears to trim the hedges surrounding the overturned sod. The foot-tall green hedges framed the small flower garden in front of a large street-facing picture window.

At the completion of these tasks, I hosed down the front porch and sidewalks. I never informed Mr. and Mrs. Catholic that, after finishing the exterior tasks, I also cleaned the interior. This semi-deep cleaning process included sweeping the carpet areas with a straw broom, mopping the kitchen linoleum floor with a rag mop, and washing, hanging, and ironing our clothing and bedding.

I knew the results of these assorted household chores would

bring a smile to my mother's face, and that smile was the only reward I needed after her daily routine of processing the University of California at the Blue Pacific (UCBP) undergraduate admissions applications.

To return to the pharmacist's parting remarks, I was told that Jerome, the former evening manager, was lazy; if he weren't already deceased, he would fire him because he could have lost his liquor license; and it would behoove me to exit his store immediately before he decided to call the police.

There I was, an honor student at Thomas Jefferson High (TJH), *ratted out* by an elderly former neighbor, with this middle- aged man threatening to press legal charges against me and kicking me out of his establishment. The discouraging response from the owner reminded me of the way the pharmacist talked to George Bailey in the Christmas classic *It's a Wonderful Life*, starring James Stewart and Donna Reed. So, upon hearing the owner's disappointing comments, I turned and with a heavy heart headed towards the front screen door. I exited the store, silently vowing never to return again.

My mother had decided to accept my recommendation that the family relocate from 46th Street to the new Towne Avenue apartment building primarily because the move would allow me to complete my senior year at TJH. From the perspective of transporting heavy furniture, she also found the apartment to be very practical because the unit was just around the corner from the Forty-Sixth Street rental. For several months, I had been observing the progress at the construction site. The two-story, three-unit complex was being built on a rear lot behind the owner's main residence.

I'll never forget the day my mother appeared particularly despondent about being displaced from still another rental property. Her spirits seemed to rise when I reassured her by saying, "Mom, wherever you are, that's where home is." *My mother was loving, caring, nurturing, and kind. And rarely a day goes by when I don't give thanks to God for having been blessed with her presence.*

It was a Thursday afternoon in September 1964, and I had begun the fall semester of my senior year at Thomas Jefferson High, or

TJH as it was affectionately called. The public high school was part of the Los Angeles Unified School District. It was located in South Los Angeles and, in general, its student body matriculated from the surrounding communities of downtown LA, Florence, historic South-Central LA, and South Park. Gazing down the long stretch of polished tan-brown linoleum hallways, I couldn't help but recall the phrase, "Home of the mighty Democrats—or Demos for short." And as I traversed the corridors, I certainly gave credit to my Uncle Jake for helping launch my academic career.

My brother Bob and I were invited to stay with his family in Galena Park, Texas. Galena Park was a small, closely knit and predominantly Black middle-class community on the outskirts of Houston. The visit to Galena Park occurred during 1959–1960 when I was in seventh grade. My Aunt Anne (Anne P. Lilly) and Uncle Jake (Julius C. Lilly) had two daughters, and Connye Yvette and Judlyne were more than just my first cousins. To the contrary, I viewed them as adopted sisters. Without them, all the excitement and joy experienced while interacting with new personalities and navigating a broad spectrum of preteen adventures would have been incomplete.

Until then, I had always thought of myself as being an average student. Well, Uncle Jake was the woodshop instructor and photographer, and he also officiated Fidelity Manor High School (FMH) football games. The student body for FMH was comprised of pupils enrolled in grades seven through twelve. Uncle Jake's brother was the high school principal. Aunt Anne, my mother's sister, taught at the adjacent Fidelity Manor Elementary School. Uncle Jake took serious offense to the statement that I was just an average student. He said, "Negro, I've seen your test scores—and you are not average.

My brother and I sometimes rode the school bus to the Friday night football game skirmishes. Glancing around the bus, I couldn't help but notice the contrast between some of the jumbotron-sized players and the petite, yet smoking-hot cheerleaders. We sat in the front of the bus, right next to an open one-gallon container of heat balm. Upon entering or exiting the bus, the players used to dip a few fingers into the balm and smear it all over whatever ailed them. And because Fidelity Manor High was a combined junior and senior high school, we often attended the sometimes-raucous varsity basketball games on Friday nights. A particular basketball game played against a crosstown rival illustrated just how rowdy things could get.

As time wound down on the tied basketball game, a fight broke out in the wooden bleachers. Apparently, two staunch opponents had a difference of opinion regarding the pending outcome. My brother and I were seated close to where the scuffle originated. As the battle ensued, girls began to scream frantically.

The astonished onlookers seemed to be equally divided between wanna-get-aways and lookie-loos. Some idiot thought it would be cool to pull the master power switch, plunging the entire gymnasium and its occupants into sudden darkness.

The unexpected blackout prompted some members of the audience to run out onto the hardwood floor. The accidental jostling of hyperexcited parties in the dark, in turn, led to sporadic outbreaks of additional skirmishes. Desperately seeking an escape from the chaos and observing the stampede of students rushing toward the main exit, I shouted, "C'mon, Bob. Let's go!" I selected a path that led us across the hardwood floor and toward the elevated stage area. We scrambled up onto the platform and took refuge behind the closed floor to ceiling stage curtains.

When the lights came back on, Uncle Jake was weaving his way through the crowd of totally freaked-out students. Apparently on faculty-appointed MP duty and armed with a baseball bat, he shouted, "Son! Son! Come here, son. I want to talk to you. Naw, naw, son! Don't you! Don't you run away from me!"

My aunts and uncles also played major roles in the shaping and development of my world view. My mother came from a rather large family that was comprised of five girls and six boys. The Pittman family home was located on Bringhurst Street in Houston's Fifth Ward. Of this group, Foster Pittman (Uncle Brother), Robert Pittman (Uncle Bobby), and Walter Pittman (Uncle Abbey) migrated from Houston to the Los Angeles area.

My mother was well into her teenage years in 1939 when the

Great Depression ended. The Great Depression has been referred to by historians as the longest, deepest, and most widespread depression of the twentieth century. According to some economists, the country's entry into World War II led to an increase in industrial and labor production for the war effort that contributed to the end of the Depression.

Lynette and Rowena, my sisters, were born in Houston, Texas. My mother decided to move to Los Angeles to join Robert Harris Sr. Following an honorable discharge from the United States Army, he established residency in the Los Angeles area. So, after migrating to LA, it wasn't long before my mother introduced me—and later my brother Bob—into the world.

I experienced a wide range of interactions with each of the California- based Pittman men. This assortment of positive and mixed role model encounters began in early childhood and continued throughout my adult life. However, it was the Houston-based James Pittman (Uncle Jim) who would later become the last living Pittman brother.

Uncle Jim is survived by a son, Jimmy, who also migrated from Houston to LA, and a daughter, Darilyn. Similar to my mother's sisters Maud, Anne, and Geraldine, my cousin Darilyn chose to remain in Houston and raise a family. Geraldine Pittman (Aunt Geri) was the second youngest of the eleven Pittman children. She passed away at age 92 in 2020. Aunt Geri was the only remaining member of the eleven Pittman siblings. I always looked forward to spending quality time with Uncle Jim when he visited the LA area for vacations and/or family affairs.

In his earlier years, Uncle Jim was an avid golfer. Later in life, he transformed into an even more enthusiastic observer of the sport. I certainly have fond memories of evenings spent watching movies in my townhouse living room with Uncle Jim and his son, Jimmy. The wide-screen productions included classics such as *Midnight in the Garden of Good and Evil* (1997), *Devil in a Blue Dress* (1995), *The Bridges of Madison County* (1995), and *The Shawshank Redemption* (1994).

Uncle Jim enjoyed most of the movies, but he seemed particularly impressed by *The Legend of Bagger Vance* (2000), which starred Matt Damon, Will Smith, and Charlize Theron. I sometimes reflect on the various themes, motifs, and underlying plots that were woven throughout *The Legend of Bagger Vance*.

"There's a perfect shot out there tryin' to find each and every one of us. All we got to do is get ourselves out of its way to let it choose us." That quote pretty much summarized the wisdom Uncle Jim shared with me when it came to various decisions such as the selection of possible mates, goals to be achieved, and future career aspirations.

I celebrated my seventeenth birthday in November 1964. Earlier that milestone year President Lyndon B. Johnson signed the *Civil Rights Act*. The *Civil Rights Act* was the most sweeping civil rights legislation since *Reconstruction*. Essentially the *Civil Rights Act* prohibited discrimination of all kinds based on race, color, religion, or national origin.

If someone were to try to sketch an eight-by-eleven-foot mural to highlight some of my achievements since I left Galena Park, Texas it would need to include the mile-swim merit badge at age fourteen, graduating valedictorian from Carver Junior High in 1962, and the challenges that lay before me, and the magnitude of the project would soon become overwhelming. As I saw it, the journey before me would be strewn with forking paths and winding trails. The complexity of the journey would be as diverse as some of the topics addressed in the wood-framed, glass hallway displays, their background often decorated in the distinctive school colors of Kelly green and gold.

In many ways, there was no map for navigating the path toward my future goals. For example, there was the academic goal of improving my overall GPA and perhaps graduating as valedictorian from TJH. Then there was the athletic goal to better my time in the two-hundred-yard individual medley (especially the butterfly leg), the hundred-yard breast stroke, and the relays. In addition, there was the need to improve my ability to flip-turn a skinny, five-foot-eleven- and-a-half-inch frame at the walls.

There were the short-term goals to gain admission and financial aid offers from undergraduate colleges like the University of California at the Blue Pacific (UCBP), one of the private colleges in Clareville, California, a nickname given by its students, or a historically Black college (HBCU) in Georgia. Beyond that, there were the long-term goals of gaining admission and aid offers from medical schools such as the UCBP, the First Southern Medical School, and an East Coast HBCU medical school. On top of all these goals, there was peer pressure to score a date for the spring 1965 prom.

There were days when the latter task seemed to be the most formidable. It seemed like most of the girls I was interested in taking to the prom were already going steady or were hooked up. Complicating matters was the fact that I didn't have a driver's license. It just wouldn't do to roll up to the set burning rubber on a pocket scooter. Overall, it seemed like the tsunami-like surge of goals to be achieved, some of them almost simultaneously, was almost insurmountable.

The music that often permeated my surroundings provided a sanctuary from the ongoing pressures. Pulsating, often dramatic beats everywhere issued from home hi-fi systems, storefronts, and the occasional green and gold, metal flake-trimmed 1965 Ford Mustang with tricked-out rims. The owners of the Mustangs were mainly TJH graduates or dropouts who parked curbside outside the main entrance, probably hoping to pick up the honeys.

Generally, the music had its roots in Detroit or Philadelphia. A unique characteristic of the melodies, were their signature up-tempo, back beat, percussion and Southern-styled soul influence. To further enhance our listening pleasure, many of us preferred to bump the base. That rhythm often served as my personalized Hollywood-style soundtrack as I made my way to and from TJH. It was a rhythm that would probably be termed "classic Chevrolet music," as the swim coach would say.

I smile when I recall the antics of the six-foot-two, ebony-toned, 220-pound swim coach. For example, when using the term "Chevrolet," Coach wasn't referring to the Chevrolet automobile. Rather, he meant "sheave" one foot and "lay" the other as in a forward progression walking motion. Then there was the time Coach tried to

13

simulate the proper way to execute the butterfly.

He stood on the ceramic tile border above the water and simulated a gyrating motion from his knees to his hips to his chest. Judging by the ensuing laughter and high-fives, most of us thought his butterfly simulation looked like he was getting some in the standing position. In response to our laughter, Coach said, "You people need to get your minds out of the gutter."

One of the guys leaned toward me, rocking a mouth full of silver braces, and whispered, "Man, once Coach gets hold of a woman, I'll bet there'll be no doubt in her mind that she'd been properly laid!"

The coaches' response was quite similar to one given by a female Spanish II instructor. On that day the instructor asked a male classmate, in a coed setting, to conjugate the verb poner (to put, place, set) in the preterite tense (e.g. *puse, pusiste, puso, pusimos, pusisteis, pusieron*).

After I navigated the crowded hallways at the end of sixth period, I merged with the exiting students onto a bustling Forty-First Street and began the two- mile journey home. I tuned into the music that was preprogrammed in my mind and not a Chevrolet radio. The music reverberated throughout the very fabric of my persona: "Dancing in the Streets" by Martha and the Vandellas, "Baby, I Need Your Loving" by the Four Tops, and "Walk On By" by Dionne Warwick.

In geometry class, I learned that the shortest distance between two points was a straight line. In a rough approximation of a straight line, the traditional route home from TJH took me south on Central Avenue, west on East Vernon, and east on Towne Avenue. My mother's favorite beauty shop was located at the corner of Towne Avenue and East Vernon.

Each leg of the journey evoked a wide variety of visual and auditory stimuli, interspersed with assorted memories. Similar to a marathon, aid stations were strategically located along the route.

One of these aid stations was the Taco Bell on Central Avenue. The hamburger, cake, and milk I had for lunch had long since lost their kick. En route to dinner, I sometimes frequented the taco stand. Since I was often accompanied by several hog-freak-mooching swim team buddies, I generally ended up with just an appetizer, maybe a piece of a bean burrito. The Taco Bell pit stop was prompted by hunger pains generated by a rigorous swim practice at the Twenty-Eighth Street YMCA.

Another aid station was Thrifty's Drugstore, famous for its single-dip, double-dip, and triple-dip mix-and-match cones. Just a few blocks down from Thrifty's was the S. H. Kress & Co. five-and-dime department store. Here you could purchase a twenty-five-cent bag of broken pieces of candy, white-and- pink shredded coconut or peanut brittle.

All along the way, Black-owned-and-operated businesses seemed to thrive on both sides of Central Avenue. There was a barber college where you could get a Quo Vadis haircut for seventy-five cents. The trim reminded me of a military buzz cut, complete with signature hairline indentations and truncated sideburns. The Quo Vadis, once received at the beginning of summer vacation, generally lasted until the first day of school in the fall.

The barber college had a series of benches that were pushed together right down the middle of a very large room. In fact, the college had the ability to seat at least fifty clients at a time. In addition, there were long rows of barber chairs on either side of the benches. Each chair was manned by a barber college student dressed in a white smock. When you walked into the college for a cut, you pulled a number from the dispenser and took a seat on the bench. It didn't take long before your number was called.

Unique to the barber college experience was the jazz music that reverberated throughout the large room. A sample playlist that emerged from the stereo speakers in 1964 included classic tunes such as "Tequila" by the Champs, "Take Five" by the Dave Brubeck Quartet, "Watermelon Man" by Herbie Hancock, "Flight Time" by Donald Byrd, "Poinciana" by Ahmad Jamal, "The In Crowd" by the Ramsey Lewis Trio, "Bumpin' on Sunset" by Wes Montgomery, and "My Love Has Butterfly Wings" by John Klemmer.

Little did I know at the time, but Leslie, a neighbor and close friend from my Forty-Eighth Street days, would move on to an outstanding funk, rock, and jazz musical career. His future musical scores would have easily qualified for a featured slot on the barber college playlist. Leslie became a founding member of Earth, Wind & Fire. He played in the orchestra pit of the Hollywood production of the counterculture musical *Hair*.

Leslie also arranged and conducted sessions for Nancy Wilson and New Birth, and served as music director and conductor for Marvin Gaye and Sylvester. He played big band jazz with the Cab Calloway, Gerald Wilson, and Louis Bellson orchestras. Among his extensive list of lifetime credits are the albums What It Is, Is What It Is (1987), Unfinished Business (1990), Until Further Notice (1994), Jazz House Party (1995), and Urbanesque (1998).

I would walk out of the barber college after an hour and a half, Looking sharp and feeling a little bit sophisticated. In some circles, jazz was considered a step above rhythm and blues and rock and roll.

In many ways, I also got a preview of what it must have felt like to be a grown-ass man. The barber attendants patted the astringent Cool Water along the edge lines of my closely shaven head and down the back of my neck. I distinctly recall the brief sting of the fragrant aftershave. The pain occurred when the alcohol base in the mixture came in contact with minor abrasions in my skin—probably caused by the sharp edges of the barber's clippers.

Next door to the barber college on Central Avenue was a White-owned pawn shop. Each time I walked by the glass-enclosed displays of the storefront, I paused to gaze through the window. I dreamed of the day when I would have enough money to purchase the medium-sized, Royal portable typewriter in the window. I had completed a year of typing at TJH and scored fifty-six words per minute on my most recent time trial. I would definitely need a portable manual typewriter when it was time to pack up my belongings and move on to college.

As I rounded the corner at the intersection of Central and East Vernon Avenues, I passed in front of the Black-owned Dolphins of Hollywood record store. A live DJ often spun platters from a sound booth in the front window. That day, outdoor speakers were playing "The Way You Do the Things You Do" by the Temptations.

Across the street from Dolphins was the Evans Photography

Studio, upstairs in a building of light-tan and dark-brown brick. Among other contracted jobs, the proprietor was the photographer for the TJH yearbook and senior class graduation. And catercorner from Dolphins was the Vernon Branch Library, a location I often credit with helping jump-start my academic career.

I happily spent many late afternoons and early evenings perusing books in the library. The two young and attractive female librarians were strict enforcers of the no-talking rule. The dreaded bathroom was located in the basement, or the dungeon, as I used to call it—dreaded, because once you descended the wide, winding stairway, it was dimly lit and isolated down there.

In a flashback memory from age eight, I experienced one of my first views of a vagina in the Vernon Branch Library. The incident occurred when I discovered a large medical reference book on a tabletop book stand. As I turned the pages and looked up words like *syphilis* and *gonorrhea*, to my surprise graphic displays of diseased vaginas appeared. It was mind-blowing. I motioned for my brother Bob, who was a year and a half younger than me, to come over.

Bob came over to the book stand and viewed the graphics. I whispered, "At ease, disease. There's fungus among us."

He released an inappropriately audible laugh, which prompted an equally loud "Shhh!" from the nearby librarians. Now, during my TJH days, I was once kicked out of Lee's house for chugging a brain freeze-inducing, ice-cold cola that caused me to belch and made foam ooze from my nose. But it was a horse of a different color to get kicked out of the Vernon Branch Library at the age of eight for excessive levity!

Needless to say, the visuals of infected vaginas didn't really help get me in the mood for the real, non-diseased deal. Fortunately, I remained optimistic that in the not-too-distant future, there would be a change in my perception.

Although the graphic visuals were eye-opening, the medical reference text probably was not the best prelude to concepts linked to Jack and Jill Went up the Hill 101. By age seven, the only indirect reference to the vagina that had ever been made in my household was a favorite memory first relayed by my mother, Florence.

I have always had a great deal of respect and admiration for my mother's sheer tenacity. As a single parent, she accomplished the miraculous task of nurturing and raising four children on her own. She even deferred her own higher education goals until the four of us reached maturity. As an elementary school instructor, she specialized in teaching arts and crafts to the developmentally disabled. To underscore her commitment to the field of education, in her sixties she obtained a master's degree in special education from a California-based private nonprofit university.

Several years ago, my mother's Houston-based sisters Maud, Anne, and Geri visited. From all accounts, my maternal grandmother, Elma Edwards, was a small-framed woman. She was also the matriarch of the family abode, located on Bringhurst Street in the Fifth Ward of Houston, and in that capacity, she was often described as strong-willed and determined. The latter characteristics complemented her very affable personality and warm, caring heart. However, as I have been told, from an educational perspective, there were a few occasions when she might not have been the most book-wise person in the room.

As the story goes, my grandmother was taking her eldest daughter, Maud, for a required elementary school vaccination. The administrator informed my grandmother that Maud would have to be vaccinated in her precinct.

My grandmother replied, "What! Why, all the other girls get vaccinated in the arm, and you want to vaccinate my daughter in her precinct!"

From that day forward, whenever the concept of a vagina was referred to in my household—which was rarely—my mother would reply, "What? In her precinct!" She would emit a hearty laugh at this insider-only, family joke.

The second leg of the two-mile journey from TJH to Towne Avenue took me past Carver Junior High School, my old alma mater, on McKinley Avenue. Then it was onward past the major intersection of Avalon Boulevard and East Vernon Avenue. I crossed the street and headed south on Towne Avenue, passing the beauty shop at the southwest corner of Towne Avenue and East Vernon. For a year, my family had been staying in a new three-unit apartment building, located in the rear of the owner's single-family residential property.

When I arrived at the Towne Avenue address, I traversed the long driveway that stretched behind the residential property and climbed the stairs to our apartment. As soon as I reached the front door, it was clear that something was wrong. One of the glass wings in the louver window next to the door had been broken. I turned the knob to the right and discovered that the door was unlocked. I opened it and entered the living room. To my surprise, a man was sitting on the couch with his back to the large picture window. He was wearing a brown sports coat, and black slacks.

"Who are you?" I asked.

"I am an old friend of your mother from Houston. My name is John—John Smith."

Observing the broken glass on the floor, I said, "It looks like someone broke in here."

"Yeah, Sherman. I arrived a short while ago, and your mother was really upset about the break-in. However, she had to leave for a beauty shop appointment and asked me to stay here until she returned."

I was puzzled because one of the last things my mother had said to me before I departed for TJH that morning was that she had a beauty shop appointment. She was a single mom, and she had the occasional male visitor. However, leaving a strange man in the house—without a proper introduction to the family—was something she would never do. Confounding matters, this particular stranger seemed to be aware that my family had roots in Houston.

The plot thickened when John, as he called himself, kept referring to me as Sherman. Sherman wasn't my name. My impression was that he was a little high on something. The parts of John's story that didn't add up outweighed the parts that did, but there was just enough to make his story halfway believable. However, if this man was a burglar and had harmed my mother, I fully intended to do my best to put a serious hurt on him.

I took a few steps toward the hallway that led to the bathroom and the adjacent bedrooms and glanced around. I noticed fragments of my sister Lynette's broken piggy bank on the floor. It didn't help that John, who stood about six foot two and looked like he weighed about 190 pounds, got up from the couch and followed me into the hallway. For a brief moment, I had my back to him. At that point, he could have easily gotten the drop on me and taken me out.

I pointed to the piggy bank fragments on the floor. "That's my sister's piggy bank."

"Yes, it appears that someone took some money from the piggy bank."

A sixth sense told me not to continue deeper into the bedroom area. The kitchen to my right had a sliding door that led to a small utility porch with a double-sink basin.

I turned to John and said, "You know what, I forgot something downstairs. I'll be right back."

John shrugged and stepped aside to let me pass. I exited the apartment and hastily scampered down the stairs.

Upon reaching the driveway, I began to jog toward the landlord's residence. At the sidewalk, I accelerated into a hundred-meter top-end sprint speed toward the beauty shop at the end of the block. I entered the shop, probably looking a little wild-eyed and sweating profusely. I did my best to calm down as I approached my mother.

"Hi, Joe," my mother said with a smile. She was sitting under one of the dryers.

As calmly as I could, I asked, "Mom, did you leave a man sitting in the living room?"

Her look of shock and dismay clearly answered my question. "What man!" she shouted.

Similar to the cartoons I used to watch when I was much younger, I felt like a big neon sign had just appeared over my head spelling out "Sucker!" *Obviously, I'd been played! The only thing missing from this picture was the TJH marching band!* Without uttering another word, I nodded toward my mother, exited the beauty shop, and began sprinting back to the apartment.

Clearing the long driveway, I scrambled up the stairs and opened the door. To my surprise, John—or whatever his name was—was still there. He was unscrewing the legs from the stereo hi-fi unit.

I confronted him. "You lied to me. Who the hell are you!"

John mumbled something and—seemingly empty-handed walked toward the front door. He exited the apartment and proceeded down the stairs.

Halfway down, John was confronted by my mother. She said, "Mister, who are you?" She was accompanied by the landlord's wife and the lady who lived downstairs.

I had often observed my mother privately styling her own hair and was used to seeing her in the kitchen with a hot comb steaming on one of the stove burners. I was still surprised by her appearance that day. It seemed to me that she was the inventor of the natural hair style. Like me, my mother had a smooth ebony complexion and narrow lips. She was still wearing the white smock from the beauty shop, and her hair flared out in all directions.

Apparently, the unexpected visual of my five-foot-four mom in her full- blown Afro glory prompted John to pause. After he regained his composure, John started to mumble to himself and continued until he reached the end of the stairway. He made an abrupt right turn and started walking toward the rear of the apartment complex, where he encountered a six-foot cement block wall, John hoisted himself up and over the wall and down into Lee's backyard.

I followed and tried futilely to get him to come back. My commands fell on deaf ears. To my mother's dismay, I turned around, gave her a wink, hoisted myself up over the wall, and continued my pursuit of John. I heard my mother pleading for me to come back, but I felt like I had an obligation to handle the situation. Unfortunately, it appeared that Lee wasn't home. If reinforcements weren't available, I was on my own. It would have helped if Lee had a vicious pit bull roaming the yard, but that was not the case.

I continued to follow John north up Crocker Avenue toward East Vernon. In spite of my persistent urgings, John was definitely not coming back. I followed him across East Vernon and into an alley that stretched east toward Avalon. Halfway through the alley, it became clear that my efforts to persuade John to return to the Towne Avenue location had failed. His only response to my frequent requests was, "Sherman, what you following me for? You need to get on back home."

At that point, I realized I was too deep in the alley for comfort. I Paused long enough to pick up an empty Purex bottle. I tried to hide the dark-brown glass bottle behind my back, grasping it tightly in my right hand, and continued to follow John.

Drawing upon flashback memories from combat scenarios in elementary and junior high school I recalled that it was important to draw a distinction between heavyweights, lightweights, and featherweights. After elementary school, I had somehow managed to defuse quite a few situations that could have resulted in physical altercations. This was accomplished as a result of improvements in what police would term my "verbal judo skills." The only exception to my near-perfect combat-avoidance record occurred in the summer of 1964. That's when I had an altercation with an oversized, heavyweight teenage thug.

The thug was accompanied by four of his half-pint cronies. I had been sitting on the concrete steps of an elementary school, waiting for the scoutmaster to arrive for the weekly Boy Scout meeting. The scoutmaster generally arrived early to unlock the doors and get the evening's activities underway. However, on that particular afternoon, he was uncharacteristically late. And wouldn't you know it? That's when the thug showed up and accused one of the younger scouts of liberating his pigeons. The *young blood* denied the allegations, but the thug called him a liar and proceeded to bitch-slap him hard upside his head.

Still seated on the steps, I glared at the thug and said, "What did you do that for?"

The thug replied, "What?"

One of his cronies piped in and said, "Now ain't this about nothing! That little GG think he bad!"

I shifted my attention from the thug and briefly glanced up the street, hoping to see the scoutmaster's vehicle on the horizon.

That split second was all the thug needed. He went airborne, and the sheer force of his weight caromed me off the stairs and into the surrounding bushes. By all accounts, what transpired next was nothing short of embarrassing.

Although there was little time to react and even less time to think, I recall thinking, *This must be what it's like to get mauled by a bear! I can't even get my arms free to throw a punch.*

As it turned out, throwing a punch wasn't the thug's objectives.

He simply flung me around and shook me back and forth like a possum trapped between the vise-like jaws of a black Labrador retriever mix.

The bell finally sounded after just one round of the "Rumble in the Hood." My feelings may have been a little hurt, but as the great Muhammed Ali once said, "I was still pretty."

In a final show of disrespect, the thug ordered me to sit down.

Out of sheer defiance, I continued to stand and glare at him, fully expecting the bell for round two to ring.

In retrospect, the lyrics to the 1996 gospel hit "Stand" by Donnie McClurkin, like rays of sunlight from a rotating prism, would have appropriately captured my mood: "Tell me what do you do when you've done all you can, and it seems like you can't make it through."

Upon observing my resolve, the thug shrugged, turned, and walked away with his crew.

That's what you get, I thought, *for asking that doggie-breath hothead a rhetorical question.*

Although I was too preoccupied to notice, apparently my brother Bob, did try to intervene. Bob informed me that one of the thug's cronies neutralized him by knocking the wind out of his stomach with a walking stick.

I thought my fighting days were over. I was on track to becoming valedictorian of my high school and well on my way to college. Over the years I had managed to bluff my way out of quite a few combat situations, and that ability explains why my last major bout had been in elementary school. Apparently, however, there were still people in the world who would say, "Your fighting days aren't over until I say they are over!"

Perhaps if I had had proper training in boxing and self-defense, I would have qualified for a Boy Scouts of America athletics merit badge. In any case, the missing pigeons incident represented a major setback to my mastery of the fine art of verbal judo.

Not long after the thug and his posse departed, the scoutmaster drove up. And shortly thereafter, Chuck (aka Butch), one of my best friends, and his younger brother Tonic showed up too. Chuck was the Troop 182 senior patrol leader. At Manual Arts High School, Chuck lettered in track and field. His six-foot, muscular frame played a major role in those achievements. Chuck also had a kind of no-nonsense, take-no-prisoners approach to unnecessary foolishness. When it came to looking out for me, he fully embodied the expression "my brother's keeper."

After Chuck saw me looking like I had come up on the short end of a long dogfight, he asked the scouts a few questions and took off down the block in search of the thug. He was accompanied by his little brother Tonic, another bad-ass, and a few of the others. I decided not to volunteer for this second tour of duty since I was recovering from a temporary case of "no mas-itis." The phrase is a reference to the rematch between Sugar Ray Leonard and Roberto Duran in 1980. Duran withdrew during the eighth round by turning his back on Leonard and allegedly saying to the referee Octavio Meyran, "No mas."

When Chuck located the thug, a confrontation ensued. Upon his return, he said, "He said to tell you he was very sorry."

About a month later, I was walking down McKinley Avenue en route to an early morning Jefferson Knights meeting. The Knights were a TJH honor society. Admission was generally based on academic scholarship and strength of character. Whenever we were assigned to TJH stations or attending weekly meetings, the Knights wore Kelly green wool vests. Each of the vests had a distinctive round Golden Knights emblem sewn on the front.

When I noticed the thug and his cronies standing across the street, I briefly raised my right palm in a gesture of hello. One of the cronies pointed in my direction and said, "Look, you beat up a Knight!" Perhaps I was imagining things, but I think I saw what appeared to be a sincerely apologetic, almost remorseful expression on the face of someone I had once labeled a thug.

Returning to my pursuit of John in the alley. I was five foot eleven and weighed 135, and John was six foot two and 190. It was clear that I was a lightweight. Short of mixed martial arts training, which I did not have, the only ammunition at my disposal was that empty Purex bottle.

Glancing back at me, John noticed that I had one arm behind my back. He stopped, turned toward me with a scowl on his face, and said, "Sherman, what you got there behind your back?"

"I asked you to come on back!" I replied defiantly.

John reached into his pocket, pulled out a pocketknife, and unlocked the blade.

In retrospect, I see the comparisons between my 1964 alley encounter and the attempted mugging of Nick in the 1986 comedy *Crocodile Dundee*. In response to the perp's demand for his wallet, Nick said, "That's not a knife. That's a *knife*!"

We began to circle each other, and I knew I only had one move left. I hurled the bottle with as much force as possible, hoping to make contact with John's face and jam his control tower. However, my aim was altered by nervous tension, and the Purex bottle ended up shattering against his chest.

John took one step backward and shouted, "Ow! God damn you, Sherman!"

The blunt force of the bottle ricocheting off his chest had served its purpose. It provided the shock value I needed to execute a reverse pivot maneuver. I combined that move with what can best be described as a Roadrunner windup, followed by a shot out of the cannon, and a hundred-meter top-end sprint down the alley.

Probably the only thought running through my mind was, *If this jive turkey catches me from behind, maybe I deserve to be cut!*

John attempted to give chase, but he was no match for my adrenaline- fueled acceleration. At the end of the alley, I encountered two men on the porch of a duplex. I was winded and sweaty, and I probably looked a little wild-eyed. I tried to calm myself down and said, "Please call the police. I need help!"

The men glanced at each other, and one of them responded, "We don't have no phone."

The other one said, "Yeah—take it somewhere else!"

I thought, *Now, that's just cold.* I could clearly see the lines running from the main telephone poles to their duplex.

I shrugged and started jogging down the street, across East Vernon, and down Crocker. Upon reaching the gate leading to Lee's front door, I continued jogging toward the back yard and climbed back over the six-foot wall.

To my surprise, a police squad car was parked in the long driveway. There was a reciprocal look of astonishment on the faces of the two White officers. At the time, the officers were talking to my mother in front of the apartment building. The reunion glances exchanged with my mother reminded me of a previous flashback memory in my life when I was four-years old. In both instances, she was too happy to see me again to scold me.

The officers ceased their discussions with my mother and turned their attention to me. At their request, I briefly explained what had transpired with John. The officers asked if I would be willing to ride with them for a while to see if they could locate John. I agreed and climbed into the squad car.

We drove north on Towne—toward the alley where the confrontation had taken place—and I pointed to the spot where the incident had occurred. The officers observed the broken bottle, and one of them cautioned me that, it would be difficult to bring assault charges without witnesses. We reentered the squad car and continued east down the alley toward Avalon.

The officers decided to park and take a closer look inside of a bar. The bar was located at the southwest corner of Avalon and Forty-Third Street. It was directly across the street from a private medical office. The doctor who practiced there had once given me a tetanus shot.

At the entrance to the bar, I said, "I know for a fact that I am not allowed to go in there."

One of the officers laughed and said, "It's okay. You are with us."

The bar had a salon door that looked like it was from an old cowboy movie. In the dimly lit bar, it took a few seconds for my eyes to adjust.

One of the officers said, "Do you see the man we are looking for in here?"

About eight men were sitting at the bar, and they took turns nervously glancing back at me.

I slowly moved my head from side to side. Unfortunately, John was not among the men at the bar.

One of the officers said, "Sometimes this process is a lot like finding a needle in a haystack."

I slowly nodded my head up and down.

We exited the bar, climbed back into the squad car, and headed east across Avalon.

That's when I saw the back of a man walking slowly down the street near the rear of the medical office. The man was wearing a brown sports coat, and black slacks.

As we drew closer, I said, "I can't believe it! That's him! Oh, quick, get him, get him!

One of the officers said, "Now, take it easy. Are you sure that's him?"

"I'm positive!" I replied.

They pulled over next to John, and the officer on the passenger side motioned for him to halt. He also informed John that they wanted to ask him a few questions.

John stopped, turned toward the officers, and seemed to signal that he knew the jig was up when he saw me in the back of the squad car.

The police asked John a few preliminary questions. Shortly thereafter, he was taken into custody.

When we drove back to Towne Avenue, my mother was talking to one of the neighbors in the driveway. It appeared that the case was a slam dunk since my mother was able to provide a second positive ID.

The officers completed some preliminary paperwork and informed us of the next step in the legal process.

We thanked them for their assistance, and the officers departed.

My mother said, "Joe, you got to learn how to *mitiblende*! I didn't like any of that—that man could have hurt you."

I just shrugged. I definitely was familiar with the term. *Mitiblende* was a word coined by Uncle Bobby, lead tenor for the Ink Spots. Among other melodic contributions, he provided the vocals for the hit song "If I Didn't Care." When Uncle Bobby used the term *mitiblende*, he meant make the brains grow smarter.

My mother and I headed upstairs to the apartment. Inside, I discovered a small piece of paper on the living room floor. I picked it up, turned it over, and read the note.

My mother had written the note in her distinctively elegant penmanship and left it attached to the outside of the door: "I have gone to the beauty shop. See you later. Love, Mom."

It appeared that John had read the note and viewed the apartment as an easy target for a break-in. I got extra helpings of everything for dinner that night.

Later that evening, I was studying in my bedroom.

Bob walked in and said, "You are unbelievable. You know that, don't you?"

I just shrugged.

As he put his pajamas on, Bob asked, "Were you scared?"

I shook my head, but I probably should have been frightened by the ordeal because things could have gone south really quickly.

I was more ticked off at John—or whatever his name was—for the events of the day. When a home is broken into, the inhabitants often feel violated. The traditional sense of warmth and security that a home generally provides are greatly diminished.

That pretty much captured the sentiments that were expressed by my family that evening, including Lynette. A kind of pain in the pit of your stomach that often goes hand in hand with feelings of loss and vulnerability.

In response to the break-in, my mother decided to reach out to her now- divorced husband, Robert Harris Sr., and he agreed to spend the evening with us. His assignment was to sleep on the couch next to the broken leveler windows. Since most of the glass-repair businesses were closed, the window couldn't be fixed until the next day.

He said, "What do you need me here for? You've got Joseph!"

She said, "He's just a boy! Tonight, I need a man sleeping by that window!"

The next day, after the end of sixth period, I took a short walk to Central and Santa Barbara Avenues. I boarded the metro bus and headed west for a two-mile journey up Santa Barbara. Departing the metro at Santa Barbara and Figueroa, I walked north on Figueroa toward the First Southern University Law School Library. My goal was to learn a little more about the pending court case against the suspect.

At the law library, I walked over to the reference librarian and shared my research topic.

The librarian directed me to the aisle that contained mock trial transcripts. She understood that I was a layman when it came to legal issues and felt that the transcripts would provide the most user-friendly overview of terminology and procedures specific to my case.

I thumbed through the pages of one of the mock trial transcripts, and it read like the dialogue in a Shakespearean play.

In one of the volumes, I learned the following about California burglary laws. California's burglary statute, Penal Code 459 PC, defines burglary as entering any residential or commercial building or room with the intent to commit a California felony, a grand theft, or a petty theft. California burglary is divided into "first-degree burglary" and "second-degree burglary."

First-degree burglary is burglary of a residence. Second-degree burglary is burglary of any other type of structure (including stores and businesses). An example of behavior that could lead to charges under California burglary laws is breaking into a house while the owners are not home to steal electronics and jewelry. In California, first-degree burglary is a felony. The potential consequences include a state prison sentence of two, four, or six years. Common legal defenses that are most useful for fighting PC 459 burglary charges include not having the intent to commit a crime when entering the building, claims of ownership of the stolen items, and having a legitimate claim to them. It can also be a case of mistaken identity.

Armed with copies of the mock court proceedings, my mother and I patiently awaited the assigned date and time for our court appearance. It wasn't long before the summons to appear in court arrived in the mailbox.

On the assigned day, my mother and I departed the apartment. With my mother at the wheel, we sidestepped the bumper-to-bumper northbound Harbor Freeway traffic. Instead, my mother took a northbound route on Figueroa. Our destination was the Superior Court of California, County of Los Angeles building. After parking in the assigned structure, we entered the building and were screened by the guards. We took the elevator to the designated courtroom on the eighth floor.

A retrospective reenactment of the events that transpired in the Superior Court that day is provided below.

Bailiff: All rise. Department One of the Superior Court is now in session. Judge Anthony presiding. Please be seated.
Judge: Good morning, ladies and gentlemen. Calling the case of the People of the State of California versus John Smith. Are both sides ready?
District Attorney: Ready for the People, Your Honor.
Public Defender: Ready for the defense, Your Honor
Judge: It is my understanding that the defendant has waived his right to a jury trial.
Public Defender: Yes, Your Honor

From my law library research, I was aware that the first thing that happens in a trial is opening statements. That is when each attorney can tell the jury what evidence they will present during the trial. According to the mock trial script, the deputy DA goes first and the public defender goes next.

I was also aware that the deputy DA would stand up and talk to the jury at that time. However, I was surprised to learn that the defendant had waived his right to a jury trial.

Deputy DA: Your Honor; the defendant has been charged with the crime of entering an apartment where he did not reside—without the permission of the residents. The evidence will show that approximately fourteen dollars in loose change was stolen from the property. The defendant's fingerprints were on pieces of a broken piggy bank. The evidence I present will prove to you that the defendant is guilty as charged.

From my law library research, I was also aware that, had the jury trial not been waived, the public defender would generally stand up and speak to the jury at that time.

Your Honor, under the law, my client is presumed innocent until proven guilty. During this trial, you will hear no real evidence against my client. You will come to know the truth: that the defendant was just waiting in the apartment until the coplaintiffs could arrive home. After determining that the apartment had been broken into, my client was just trying to do the right thing by safeguarding the premises until the owner could arrive. Therefore, my client is not guilty.

I turned the pages in the copied mock trial transcript and determined that, after opening statements, witnesses are called to testify about what they know about the case. According to the transcript, the attorneys may wish to show physical things—like a photograph of the broken piggy bank—to the jury or the judge. I was also aware that these things were called exhibits. If it were a jury trial, the jury would only consider an exhibit if the judge admitted the exhibit into evidence. The latter step would occur when the jury met to decide if the defendant is guilty or not guilty.

Judge: The prosecution may call its first witness.

Deputy DA: The People call Joseph Harris, the son of Florence Harris, the apartment lease holder.

I stood up and moved toward the middle aisle, and the bailiff escorted me to the witness stand.

Clerk: Please stand. Raise your right hand. Do you promise that the testimony you shall give in the case before this court shall be the truth, the whole truth, and nothing but the truth, so help you God?

Me: I do.

Clerk: Please state your first and last name.

Me: Joseph Harris…but everybody calls me Joe.

Clerk: You may be seated.

Reporter: Please spell your last name for the record.

Deputy DA: Joe, where do you attend school?

Me: I am a senior at Thomas Jefferson High School

Deputy DA: What is your address of residence?

I replied: 4444 Towne Avenue, Apartment 2, Los Angeles, CA 90011.

Deputy DA: Were you residing there on September 10, 1964?

Me: Yes, sir.

Deputy DA: At approximately what time did you arrive to your address of residence on September 10, 1964?

Me: At approximately 5:00 p.m.

Deputy DA: Did you observe that a break-in had occurred at your place of residence?

Me: Yes, sir. I did.

Deputy DA: Was there someone present in the living room of your apartment when you arrived?

Me: Yes, sir.

Deputy DA: If that person is sitting in this courtroom, would you kindly point him out?

I paused. An episode from Mark Twain's *The Adventures of Tom Sawyer* flashed through my memory. When Tom Sawyer was in the witness box, the DA asked, "If that person is sitting in this courtroom, would you kindly point him out?"

Injun Joe jumped up and said, "You're dead, boy, dead!" With all his might, Injun Joe hurled a hunting knife at Tom.

Tom instinctively swerved to his left, and the knife flew past to his right. The projectile barely missed Tom's head and stuck, quivering, in the wall behind the witness box.

Regaining my composure, I pointed at the defendant. I was slightly embarrassed because my hand trembled when I pointed.

Deputy DA: The record will show that the witness has identified the defendant, sitting at the defense table.

Deputy DA: Did you exchange words with the defendant at that time?

Me: Yes, sir. I asked him who he was.

Deputy DA: And what was his answer?

Me: He said he was an old friend of my mother from Houston. That there had been a break-in. That my mother had a beauty shop appointment, and that she had asked him to stay there until she returned from the beauty shop.

Deputy DA: Upon her arrival, did your mother confirm that he was an old friend from Houston?

Me: No, sir. She did not.

Deputy DA: Prior to your mother's arrival, what further evidence did you observe of a break-in.

Me: I noticed broken pieces of my sister's piggy bank on the floor in the hallway leading to the bedrooms.

Deputy DA: At that point, what did you do?

Me: I indicated to the defendant that I had forgotten something and exited the apartment. I ran to the end of the block and asked my mother if she had left a man sitting in the living room.

Deputy DA: And what was her response?

Me: She shouted, "What man?"

Deputy DA: And then what did you do?

Me: I ran back to the apartment, and he was unscrewing the legs off the stereo hi-fi unit, and so I confronted him.

Deputy DA: And what occurred next?

Me: He started mumbling something to himself and began to exit the apartment.

Deputy DA: And what occurred next?

Me: By then, my mother had arrived and was standing at the bottom of the stairs, and she said, "Mister, who are you?"

Deputy DA: And what occurred next?

Me: He continued walking toward the back of the apartment, climbed over a six-foot wall, and started heading down Crocker Avenue toward East Vernon.

Deputy DA: And what occurred next?

Me: I climbed over the wall and followed him into the alley, trying to get him to return.

Deputy DA: And what occurred next?

Me: He got really irritated with me and pulled out a pocket knife, and that's when I hit him in the chest with a Purex bottle!

Upon hearing my response, the courtroom audience burst into laughter.

The public defender turned and glared at the defendant.

The judge hit his gavel on the desk and called for order. The defendant had a funny scowl.

Public Defender: Your Honor, I object. There were no witnesses to the Sequence of events described by the witness.

Judge: The objection is sustained. The last comment by the witness will be stricken from the record.

Deputy DA: Thank you, I have no further questions.

Judge: Does the defense have any questions?

Public Defender: Not at this time, Your Honor.

Judge: The witness is excused.

I exited the witness chair and took my place in the audience next to my mother.

Judge: The prosecution may call the next witness.

Deputy DA: The People call Sergeant Don Murphy, the lead arresting officer.

The bailiff escorted the officer to the witness stand.

Clerk: Please stand. Raise your right hand. Do you promise that the testimony you shall give in the case before this court shall be the truth, the whole truth, and nothing but the truth, so help you God?

Officer: I do.

Clerk: Please state your first and last name.

Officer: Don Murphy.

Clerk: You may be seated.

Reporter: Please spell your last name for the record.

Officer: M-u-r-p -h-y.

Deputy DA: Officer, where do you work?

Officer: I have worked for the Los Angeles Police Department, the Central Bureau, the Newton Division for the past twelve years.

Deputy DA: Were you on duty on the afternoon of September 10, 1964?

Officer: Yes, I was patrolling the streets near Avalon and East Vernon.

Deputy DA: Did you receive a call from a dispatcher regarding a possible break-in in progress at 4444 Towne Avenue, Los Angeles, CA 90011?

Officer: Yes, I did.

Deputy DA: What did you observe upon arriving at the scene?

Officer: I observed the coplaintiff's mother, standing in the driveway of the apartment complex. She seemed to be quite distraught.

Deputy DA: Did she provide you with a reason for her visible concerns.

Officer: Yes, she did. Apparently, there had been a break-in in apartment 2, and her son had climbed over a wall behind the apartment complex in pursuit of the suspect.

Deputy DA: After you spoke with the coplaintiff's mother outside of apartment 2, did you enter the premises and review the scene?

Officer: Yes, I did.

Deputy DA: And what did you observe?

Officer: The first thing I noticed was the broken glass from a louver window scattered on the floor near the front door. Photos were taken. A determination was then made that, once the windowpane had been broken, someone could have easily reached in from the outside and unlocked the front door. I also saw pieces of a broken piggy bank on the floor in the hallway leading into the two-bedroom, one-bath apartment. Photos were again taken. a request for the services of the LAPD fingerprint examiner was made. It is my understanding that, upon arrival, the examiner collected the broken piggy bank pieces and placed them in a secured container.

Deputy DA: Your Honor, I would like to have these photographs of the broken louver window marked as People's exhibit number one, the container housing the broken piggy bank pieces as People's exhibit number two, and the report from the LAPD fingerprint examiner marked as People's exhibit number three. I would also like to ask that they be admitted into evidence.

Judge: Does the defense have any objection?

Public Defender: No, Your Honor.

Judge: The photographs, the container housing the broken pieces of the piggy bank, and the findings from the fingerprint examiner will be admitted as People's exhibit numbers one, two, and three.

Deputy DA: After completion of your review of the premises, what happened next?

Officer: At the time, I observed the coplaintiff's son climbing over a six-foot wall from the western Crocker side at the rear of the complex.

Deputy DA: And then what occurred?

Officer: My partner and I asked him a few brief questions regarding the events that had transpired. Then we asked if he would be willing to take a ride around the surrounding neighborhood in an attempt to possibly apprehend the suspect.

To which he agreed.

Deputy DA: And then what occurred?

Officer: Following the directions of the coplaintiff, my partner and I drove north on Towne Avenue, made a left onto East Vernon, drove one block, and then made a right into an alley which, eventually would lead to Avalon Boulevard.

Deputy DA: And then what occurred?

Officer: At the coplaintiff's request, we stopped midway through the alley and reviewed an area where he indicated an altercation had taken place.

Deputy DA: And what did you observe?

Officer: I saw broken pieces of a Purex bottle scattered about the dirt alley and footprint evidence of a possible scuffle.

Deputy DA: And then what occurred?

Officer: I informed the coplaintiff that, without a witness to corroborate his story, it would be difficult to uphold possible assault charges in a court of law.

Deputy DA: And then what occurred?

Officer: We reentered the squad car, continued eastbound through the alley, and reached Avalon Boulevard. At that time, we conducted a brief search of a bar located at the corner of Forty-Third Street and Avalon. However, it was determined that the suspect was not present in the bar.

Deputy DA: And then what occurred?

Officer: We drove east across Avalon and, owing to a positive ID from the coplaintiff, were able to apprehend the suspect walking east on Forty- Third Street near Avalon.

Deputy DA: And as part of the process of arresting the suspect, did you search him?

Officer: Yes, we did.

Deputy DA: And what did you find?

Officer: Among other things, we found a pocketknife, and approximately fourteen dollars in loose change.

Deputy DA: Is this the pocketknife you found?

Officer: Yes, it is.

Deputy DA: Your Honor, I would like to have this pocket knife marked as People's exhibit number four and ask that it be admitted into evidence.

Judge: Does the defense have any objections?

Public Defender: No, Your Honor.

Judge: The pocketknife will be admitted as People's exhibit number four.

Deputy DA: I have no further questions.

Judge: Does the defense wish to ask any questions?

Public Defender: Yes, Your Honor. Officer, when you stopped in the alley, did you advise the coplaintiff that, without a witness, the broken pieces of a Purex bottle may not be admissible in a court of law as possible evidence of an alleged altercation?

Officer: Yes, I did.

Public Defender: So, the coplaintiff was aware that without a corroborating witness, a charge of assault would more than likely not be admissible in a court of law?

Officer: Yes.

Public Defender: Thank you. I have no further questions.

Judge: Thank you. The witness is excused. Does the prosecution have any other witnesses?

Deputy DA: Yes, Your Honor. The People call the Los Angeles Police Department fingerprint examiner.

The bailiff then escorted the fingerprint examiner to the stand.

Clerk: Please stand. Raise your right hand. Do you promise that the testimony you shall give in the case now before this court shall be the truth, the whole truth, and nothing but the truth, so help you God?

Expert: I do.

Clerk: You may be seated.

Reporter: Please spell your last name for the record.

Expert: P-o-w-e-l-l.

Deputy DA: James, where do you work?

Expert: I am employed by the Los Angeles Police Department. I have been a qualified fingerprint examiner for twelve years.

The deputy DA took the container housing the broken piggy bank pieces to the examiner.

Deputy DA: Have you ever seen these broken pieces before?

Expert: Yes, I was asked to check them for fingerprints in my lab.

Deputy DA: Did you find any fingerprints as a result of your testing?

Expert: Yes, there were several rather clear fingerprint impressions.

Deputy DA: Were you able to identify the defendant's prints on the pieces?

Expert: Yes, the prints I took from three of the pieces were identical to the fingerprints taken from the defendant.

Deputy DA: Thank you. I have no further questions and no further witnesses, Your Honor.

Judge: Does the defense have any questions?

Public Defender: Yes, Your Honor. James, according to your report, you also found fingerprints on pieces that did not belong to the defendant. Is that true?

Expert: That is correct.

Public Defender: To whom did they belong?

Expert: I don't know.

Public Defender: Thank you, I have no further questions.

Judge: The witness is excused.

Deputy DA: Your Honor, the People rest their case.

Judge: Is the defense ready for its case?

Public Defender: Your Honor, at this time the defense rests.

Glancing at the mock trial transcript, I saw reference to the fact that, under the Bill of Rights, a person who is accused of a crime cannot be forced to testify at their own criminal trial. In addition, I read that the prosecution cannot make any comment about it if the defendant doesn't testify. Also, if this were a jury trial, which it was not, the jury cannot hold it against the defendant. Therefore, it appeared to me that, in this particular case, the defendant had decided not to testify.

A review of the mock trial transcript also revealed that if the defense had opted for a jury trial, the judge would have provided the jury with specific instructions. Included among the instructions were the three things that the prosecution needed to prove.

Since a jury trial had been waived by the defense, I sketched out on a legal pad a hypothetical script containing language the judge might have used if the defense had opted for a jury trial.

Judge: Ladies and gentlemen of the jury, I am now going to read to you the law that you must follow in deciding this case. To prove the crime charged against the defendant, the prosecution must prove three things to you. First, that the defendant broke into the apartment where the coplaintiffs resided. Second, that the coplaintiffs did not give the defendant permission to enter the apartment. Third, that the defendant intended to take away the coplaintiffs' right to retain custody of their possessions either permanently or temporarily. If each of you believes that the prosecution proved all three of these things beyond a reasonable doubt, then you should find the defendant guilty. But if you believe the prosecution did not prove any one of these things beyond a reasonable doubt, then you must find the defendant not guilty.

Glancing at a copy of the mock trial reference materials, the concept of proof beyond a reasonable doubt does not mean beyond all possible doubt. To the contrary, it means that the jury must consider all of the evidence and that the jury is very sure that the charge is true.

A review of the mock trial transcript also assisted me in understanding that, at this stage of the trial, the judge generally asks the deputy DA and the Public defender if they are ready with final arguments. The transcript copies also indicated that the final arguments were the attorneys' last chance to talk to the jury. The public defender would probably remind the jury that, under the law, his client was presumed to be innocent.

In the next step of the trial, the jury decides whether the defendant is guilty or not guilty. According to the transcript, not guilty is not the same thing as innocent. If all twelve of the jurors are unanimous in their decision, that will be the jury's verdict. Next, it will be up to each jury member to decide if he or she believed a witness was telling the truth or not. In addition, each member of the jury should consider how the witness behaved on the stand.

Finally, each jury member will also be expected to use their common sense in deciding whether or not a witness was telling the truth.

Several concepts in the mock trial transcript perplexed me. I read that it is up to the prosecution to prove the defendant is guilty. In other words, the defense does not have to prove the defendant is innocent. Therefore, as I interpreted the transcript, if the prosecution has not proven its case, the defendant is not guilty. The transcript copies provided the following guidelines for determining guilt: you can only say the defendant is guilty if the prosecution has proven all three of the things, identified by the judge, beyond a reasonable doubt.

Another finding from the mock trial transcript that perplexed me was the concept of reasonable doubt. From my perspective, the concept of reasonable doubt meant that you, as a jury member, must be very sure. That means that you will still be sure next month, next year, or two years from now. The transcript also indicated that reasonable doubt does not include any possible doubt you can come up with.

From my review of the transcript copies, I knew that, if the defense had opted for a jury trial, the jury foreperson would be selected. The deliberations would occur in the jury chambers. On the legal pad, I sketched out the dialogue that would emerge from this hypothetical scenario.

41

Judge: Will the jury foreperson please stand? Has the jury reached a unanimous verdict?

If the foreperson said, "Yes, the jury has reached a verdict," the clerk will retrieve the verdict form from the foreperson and hand it to the judge.

The judge will read the verdict silently before handing it back to the clerk to read aloud.

According to the mock trial transcript copy, at this stage of the trial, a finding of hung jury may have been reached. Glancing at the transcript, I also learned that the jury might not find the defendant guilty or not guilty. A hung jury would be declared if the jury could not reach a verdict.

If a hung jury occurred, the judge might elect to send the jury back for further deliberations. The goal would be to see if they can reach a unanimous decision. However, if the jury still could not reach a unanimous decision, the judge would declare a mistrial. If a mistrial is declared, the district attorney's office would decide if they wanted to have another trial. If the verdict was guilty, the defendant would return to the court on another day. the defendant would find out what the punishment would be. However, if the verdict was not guilty, the defendant would be free to depart and would not have to come back to court for that particular case.

Finally, the judge would say, "The jury is thanked and excused. Court is adjourned."

My mother and I exited the courtroom and walked toward the elevators. The arresting officers were about ten yards ahead of us. One of the officers glanced back at me a few times, shook his head, and said something humorous to his partner.

My mother whispered, "I guess they are having a hard time figuring out how a skinny little Black teenager was able to help bring down a known felon."

A court representative later called my mother and informed her of the hearing results. Apparently, after reviewing the testimony and the evidence presented in court, the judge had sentenced the defendant to the six-year maximum term in state prison. According to the representative, the judge's decision was based on the fact that the defendant had a rather lengthy history of performing similar acts of burglary.

It was more than a week after the courtroom experience before I finally allowed myself to breathe a sigh of relief. Since it was just the beginning of my senior year, I was sure it would be hard to top the "Case of the Knock- Knock Burglar."

The next day, I received a letter in the mail. It was from the Troop 182 Sea Explorer Unit. Apparently, a friend from Manual Arts High and I had been invited to a weekend camping trip with the Sea Explorer Unit.

Chapter 2

Heavy winds and torrential rain—an atmospheric river fostered three days of downpours and blustery conditions. According to the Southern California evening news meteorologists, the seldom-occurring river, nicknamed the Pineapple Express, was created by two weather systems that were dominated by winds moving away from each other. The divergent surface air flow left an empty space between the winds that needed to be filled. Moisture was then concentrated in the resulting long, thin corridors. When the gap between the diverging weather fronts appeared, it provided a rapid route for water to ascend into the atmosphere, generating an atmospheric river.

The meteorologists believed that the river was a manifestation of a low-pressure void that was predisposed to capturing whatever lay beneath it. For example, if this scenario occurred over the sea, the void would naturally capture huge quantities of water vapor.

In addition to mountain, desert, suburban, and inner-city

environmental impacts, a storm of that magnitude had the power to cause coastal alterations in the surface of the ocean floor. The front that had brought torrents of rain to the entire Southern California area had given way to a mild Indian summer afternoon in South Central Los Angeles.

Chuck and I were looking forward to the weekend trip to the San Pedro Sea Explorer Base. Although, still members of the Troop 182 Boy Scout Unit, we had been invited to the base as guests of the *Dolphin* Sea Explorer Unit. Devon, the *Dolphin*'s bosun, and Carl Toon, the *Dolphin*'s bosun's mate, rode in the truck's front cabin with Mr. Hines. Mr. Hines was the skipper for the Troop 182 Sea Explorer Unit.

Chuck and I tossed our duffel bags into the truck bed. Prior to departure, we were informed by the skipper that the first order of business was a trip to Ralph's for supplies.

I hadn't given much thought into how much food would be needed to provide breakfast, lunch, and dinner for a group of ten for two days. However, it wasn't long before I received my first crash course in bulk purchasing. I began rolling my basket down the canned goods section of the market's aisle as Chuck, Devon, Toon, and the skipper fanned out down separate aisles. Each member of the group pushed his own basket and was responsible for a portion of the master shopping list.

It wasn't long before the cumulative inventory of supplies retrieved from the shelves started to multiply. Among other items, the five baskets contained several five-pound bags of potatoes, powdered milk, concentrated orange juice, family-sized cans of green beans and pork and beans, chili beans, several cases of drinking water and canned soft drinks, several bags of ice, instant cocoa and coffee, chicken, ground round, spaghetti, white rice, hot dogs and buns, condiments, wheat bread, hash browns, grits, sausage, bacon, eggs, pancake mix, Bisquick mix, several varieties of syrup, several flavors of preserves, margarine, Hawaiian Punch, a variety of chips, corn husks, apples, oranges, assorted pies, cookies, and danish rolls, Crisco oil, tomato sauce, tomato paste, dishwashing liquid, and SOS scouring pads.

I was perplexed, however, by the addition of three bottles of red, yellow, and blue food coloring to the list. It seemed like we had accumulated enough supplies to feed a small platoon.

At the conclusion of the shopping spree, and to help speed things up, the skipper paid for the entire haul in cash.

Chuck and I climbed into the truck bed—amidst the boxes of pots and pans and bags of groceries—and the crew headed for the nearby Harbor Freeway. It was approximately a twenty-two-mile journey down the freeway to San Pedro.

To help pass the time, Chuck turned the volume up on his transistor radio. It didn't take long before the truck was out of range for the Eastside Motown beats and into American Bandstand territory. Soon, we found ourselves listening to music like the Vince Guaraldi Trio's "Cast Your Fate to the Wind" and Santo and Johnny's "Sleepwalk."

When the Four Season's "Sherry" came on the air—to Chuck's amusement—I chimed in with a high-pitched falsetto: "You, oh, better ask your mama (Sherry baby), tell her everything is all right."

Chuck turned the volume all the way down on the portable radio and said, "Hey, Joe. Earlier today, you mentioned that you've been working on several new editions to your poetry collection. Well, let's hear it. Go ahead. Now's as good a time as any to lay it on me."

Pulling a well-worn journal from my duffel bag, I said, "Okay, but you have to remember that the entries are just rough drafts." And with that, I began to read my most recent poem.

Reflections

Eyes the shade of foamy ocean-green,
Hazel as a smoke-covered ice-blue sky

Hair that reflects the chill of a wintry night,
Sparkling and glistening in a halo of moonlight

A light-complexioned Sista, with a welcoming smile,
Beckoning arms, knowing eyes, and teasing lips

A body soft and firm,
Womanly and tender

The smile and warmth and being,
Of one who loves, and is loved

Though we be separated by many miles,
Our hearts and minds, are joined as one

I live for you, and only you
My life is yours, you are my life

Wait for me my darling,
I will come soon

Remember me my darling,
Forever, and always

After a moment, Chuck said, "Now, that's deep. I mean, that's really good stuff. Sounds like you got a little bit of Pepe Le Pew stored up inside of you."

"Yeah," I replied. "As Pepe would say,
'You have the aroma of spring flowers, that bloom in the spring.'"
We both laughed.

Chuck added, "Well, whatever you do, don't stand up on a bench in the swim team's locker room and recite that nonsense. I mean, somebody's gonna chunk a wet towel and smack you square in the face! You hear what I am saying?"

"Right on, brother. I hear where you're coming from."

Chuck said, "Well, since you are on such a creative roll, how about sharing another entry from your journal?"

"Okay, but after this one, I think it's time to slide that bad boy back into the duffel bag. Every time I read one of my drafts, I have an uncontrollable urge to edit. And riding in the back of a jostling truck at sixty miles an hour doesn't make for ideal editing circumstances."

With that, I began reading the rough draft of another poem.

Ebony Lady

Ebony lady, "Are You Going My Way?"
Bringing your world of joys, sorrows, and happiness,
Pull me close, gentle bliss,
Let your tears fall upon my chest,
Hold me long, moistly linger on,
Golden sunrise, coral sunset, never gone

Ebony lady, look at me,
Shapely, firm tender breasts,
"Mind-Blowing" smile, tease me dove,
Sweetly fresh, squeeze me hug,
Promise to love, honor, and cherish,
Parting breath, never perish

Ebony lady, "Don't Keep Me Waiting,"
Don't lie, don't cheat, don't deceive, believe,
That for you, I give my heart,
I share my life, I lay my strife
Forever surround me, in the afterglow
Of your completeness,
For you I hunger, I kiss, I caress

Once again, Chuck was silent for a few moments. And then he said, "Ah, Joey! You wrote one poem about a light, bright, almost White Black woman and then another about an ebony-toned chick. You do realize that if you turn state's evidence with this nonsense, the Sistas are going to tag you as an international lover!"

I smiled as I reflected on Chuck's comments.

Reverend Cecil Murray, my minister at First African Methodist Episcopal Church of Los Angeles (FAME) once said, "Can't nobody make brown sugar like God can make brown sugar!"

Chuck said, "You know what, Joe? When I first heard Ebony Lady, my first thought was now there are a woman I would like to have sex with!"

I laughed and replied, "As they say in the TJH locker room, your eyes may glitter, and your teeth may grit—"

Chuck said, "But none of Miss Ebony Woman is you gonna get!"

Following that witty exchange, Chuck turned the volume back up on the transistor radio. To our surprise, soul music had managed to hijack the early evening airwaves.

Chuck pumped up the jam when "Twist and Shout" by the Isley Brothers started playing.

Feeling the pulsating rhythm, I began nodding my head, moving my hands and waist from side to side, and simulating the Twist. I chimed in with another high-pitched falsetto: "Come on, come on, come, come on, baby, now. Come on and work it on out."

A brisk wind flowed throughout San Pedro Bay, carrying the briny smell of the nearby Pacific. The fire-engine red late-model 1957 Ford truck rambled slowly along the half-mile stretch of the winding dirt road. The unpaved, unlit dirt road was the only route into and out of the San Pedro Sea Explorer Base.

I unbuttoned my bulky, warm, dark blue, Navy peacoat and lifted my black wool knit hat off my glasses. Chuck was wrapped in a warm army green blanket.

"Damn that was a windy, Frosty Freeze ride!" I said.

"You ain't jiving!" It was colder than a mosquito's *tweeter*." Chuck replied.

I suddenly recalled what one TJH classmate said while selling wolf tickets during a fifteen-minute nutrition break: "Hey, man. When the wind blows, your address changes!"

Tweedledee and Tweedledum were from Walt Disney's 1951 animated feature film *Alice in Wonderland*. In the wolf sessions, Tweedledee would start by criticizing Tweedledum's shoes.

Tweedledum would critique Tweedledee's face, and a negative statement would eventually be made about one or the other's mother. At that point, and to the delight of the encircled crowd, some of whom egged the adversaries on by shouting, "Fight, fight, and fire to the membrane," the discourse generally ended in a physical altercation. "Not bad—a cinnamon roll, milk, and an animated throw down all in fifteen minutes."

"Hey! Check it out! Remember that?" I pointed toward a stretch of beach just north of the Cabrillo Boathouse. Both of us burst into laughter as we recalled a recent incident on the beach.

"Right on!" Chuck replied. "I'll never forget last summer. We snuck off the base with that signal flare gun for a midnight snoop-and-poop, virgin-patrol expedition."

"Yeah!" I continued. "The bright rays from the flare gun were visible for up to a mile and came in handy for the half-mile trek up the dark road to the park."

"Really!" Chuck added. "There was nothing out there but the sound of crickets and footsteps crunching in the gravel as we made our way up the dirt road."

I recalled the outing as though it were yesterday. "I remember the intoxicating scent of star jasmines that grew wild in the surrounding brush and then spiraled up along the edges of the overhanging cliffs."

Chuck continued, "Except for the occasional headlights from a slowly approaching vehicle that prompted us to fan off to the side of the road."

"Probably a Sea Explorer returning from a late-night movie on the army base." The army base was adjacent to the twelve acres that were set aside for the Sea Explorer Base. However, the approaching vehicle was definitely not the Troop 182 scoutmaster because he was kicked back in his tent and knocking down some serious Zs.

Chuck added, "As we neared the park, you raised your left hand and moved your index finger across your throat. I needed to kill the light."

"And that's when we spotted a lone car parked on the beach, and I put my index finger to my lips. We fanned out and moved in on the driver's side of the vehicle. As we neared the vehicle, we observed that all the windows were steamed up. We heard a pulsating beat coming from the car radio."

Chuck continued, "I whispered, 'Well, well, well. It looks like we got ourselves a situation here!'"

I replied, "As the police might say, 'It looks like we are about to witness something that may be illegal, immoral, and unethical."

Chuck laughed. "No comment on matters pending further investigation! You motioned for silence and began the countdown to fire in the hole."

"And man!" I continued. "That guy was surprised when you lit up the vehicle with the flare! The girl screamed, and he jumped up. The visual wasn't pretty. I mean, I am talking about a beet-red, half-naked, blond-haired, wide- eyed perp with both hands raised in the air."

Trying hard to hide his amusement, Chuck added, "After seeing his hands up, I said, 'I see he knows the routine!'"

"No telling what he was thinking," I added. "Maybe he figured we were from Take Back Auto!"

Chuck continued, "I guess he really thought we were the police and figured he was going down on charges like an alleged inappropriate relationship with an underaged minor."

"That's right!" I replied. "Or maybe he thought he would be booked on suspicion of lewd or lascivious acts with a minor. I am sure there is a penal code statute for adolescence interruptus, aka statutory rape!"

We both laughed.

Chuck said, "Or annoying or molesting a child under eighteen."

"Wow, I added. "That person of interest was ticked off when he heard us laughing and figured out we were just a couple of unorthodoxed blockers."

Chuck continued, "He was so enraged that he gunned the engine and tried to run us over. All that action while we sprinted down the shoreline and scrambled willy-nilly, seeking cover in the bushes near the beachfront."

"Case in point!" I added. "Confucius would probably say, 'Man should take no shame in getting butt in wind!'"

My analogy to the Chinese teacher, editor, politician, and

philosopher of the spring and autumn period of Chinese history drew a loud laugh from Chuck who chimed in,

"I mean, we were like, see you later, alligator! After while crocodile, or on the further, brother!"

"No, I answered, as the police might say, just what part of git your narrow *gluteus maximus* in gear, didn't you understand?"

"Wow! Chuck proclaimed. "Where was the pursuit-intervention technique when you needed it?"

"No wait! My kingdom for a spike strip!" I replied.

"Forget about the spike strip! I'd call for a *blitzkrieg!* Because this was definitely an extreme *pucker factor* situation." Chuck answered.

The ensuring uncontrollable laughter hurt my sides.

I said, "Then the perp's tires lost traction in the wet sand, and from a strategic vantage point in the bushes, we could see him displaying some pretty angry body language. From a situational awareness perspective, he was glaring back in the general direction of where he thought we might be hiding."

"Yeah," Chuck added. "He was flipping the bird in the air like he just didn't care and high tailing it toward a telephone booth— probably to request a tow truck because assault with a deadly weapon in response to something as minor as a teenage prank would be deemed highly inappropriate. *Namaste!* To quote the police, *we have enough evidence and probable cause to suggest that he intended to act with malice.*"

"Quiet is kept," I concluded. He needed to move that vehicle before it got *field stripped*. Of course, no nooky for him that night! She probably told him *niche a noche!*" I intentionally mixed my rather sparse knowledge of Spanish and German.

Chuck smirked. "I am hip. Score one for the virgin patrol—at least for that night. We done her mama proud!"

The truck was entering the gated area of the Sea Explorer Base. A single line of eight worn army green tents stretched across the clearing, and a boathouse containing several rows of uniformly stacked sabots and catamarans was positioned near the pier.

The skipper stopped in the clearing near the base commander's

Quonset hut business office. A trailer that was used as the commander's portable living quarters was positioned next to the hut. About twenty yards in front of the hut, a large American flag flew from sunup to sundown, atop a towering flagpole.

Devon, Carl Toon, and the skipper climbed out of the truck's cabin. Toon had a slender frame, stood only about five foot five, and had a fair-skinned complexion and short, curly brown hair.

Toon said, "All hands-on deck, homeboys! Time to un-ass that truck bed and help us carry in this equipment!"

At Toon's prompting, Chuck and I abruptly got up and started unloading the groceries and supplies over the sides. The first order of business was to route the cold items to the giant refrigerator storage units that were positioned adjacent to the indoor showers.

"Careful with that stuff, homies!" Toon shouted. "Didn't the Girl Scouts teach you nothing?"

Toon's abrasive way of speaking was starting to wear thin on Chuck, so I gave Chuck a friendly nudge with my elbow and followed it up with my best imitation of a Cheshire cat grin.

Toon and Devon walked off toward the tents, and the skipper went up to the Quonset hut to coordinate the weekend activities with the base commander.

Chuck said, "Man, I don't know how the hell they elected that lewd, rude and misconstrued turkey with a Napoleon complex boatswain's mate, but he's really morphed into a first-class *blue falcon*!"

"Right on!" I pointed in the direction of Toon's fading exit, and said, *"Oh dey, ick fey, ugly fey!"*

"Toon deserves nothing short of a *righteous* butt-whipping!" Chuck stated.

"Damn, Skippy!" I replied. "I read somewhere in the Sea Explorer Manual that rank has its privileges, but we're still in the *Dolphin* Scout Patrol—and I don't think they can lay that stuff on us yet!"

"Heads up!" Chuck cut in. "Here comes Cartoon and the others!"

Toon was talking loud and walking in front of five of the older Sea Explorers. Some of them were nicotine junkies, and their cigarettes flickered in the starlit night. Apparently, three of the Sea Explorers had arrived around 0900 that morning.

As they drew near, I recognized Troop 182's Howard Henderson's older brother Bert, the *Dolphin*'s boatswain Devon, Dorsey High's senior class vice president Jaden, and clad in a letterman's jacket, Los Angeles High's all- conference linebacker Aaron.

"Damn!" I whispered. "Now, there are some bad GGs."

"I hear you, brother!" Chuck replied with a hushed tone.

"Hey! What's happening, lil bros!" Devon said.

"Nothing to it, man!" Chuck replied.

"Righteous brother, you got it all!" I added, looking for the Slightest opportunity to try to gain a potential ally.

"All right! All right! Knock it off, homies!" Toon cut in. "How come this truck ain't empty? And from now on, you *plebes* don't call us nothing but sir!"

Plebes! The word ricocheted through my mind like a .22-caliber shell.

Chuck and I turned and looked at each other, unable to speak.

The crew was laughing and joking about the new label.

"Yeah, *plebes!*" Toon started again. "Don't look so funny! You'll get yours tonight!"

"Go easy on them, Toon!" Devon cut in. "All right, you guys! Help them get this gear squared away!"

Chuck and I each grabbed two bags of groceries, climbed out of the truck, and started toward the tents.

"Damn!" I said. "And I wanted to get some swimming and sailing in tomorrow!"

"Ain't no way!" Chuck replied. "They brought us up here to kick our asses!"

We ran into the skipper on his way back from the base commander's office. He was a six-foot-two, dark-skinned, heavyset, elderly man. And, as usual, a cherry blend aroma trailed from his flickering pipe.

"Well, how's it going, fellas?" the skipper asked.

"Fine, sir!" we replied in unison.

"Guess you guys know about the initiation now?"

"Yes, sir. I guess we do," Chuck answered.

"Well, don't worry about it," the skipper continued. "Lots of young men have made it through." He smiled. "You fellas were scheduled to join the Dolphins next month, so the crew decided to go ahead with the initiation this weekend. Well, anyway, I'll be in my tent reading. Good luck!" And with that, he walked off.

It took a while to unload everything, but we got all the gear in place.

The quickly prepared evening meal consisted of rotisserie-style chicken, wheat bread, green beans, and a slice of apple pie.

After our assigned cleanup duty had been completed, Chuck and I quietly sipped instant cocoa out of Styrofoam cups in front of the old iron-frame stove. We took turns tossing pieces of timber onto the glowing charcoals. The other crew members had disappeared down the beach somewhere, apparently prepping the shoreline for the upcoming initiation.

"Bet they're out there scheming on us right now!" I stated.

"Yeah, I guess," Chuck replied.

"Heads up! Incoming!" I whispered as the sound of quick-paced footsteps drew near.

Devon was walking toward the redwood picnic bench. "You guys all right?" He sat next to Chuck.

"Yes, sir!" Chuck replied.

Devon was six foot-one, slender, ebony-toned, and wore gold wire-framed glasses.

"You know, it's really up to you guys whether or not you want to go through with this. But if you want into the unit, you'll have to experience this ordeal sooner or later."

"Yes, sir. We know!" I replied in a rather unconvincing tone.

"Okay!" Devon continued. "I've already passed the word to the crew to try to cut you a little slack. You know, no low blows and crap like that. Joe, you'd better put your *birth-control glasses* up somewhere. Well, anyway, beginning today and continuing through the weekend, the crew has had a rather full workload. We are trying to get them ready for the November rendezvous at the San Diego Naval Base. Earlier this morning, they scraped barnacles off the hull of *The Dolphin* and varnished it. Tomorrow, they are scheduled to run time trials for scuttlebutt and breaches buoy. The time trials will be followed by whaleboat commands and precision drill sessions. You know, the works!"

From my review of the *Sea Explorer Manual*, I knew a scuttlebutt was a barrow on shipboard used to contain freshwater for a day's use. The cast was usually suspended by a tripod. A breaches buoy was a life buoy with canvas breeches attached that, when suspended from a rope, can be used to transfer a person to safety from a ship. A whaleboat is a long rowboat with a bow at either end for easy maneuverability. Whaleboats were traditionally used in the whaling industry.

Devon added, "So, one advantage that you guys have is that the crew is already pretty damn tired!"

"Thanks for the heads-up, sir!" I answered. "But if they're going to do it to us, I figure we can take it!"

"Really?" Chuck chimed in. "Let's get it on!"

"Well, that's why I came over," Devon continued. "The crew is out prepping the beachhead, and I want both of you to steer clear of the shoreline area for a while. So, why don't you take an hour to stroll down the road toward the park area near the old Cabrillo Boathouse?" Grinning, he added,

"The crew wanted to give you a little time to figure out if you're really serious about joining the only Black Sea Explorer unit West of the Mississippi. Do you dig where I am coming from?"

"Yes, sir! We hear you!" Chuck answered sharply.

Devon rose suddenly and said, "Well, anyway! You *plebes* split! Be back by 1800. When you return, you will be under a code of silence. That means there will be no talking until further notice! And you'll obey all orders from your superior officers! RHIP! You dig?"

"Yes, sir!" We walked double-time in the direction of the old Cabrillo Beach Boathouse.

Devon grinned as we made our way off into the darkness. He knew that we were two of the best recruits Troop 182 had sent up in a long time. Joe was five eleven and slender. He was a Life Scout, assistant senior patrol leader, mile swim merit badge holder, Order of the Arrow recipient, and budding poet. His black-framed glasses seemed to underscore his image as an all- around scholar. Chuck was six-foot-tall, had a caramel complexion, and was musclebound! The Eagle Scout and senior patrol leader was a star sprinter for Manual Arts High. Devon started walking back toward the shoreline to continue supervising the crew.

It was quiet along that stretch of the beach at night. And although a somber veil had been dropped over the weekend, I couldn't help but marvel at the deep green expanse of land that flowed out toward the beach. Neatly spaced pine trees and tall magnolia bushes stretched from one end of the grassy beachfront to a massive wall of jagged cliffs. At the top of the cliff were the lime green walls of Fort MacArthur. We made a beeline across the beach and headed toward the old boathouse.

The concrete walls were painted from stem to stern in white and sprawled along the sandy shoreline like a small, Spanish cobblestone fortress. It guarded the beach from foreign invasion. I found a spot under the boat house in the cool, moist sand. It was next to the beams that supported and anchored the boathouse foundation. I scooped up some of the shells that were scattered in the sand.

Chuck went off to *hit the head* and then sat beside me. We watched the waves lapping up on the shore. The waterline stopped only a few feet from us. A foaming mass of dark brownish-green waves churned and shifted up the rocky coast. Then, hissing and spraying, it reluctantly flowed back, only to repeat the cycle again.

"What do you figure they'll do to us?" I asked.

"Aw! Work us over real good for one thing!" Chuck replied. "But I figure all you got to do is be cool, keep your mouth shut, and try not to retaliate on them. From what I hear, it don't take long."

"Yeah, I guess," I replied. "That sure was a dubious trick they pulled getting us down here and then laying all this on us!"

"Yeah!" Chuck answered. "But they would've got us sooner or later!"

"Right on! Sooner or—look out!" I shouted.

We both jumped back to avoid the spreading foam.

"Damn!" I stated. "It looks like high tide is rolling in!"

"Don't matter," Chuck said. "About time to be getting back anyway."

"Yeah? What time you got!" I asked.

"Oh, I figure it'll take about twenty minutes to get there," Chuck replied.

After a quick trip to the head, we walked down the beach. Our route took us across an empty expanse of asphalt and onto the winding dirt road.

As we approached the gates to the base, Toon shouted, "Hey! Here they come! Here come the *plebes*! Oh! Wee!"

"Damn!" Chuck mumbled. "That GG is really tripping. I mean, he just can't wait to take us out!"

"Really!" I replied. "I'd like to have a rumble in the jungle with him someday."

We joined the rest of the crew, quietly took off our jackets, and submitted to the blindfolding.

Toon continued to whoop and holler like a psycho, giving me second thoughts about the pending festivities.

Devon said, "Be cool, Toon. Man, you don't want to upset the little bros.'"

Toon said, "Naw! Naw! Where's my licking stick! We gonna do this thang! It's oops upside your head time! Somebody's ass is gonna be grass tonight! Time to Get on down to the real nitty gritty!"

Devon raised the volume of his voice while providing instructions for navigating the seven doors. His elevated tone was no match for Toon's ongoing trash talk.

Devon was saying something about a different crew member serving as the designated guardian of each door. I felt a swift, Alpha Phi Zeta board swat to my rear end and jumped forward. What made the Zeta board particularly vicious were the distinctive suction holes dotted on its surface.

Chuck let out a grunt, apparently the recipient of a whack from another Zeta paddle.

"All right, you two. Fall in *nut to butt*!" Devon said.

I placed my right hand briefly on Chuck's right shoulder to make sure we were properly lined up.

With Devon sounding off the cadence count, we started marching down the beach.

"Hup! Two! Three! Four! Hup! Two! Three! Four! Yo left! Yo left! Yo left! Right! Right! Right!"

Toon shouted, "C'mon, *plebes*! Move it! Move it! Homies! Put some pride in yo stride! Some pep in yo step! Some soul in your stroll! Hate to talk about your mama—she's a good old soul! She got a fourteen-karate diamond in her ..."

The crew could barely contain themselves in response to the muffled finish to Toon's modified cadence.

I could hear the waves flowing up on the beach, and surmised we were marching south along the dune. I also figured there was a rope climbing tower in the vicinity.

Toon said, "Hold up, y'all. Just before the start of a Southern League football or basketball game or track meet the teams huddle and kneel for a brief prayer. Tonight, I'd like to amend that ritual with a poem written by one of the *plebes*. That's right. I am talking about my homie here Joe." He placed his hand on my shoulder. "From what I hear, the brother's a poet—and he don't even know it."

The crew seemed thoroughly amused by Toon's lame rhyme.

Pulling out a pocket-sized flashlight, Toon began reading lines from "Reflections," a poem that existed in draft form only.

I had shared it with Chuck in the back of the skipper's truck. Toon must have *claimed gear adrift is a gift*, and rummaged through my duffel bag, retrieved the journal, and transcribed a copy of the poem. I was outraged because, among other things, his actions were *like a bad drug deal* - a total violation of my right to privacy. A hush fell over the crew as Toon began to read the pirated draft.

I listened to the mumbled comments that flowed from the crew.

Several of them insisted on snickering throughout the reading.

One of the crew members shouted, "Hey, Joey. I got a poem for you. Back in the day, when I was young, dumb, and full of ..."

I could tell where the mangy dog who farted that shot was headed. I held up my right hand and bowed my head slightly!

Another crew member shouted, "That poem just brung tears to me one good eye!"

Judging by the assorted feedback, I realized that—although sentimental and romantic in nature, "Reflections" would not be the crew's primary choice of reading material. In my high school public speaking class, the teacher had emphasized the importance of knowing your audience before you presented. This particular group was more of a *Penthouse* or *Playboy* crowd.

Toon said, "Great googalas boogalas, homie! Here's what I want to know. Did you hit it?"

I crossed my arms and tilted my head forward.

Ignoring my obvious irritation, Toon said, "Perhaps you don't speak the King's English. Let me break it down *Barney-style* - did you tap that ass?"

Visibly upset by Toon's rather uncouth reference to a girl's precinct, I slowly moved my head from side to side in a sincere attempt to respond to the question.

I was perplexed because the backstory of Reflections was that it was about longing for someone who, geographically, was at a great distance from me. In addition, the object of my affection had no idea that, after a single blind date, I had developed feelings for her.

Once she departed from her weekend visit, I discovered that I was actually better suited for her best friend. And that friend just happened to be geographically accessible to me.

Even if she had acquiesced to a one-night stand, which she most assuredly did not, everybody knows a gentleman doesn't tell. Furthermore, although I hadn't had an opportunity to put the advice into practice, I recalled being told by a close friend to keep a condom in my wallet in the event of an impromptu encounter. The purpose of the protection was to help avoid pregnancies and sexually transmitted diseases.

"Well, well, well, well," Toon said. "I didn't think so. Here's what I heard about you—you ain't *never* had none!"

The crew broke out in a loud chorus of laughter.

I would have preferred to simply ignore this outrageous line of questioning, but I sensed that it was not the appropriate teachable moment or place to try to impress the crew with the virtues of abstinence and delayed gratification. I slowly moved my head from side to side in denial of the allegation. That particular group wasn't trying to hear all of that, but I did experience a great deal of guilt for not adhering to my beliefs.

Toon, seemingly puzzled by an apparent disconnect between his alleged anonymous source of insider information and my steadfast denials, scratched his head. "Well, tell me this, homie—was it wet or dry?"

The crew again broke out into a raunchy chorus of laughter.

Toon continued "Raise your right hand if it was wet and your left if it was dry!"

Judging from the ensuing laughter, I could tell that the crew was truly enjoying Toon's impromptu cross-examination. His question caught me off guard because I had pondered many deep concepts in my sixteen years - algebra, geometry, trigonometry, and math analysis - but I hadn't spent much time contemplating whether the inside of a female's precinct was wet or dry.

The brief pause in my response, seemed to give Toon the Perry

Mason moment he was seeking. "You see? You see? I told you he ain't never had none!"

Figuring I still had a fifty-fifty chance of surviving this rather crude encounter, I slowly raised my right hand. Unfortunately - and judging by the comments uttered by the crew - the slight delay in response time failed to achieve the reasonable doubt standard. My only hope at redemption was that the blindfold prevented my eyes from betraying my true feelings of embarrassment and humiliation.

I think I know who the rat-faced snitch was. Probably that loudmouth Larry of the Beaver Patrol. That unit had accompanied Toon on the breakwater-to- lighthouse outing.

I was standing next to Larry after gym class and waiting for the bell to ring so I could move on to my next class. Larry started talking all kinds of smack and bragging about how much sex he got last summer. I mean, he even went so far as to say that, when he died, he planned to donate his private to the Smithsonian. That led me to suspect that he was just blowing smoke.

His comments sort of puzzled me because Larry looked like he'd been hit with the ugly stick. He was only about five foot three, had a dark complexion, and resembled a miniature version of James Brown. Similar to the alleged nickname given to James Brown, some classmates actually referred to Larry as the Monkey Man.

In a brain-freeze moment of truth I shared with him that I was a virgin and my intention was to marry another virgin someday. Well, judging by the look of shock and dismay that appeared on Larry's face, I quickly figured out that there are some personal convictions and beliefs that we all need to keep to ourselves. Other people may not be at the same level of awareness.

Larry said, "Man, you better go get you some before you go crazy!"

At the time, I didn't think it was God's will that I lose my mind over that particular issue. I was at a loss for words and held hostage by a high school bell that seemed like it would never ring.

I was grateful when the bell, which seemed to be calibrated to Dagwood Bumstead time, finally rang. The sound was my green light to try to put some distance between me and Larry with his *braggadocios* self. Whatever message I had intended to share had fallen on deaf ears.

"All right! All right, enough of this foreplay," Aaron shouted.

"Listen up, lil' bros! You are now standing at the entrance to the first door!" A sudden hush fell over the group.

"Chuck," Aaron continued, "you stand here. Joe, over there. Now hold on to this rope! I want y'all to scale Mount Kilimanjaro! And the last one back down the rope tower, well, let's just say I guess we're just gonna have to smoke his ass!"

The initiation was clearly getting worse—and we hadn't even Cleared door number one.

Aaron said, "Wait a tick! Looky here! Now, y'all didn't really think we were gonna make it that easy for you, did you? Blind man, blind man, your mama wants you."

"What does she want?" the crew chimed in.

"A cup of coffee!" Aaron added.

63

"Where's the spoon?" the crew asked.

"Feel for it!" Aaron replied.

Somebody grabbed me firmly around the shoulders and spun me around three or four times. Apparently, Chuck received the same treatment. They stuck the rope back in my hands. Dizzy, I flexed and squatted in a ready position.

"All right now, lil' bros! Aaron shouted. "Ready! Set! Go!"

I kicked up with my right leg, gripped the rope tightly, and began the grueling hand-over-hand ascent. At the beginning of the climb, a stinging Zeta board swat was applied to my rear end.

Damn! The whole ordeal is going south real fast. I strained to pull my slender frame up the rope. My head was still spinning, and even with a wraparound foot lock in place, my hands were starting to feel the burn from the rope. Without sight, the forty-foot tower actually began to feel like Mount Kilimanjaro. I wondered what would happen if I lost my grip.

"Pull! Pull!" they cried from below.

"Ain't nuthin' but a meatball, y'all!" Toon shouted.

Chuck hit the top and started his descent.

I lunged up, made contact with the top, and began my descent.

The crew shouted, "Do it! Chuck, baby with your bad self!"

We both hit the ground and bent over. We were breathing hard, Muscles tensed and strained, and sweat oozed from our bodies. Since I came in last, someone gave me a swift Zeta board swat to the butt, sending me sprawling to the ground and inhaling a mouthful of sand. Another crew member tripped Chuck, and he fell to the ground.

Bert commanded us to crawl through a series of legs that formed a human gauntlet to the second door. Although bombarded by several Zeta board swats, we made it through the gauntlet and were pulled to our feet. I felt my mask starting to loosen, and I tried to tighten it.

"Look!" Toon shouted. "He's trying to take it off!"

I wanted to say, "No, sir," but we had been sworn to an oath of silence. I felt someone tightening it.

Devon whispered, "Nice going, young man. That was the second door. Five more to go after this—and it's all over."

"C'mon! C'mon, Devon! God damn it!" Cartoon shouted.

"You're holding up the set!"

I sensed the urgency in Cartoon' voice and began to stumble forward. We made our way down the sandy embankment for about fifteen yards in spite of the constant Zeta board swats.

"All right, *plebes*!" Jaden shouted. "Hold up! We are now about to take you through the third door!"

I took a moment to suck in a few swift breaths in a desperate attempt to clear my head.

"Chuck!" Jaden continued. "You come with me!"

Half the crew went to Chuck's side, and the other half stayed with me. I heard Cartoon's piercing voice across the way and was relieved that he was on the other side of whatever they were going to do to us next.

"Hold tight, lil' bros," Jaden shouted. "This is the entrance to the third door! Down in this pit is some funky brew I wouldn't let my German shepherd dive into!"

They all laughed.

"So, hang onto this rope and pull! The man with the weaker team goes in along with some of his teammates. But, word up, I feel for the GG who takes his team down into Davy Jones's locker with him!"

Laughter again broke out among the crew.

Both teams grabbed hold of the rope and started to pull. I was at the front of my line and knew I would be going in first if we lost.

"Pull! Pull! God damn it! Pull!"

The rope grew taut as both sides strained to win.

Chuck's team was starting to give ground, and then I heard a loud splash and felt the rope slacken. As my team fell backward, Chuck's team went into the pit.

Damn! It must have been full of sea water! Judging from the commotion I heard coming out of the pit, somebody was having a field day at Chuck's expense.

"Pull 'em off!" Devon shouted. "Lighten up, Toon! Let it slide!"

I sat exhausted on the beach as they fished the soaking crew members out of the pit.

"You all right, Chuck?" Jaden asked.

Chuck just nodded slowly. I knew that Chuck shared a common feeling about what he'd like to do to Cartoon in a dark alley someday.

"Well! C'mon then!" Jaden shouted. "Move it, lil' bros! Door number four doesn't come with valet parking!"

I felt another stinging Zeta board swat to the buttocks.

Perhaps owing to a boost from an adrenaline rush or the fight-or-flight syndrome, we both managed to break loose from the group. We began sprinting down the beach, and I could hear the stampede of the crew not far behind. I recall thinking, *Maybe, I'll just keep running all the way to the San Ysidro border!*

Chuck had always been faster and stronger than me, but the wet clothes appeared to be bogging him down. I began pulling away, and then I heard a loud grunt as the crew caught up with Chuck. I experienced a brief sensation of weightlessness as I plunged into a deep pit. I fell hard against the side of the man-made crevice, and once again, I had to spit out a mouthful of sand.

"E to the T, please don't let them do that to me!" Toon exclaimed in a giddy tone. I was pulled from the pit, tripped, and swatted.

I rose to my feet, managed to break free from the crew, and sprinted down the beach. This time, I slipped the mask up a little with my right hand so I could sneak a peek at my escape route.

It's one thing for a nearsighted person to be running down the beach in the dark. However, it is a horse of a different color for a nearsighted person to be streaking down the beach at night while blindfolded!

Eventually, I was tackled by Aaron. Exhausted, I just sucked in air and wondered how long the initiation could go on.

The crew didn't drag me to my feet. Instead, Toon said, "You all right, man?"

I nodded weakly.

"Well, then! Get up! Get up, homie! This is the fifth door!

Y'all, bring Chuck over here! All right. All right! I want you two to slow dance!"

Slow dance? I thought. *This bold motor scooter must have lost his ever- loving, freakin' mind!*

But they shoved us together, and we both awkwardly tried to lead each other.

Toon starting singing the lead verse to "Please, Please, Please" by James Brown and the Famous Flames (R & B Top Ten hit single, Federal Records 1956)

Then the crew chimed in with the chorus

Please, please, please (Please, please don't go)

Darling please, don't (Go), whoa oh yeah, oh"

Toon's voice hit a high-pitched squeak like he was going through puberty.

"Ooh! Wee! Bros! Bet y'all didn't know I could blow like that!"

The crew seemed truly amused by Toon's antics, and the momentary levity—mixed with a slight dip in the hard, sandy surface—prompted me to lose my balance and slip backward.

"Now I done seen everything!" Toon proclaimed. "Check it out! That plebe thinks he's a goddamn bitch!"

Again, the crew broke out in laughter. "Hold him tighter, Chuck! Yeah, grind that bitch!"

Well, maybe all this other stuff was just borderline psycho, but I didn't sign up to be nobody's bitch! I pushed Chuck back, and broke through the encircled crew, apparently *making a hole* straight over Toon. I sprinted down the beach, and the pack hollered, "Go! Go! Go! Get! Get! Get!" I knew it would only be a matter of time before Aaron would catch me again.

I slammed into a net that whipped my head and body back onto the sand.

"Oh, wee!" Toon shouted. "That fool ran straight into the volleyball net! Now tell me you liked ta did it! Good thing we double-wrapped the support poles!"

The crew was in stiches.

Toon said, "You jive-time, finger-popping, funky piece of ...

I'm mo sheave my size 9D brogan straight up your *yeng yeng!*" Every few words, Toon forcefully shoved open-palm thrusts into my chest.

I held my hands up with both palms facing forward, but the

momentum from each push prompted me to take a step back.

"Cool it! Toon, man," Devon cut in. "Pull 'em back, guys!"

Toon continued to push me back with open-palm thrusts while spewing out a volley of curse words that would have embarrassed a sailor.

Eventually, the crew managed to separate us.

I bent forward and placed my hands on my knees, trying to regain my breath. With my right forearm, I used my sweatshirt sleeve to wipe away a small stream of blood that had started to trickle from my bottom lip.

The crew pulled me back up and led us to what felt like a smooth, wet part of the beach. Judging from the sound of the surf, I surmised that we were in an area where the waves splashed up on the sandy shoreline.

"All right!" Toon shouted. "All right! You homies wanted to run? We gonna give you a reason to get your derrieres into the wind! About twenty- five yards straight ahead is door number six.

Your task is to reach it before we catch up with you. If we do catch you, well, I am sure by now you are familiar with the routine. So, on your mark, ready, set, go!"

Once again, Chuck and I sprinted down the beach. Chuck was running strong. Apparently, he'd had time to regain his second wind. I was starting to feel the cumulative toll from the prolonged ordeal. However, perhaps owing to a sheer adrenaline rush, we still managed to outdistance the crew.

I started to experience the burn of the cool night air in my lungs. I was beginning to feel a twinge in the upper part of my left thigh, but I pressed on.

One of the crew members was gaining ground on me.

I knew the waterline was close to my left, so I zigzagged like a running back. Judging by the sound of the splash and resulting profanity, the crew member must of bit on the zig when he should have opted for the zag.

When the other crew members caught up with us, they hit us with another barrage of tackles, trips, and swats.

Chuck must have taken a major offense to a hard tackle from Aaron, and he started delivering smashing blows to Aaron's face.

I stumbled over to where they were fighting to break it up. However, Toon joined the fray and that ill-advised decision only served to aggravate the situation. I had reached my boiling point. Grabbing a handful of Toon's curly hair, I slammed a hard right into his jaw.

Shouting frantically, Devon and the rest of the crew tried to break up the brawl. When we were all finally pulled apart, Devon angrily called the crew into a huddle.

I could clearly hear him cursing out Cartoon and Aaron.

After a while, the crew returned.

Toon said, "Listen up, y'all. This is King Neptune's thang!"

The crew members placed our hands on top of a cold, metal pipe. "And these are his pubes!" Toon continued.

I grimaced as someone placed a cold, wet, slimy mass of seaweed on my head.

Judging by the muffled laughter, the crew was truly enjoying Toon's prelude to door number seven.

Toon said, "Now, I want you homies to hold on tight an pleasure da king! C'mon, do it! Do it!"

I was sure I was going to heave chow.

The crew broke out into loud cheers as we reluctantly began to rub the cold, paint-chipped pipe.

"Orgasm! Orgasm!" they all shouted.

Toon said, "Gentlemen, I believe we have satisfaction emission!"

Somebody sprayed what felt like warm shaving cream all over my face. From the way Chuck's footsteps were shuffling backwards, they were probably trying to do the same to him.

Someone took off the blindfolds, and the crew converged on us, slapping us on our backs and congratulating us on making it through the seven doors.

I sank to my knees and tried to gather myself, sucking in air while holding my sides and rocking back and forth.

Chuck, also thoroughly exhausted, knelt down next to me. We

began wiping the foamy cream off our faces with the sweaty blindfolds.

The dark silhouettes of the crew came into focused. They were all grinning, shouting, laughing, and joking.

Devon said, "You guys all right?"

We both nodded.

"Okay. We moved your bedding out there on the beach. The rule is still no talking. We'll let you sleep in late tomorrow - and then we'll come and get you for Saturday morning breakfast."

For breakfast? I thought. *Wow! You mean for the paramedics!*

The crew trailed off toward the tents.

I found my sleeping bag about a hundred yards from Chuck's, kicked off my sneakers, and climbed into the bag, exhausted, sore, frustrated, and relieved.

The worst is over now, I thought. It didn't take long before the heavy surf pounding on the shore and the quiet glow of the cool starlit night lulled me to sleep.

The sun gleamed brightly on the wide stretch of beach. Foaming, brownish-green waves pounded a steady chorus along the rocky coastline. I shifted in my sleeping bag and grimaced in pain at the aching muscles in my shoulders and legs. I reached toward my peacoat pocket and pulled out my black-framed glasses. I slowly got out of the sleeping bag and began to stretch.

Taking inventory of various parts of my anatomy, I thought, *All present and accounted for, sir! Nothing that some Neosporin and the small jar of Tiger Balm in my duffel bag can't fix.*

Down the beach, Chuck was sitting on his sleeping bag and watching a catamaran with bright red, white, and blue spinnaker sails as it glided far out to sea. I wanted to holler to him; instead, I clenched my right fist, and held up a silent power sign.

Suddenly, Chuck started pointing behind me.

"Peace, brother!" Toon said.

I stiffly turned around and nodded a hesitant hello.

Apparently, Toon had already motioned for Chuck to come over. "I just wanted to apologize for putting the hurt to y'all last night. Guess I had some unresolved issues that needed to be liberated."

The unsympathetic look in my eyes apparently made Toon a little uneasy. Also, trying hard not to laugh, I noticed that Cartoon talked as if his jaw hurt.

Toon continued, "So, well, uh, looky here, why don't you guys bring your stuff on up to the tent, wash up, and get ready for breakfast. You are going to need to be full strength to power through the rest of the day. Be cool now, lil' bros!" He smiled, turned, and walked off.

I thought, *Well, I'll be damned! He actually talked to us in a civil manner!*

Everything was ready for us when we sat down at the redwood picnic table. I glanced at my plate and thought I was going to vomit before it was over.

Chuck gave me a friendly nudge with his right elbow and followed it up with his best Cheshire cat grin.

I figured I might as well give the *soup sandwich* looking breakfast a try. *It's probably against the law for them to poison us.* I started stirring the red and green grits. The crew prepared the concoction in such a way that the end product looked a lot like someone had just experienced a serious case of Montezuma's revenge. I decided to take a sip of the green-tinted cocoa. However, it was clear that someone had sprinkled salt into what should have been a sweet-tasting brew. I pretended to accidently spill the contents of the tin cup all over the picnic table.

Chuck tilted his head toward me and stared.

"Ain't no actions like that, lil' brother!" Aaron set the tin cup upright, handed me some paper towels, and refilled the tin cup. This time, the cup was filled minus the offending granules from the salt container.

Chuck had already finished his plate and was asking for seconds. I pushed the fish eye from out of the center of my red-tinted scrambled eggs. I tried my best to ignore the green and purple sausage.

"C'mon, Joe! Eat up!" the crew urged jokingly.

I slowly chewed and swallowed a warm piece of green flapjack and then flushed it down with a sip of hot cocoa.

"At your service, my man!" Toon handed me several pieces of toilet tissue that were intended to serve as napkins.

The crew shared a good laugh.

It took a while, but we finally ate enough to please the crew members. They let out a series of loud cheers.

Toon was the first to approach me with a high-five salute.

Devon ordered the entire crew to help with the cleanup detail.

After everything had been inspected, he motioned for Chuck and me to come over. He was sitting with the skipper, who was sipping black coffee from a large tin mug.

"All right lil' bros," Devon said. "You're in now. And we're very proud to have you on board the *Dolphin*. The skipper here was telling me you can start attending Sea Explorer meetings next week. And if you meet the requirements set for you during training sessions, it'll be time to get your *blues buddies* (dress whites and dress blues) together for San Diego rendezvous duty in November."

Devon added, "Oh, and Joe, with your small frame, you might make a good candidate for the whaleboat coxswain position."

We smiled at the prospect of competing in the fall rendezvous in San Diego.

Devon said, "Rendezvous training will commence at 1300. From here on, you can talk. By the way, seeing as it's only 0900 now, I figure you can spend the rest of the morning doing your own thing! You dig?"

Both of us let out a rather hoarse hurrah and were surprised to hear the sound of our own voices again. Then we took off down the beach toward the sabot-holding area.

A sabot is a sailing dinghy no more than eight feet long that is sailed and raced singlehandedly. The sailing and racing were usually done by young sailors in various places around the world. Sailing and racing was what I fully intended to do that day.

"They're fine young men, Devon," the skipper commented.

"Right on, Skipper, sir!" Devon replied. "And they've got more spirit and drive than I've seen in a long time!"

We laughed as we jogged around the last tent at the end of the row.

Down on the beach, Chip—a tall, thin, suntanned lifeguard with medium- length brown hair—was talking with a small group of us. He went over safe sailing rules, sabot components, and other

72

requirements that needed to be addressed before sailing privileges would be granted. The first major requirement prior to sailing was proof of swimming ability. Each member of the small group, using the buddy system, had to swim half a mile out to the suspended buoy and then return to shore.

Toon ran toward the gathering and said, "Count me in. I have dibs on Joe." Running toward the water, he shouted, "Joe, last man to the buoy and back will be on call to *embrace the suck* - dishwashing duty for the remainder of the weekend!"

I shrugged, tilted my head slightly to the left, and spread my arms toward Chip.

Chip nodded for me to follow Toon.

I ran out into the surf, and it wasn't long before I began to close the gap between us. Since I was the stronger swimmer, I swam in Toon's wake for the majority of the journey. Eventually, we came within ten feet of the bobbing, barnacle-encrusted buoy.

"That's close enough," I said while treading water. "The lifeguard didn't say anything about touching the buoy." In fact, getting close enough to actually touch the wave-impacted, moving buoy could be rather dangerous. We reversed course and began our swim back to shore.

Toon chose to start the return leg first.

A quarter of the way into the return route, Toon started calling for help. Apparently, he had gotten swept up in a stretch of choppy water. The turbulence was probably the result of the meeting of currents or an abrupt change in depth.

Chip had warned us that the atmospheric river might have led to breaks in the sandbars. The breaks on the bottom of the ocean floor could lead to riptide currents. However, Toon's late arrival to the briefing meant he failed to receive the full benefit of the how-to-survive-a-riptide memo.

Toon had completely forgotten the most important rule for surviving a rip current: Do not fight the pull of the rip tide by trying to swim back to shore against the resultant current. Instead, try to stay calm and relax to conserve energy. Even if you allow the current to pull you out to sea, it will generally subside fifty or a hundred yards from shore. You could also swim parallel to the shore for about a hundred feet to escape the current.

We were too far out for Chip to reach Toon in a timely manner via the boogie board. I merged into the turbulence and took advantage of its natural power. My goal was to let the tide do what it does best and hitch a ride to Toon.

About a hundred yards from shore, Toon was waving his arms frantically in the air.

I stretched my left arm across Toon's chest and using alternating side- arm strokes and scissor kicks, I began to pull him at an angle away from the current and toward the shore. I continued the movements for about twenty-five yards.

Judging from the frequent bouts of coughing, it was clear that Toon had ingested a lot of sea water. He was exhausted from trying to swim against the rip current. "Joe, Joe, I can't make it."

The distress cry and my subsequent reaction were eerily similar to my brother's Cabrillo Beach predicament last summer. Matching the procedures followed for Bob, I rotated Toon on his back and instructed him to place his hands on my shoulders. By using the tired swimmer maneuver, I was able to use alternating breast and frog kick strokes to propel him back toward shore.

About thirty yards later, Toon regained some of his strength. He said, "Okay! Okay, man! I got this. I think I can make it."

I released him, and Toon began to freestyle back toward the shore under his own power.

Out of an abundance of caution—and to ensure that no new episodes of distress occurred—I continued to swim in the wake of his kicks.

Toon was able to reach the shore first, and I could see the dismay and concern on Chip's face. "I saw what happened out there. However, as far as I am concerned, you both passed the swimming test."

Toon turned to me and said, "Thanks, man. And by the way, you can forget about what I said before, you know, about the dishwashing detail and all." Toon had said many things the past few days that were so far out of line that they made the dishwashing reference seem rather tame in comparison. However, if nothing else, the initiation experience taught me that, in life, there are going to be some people who just don't like you.

Perhaps those people are just haters by nature—or maybe they bear some sort of deep psychological scars. Perhaps they decided to target you as the recipient of their personal bias. At any rate, there will be times when you just have to take your momentary victories and move on.

I pulled the sabot from the sandy shoreline into the water and boarded. I then shifted the rudder, and nosed the vessel into a starboard tact.

Chuck glided by along a parallel tact.

I shouted, "You know, that was a hell of an initiation!"

"You ain't jiving!" Chuck replied. "For a while there, I thought I wasn't gonna make it!

"Really?" I added. "Just wait till it's our turn to initiate new recruits. ...hopefully we'll be a lot more merciful in our actions."

"I hear you, brother!" Chuck replied.

Similar to my propensity for writing in a journal, Chuck and his transistor radio were almost inseparable. He even listened to it during 880-yard time trials. Apparently, the jams helped calm him down before and after each heat.

At any rate, in an apparent gesture of brotherhood, Chuck decided to loan the radio to me for a short while. The gesture, I thought, was Chuck's way of telling me he was my lifetime wingman and would *always have my 6. The feeling was mutual.*

I only had one day left to make the most of what I had initially envisioned to be a relaxing weekend retreat. Surely, there would be smooth sailing into the summer of 1965 graduation. Afterward, thechallenges of college await. Smiling to myself, I thought, *I hope no new traumatic episodes are in store for me before college.*

So, with the volume turned up to the sound of the Vince Guaraldi Trio's "Cast Your Fate to the Wind," the eight-foot, single-sail launch cut smoothly through the murky, greenish-brown waters. The preliminary checklist of mast, rudder, leeboard, and sail was completed. Rolling waves lapped against the sides of the vessel.

The row of military tents and the long stretch of rocky breakwater faded away to the aft. And as the mainsail gathered wind, the craft gently glided across the glistening waters of Cabrillo Beach.

Chapter 3

Reflecting on the period prior to college, I recall watching, along with my family, the May 11, 1963, telecasts of the bombings and riots in Birmingham, Alabama. I was fifteen years old at the time. I also recall viewing coverage of the August 28, 1963, March on Washington. The latter event culminated in the famous "I Have a Dream" speech by the Reverend Martin Luther King Jr.

I celebrated my sixteenth birthday in November 1963. Earlier that milestone year, I had a second opportunity to witness a fleeting moment in history. On Monday, May 27, 1963, I accompanied my mother to an event held in Bovard Auditorium on the First Southern University campus. Reverend King was the keynote speaker at the affair. In addition to providing a preview of several themes reflected in the "I Have a Dream" speech, Dr. King said, "Injustice anywhere is a threat to justice everywhere." That was not my first-time seeing Dr. King in person. He had once made an unannounced, unscheduled visit to Sunday services at Neighborhood Community Church. I joined Neighborhood Community Church at age five when my family moved to the East Side from the Rose Hills Projects.

As it turned out, John—one of my future college classmates—was also present for Dr. King's speech. Apparently, his father (a well-known religious and civic leader) and the Rev. Wyatt Tee Walker (top assistant to Rev. Martin Luther King) assisted in organizing the event. John's father also worked with the Los Angeles NAACP and the Southern Christian Leadership Conference. He became the treasurer of the Western Christian Leadership Conference in the late 1950s. In 1961, John's father chaired two of the most important civil rights movement events in Los Angeles: the April 1961 and June 1961 Freedom Rallies.

As a test of President John F. Kennedy's support of civil rights, the Congress of Racial Equality (CORE) planned a Journey of Reconciliation. The Freedom Ride consisted of interracial groups boarding buses destined for the South. At rest stops, Whites would go into Black-only areas, and Blacks would go into White-only areas.

Inside Bovard Auditorium, my mother and I selected aisle seats that were about halfway down in the center section. After the conclusion of the speech on the First Southern University campus, I caught a glimpse of John as his family followed Dr. King and his entourage up the aisle.

In the summer of 1965, I reflected on the tsunami of goals I set in the fall of 1964. Some of the goals appeared to be almost insurmountable. Sometimes in life, things just seem to work out.

For example, I did achieve my academic goal of improving my overall GPA. As a result of that improvement, I was valedictorian of TJH.

The White principal told me that he didn't believe in the policy of identifying a single person as the class valedictorian. However, if he were to select a valedictorian for the class, it would have been me. The awards listed next to my name in the June 17, 1965, TJH graduation program included Ephebians, the principal's award, the faculty award of achievement, the science departmental award, and the math departmental award.

However, things didn't work out as well for bettering my time in the two-hundred-yard individual medley, the hundred-yard breast stroke, and the relays. For a variety of reasons, my flip-turning in the Southern League Olympic-sized, indoor pools—in contrast to the more modest Twenty-Eighth Street YMCA pool—was still a work in progress.

I joined the *Dolphin* crew at the San Diego rendezvous in November. And, owing to the cumulative performance of the drill, swimming, whaleboat, scuttlebutt, and breaches buoy teams, the 182 *Dolphins* were awarded an overall score of whaleboat, which was just one level below a cutter. I was the coxswain on the *Dolphin* whaleboat crew.

I also succeeded in gaining acceptance and financial aid offers from the UCBP, a private college in Clareville, California, and one of the Historically Black Colleges (HBCU) in Georgia. Of the three offers, and as a result of a prioritized list of criteria, I selected the First Private College in Clareville (PC1).

Clareville was located among lemon and orange groves at the foot of the San Gabriel Mountains. The college was sometimes referred to as the Harvard of the West Coast. It was a liberal arts college with a total enrollment of more than seven hundred students. Freeways, highways, railroads, and buses led to the Los Angeles Civic Center thirty-five miles to the west.

Quite a few of the students who matriculated to the rather Conservative Republican setting came from private prep schools. Since I was raised with a liberal Democratic upbringing and hailed from a predominantly Black, inner- city public high school, a whole new set of challenges lay before me. Foremost among those challenges would be to gain acceptance and financial aid offers from medical schools such as the University of California at the Blue Pacific (UCBP), First Southern, and an HBCU medical school on the East Coast.

The peer pressure to score a date for the spring 1965 prom proved to be formidable. After two or three rejections, things, as the elders might say, didn't look good for the home team.

My close friend, Ava, occasionally shouted, "A raisin in the sun," as I walked by. Perhaps she was referencing the play by Lorraine Hansberry or was drawing a parallel to a poem by Langston Hughes titled "Dream Deferred." At any rate, Ava shared that contribution, with what seemed like the entire TJH Democrat student body— sometimes from two hundred yards away.

I tried to pretend I didn't hear her once, and I just kept onwalking. The uniqueness of her salutation gained the attention of all who were within hearing range. Many of them laughed and looked around with puzzled expressions. Ava shouted, "Joseph Harris, you know you hear me calling you! You better stop ignoring me—with your *high saditti* self!" The follow-up play-by-play commentary generally elicited laughter from anyone within hearing range.

She likened my ebony complexion to a raisin in the sun, and, according to her, I was an *uppity* GG to boot. Since all of this drama unfolded in an open area of campus, even the metal-framed wooden lunch benches failed to provide a sufficient hiding place for me.

However, one day, I offered to walk Ava home from TJH. Apparently, she noticed that I didn't seem to be my usual upbeat self. She asked, "Joe, why are you acting so *blasé*?"

I explained that I was experiencing difficulty getting a date for the prom.

"Well, Joe, you didn't ask me," she said softly.

The shock on my face must have been akin to the look of surprise on Einstein's countenance when he came up with the theory of relativity. I said, "You?"

Recovering from my momentary brain freeze, I asked Ava if she would go to the prom with me, and she graciously accepted. And just like that, I sighed. A seemingly unsurmountable obstacle had been vanquished.

In the fall of 1964, most of the girls I was interested in taking to the prom were already going steady or were hooked up. I subconsciously vowed to try to turn my luck around. In the spring of 1965 I, along with about twenty other students, accepted an invitation to a weekend retreat at Camp Hess Kramer in Malibu. The camp was perched 750 feet above sea level and nestled in Little Sycamore Canyon between the Santa Monica Mountains and the Pacific Ocean.

On that trip, the romance stars seemed to properly align. I just happened to take a seat on the bus next to a girl who had just graduated from Manual Arts High, and she had been invited on the trip by her aunt. Her aunt just happened to be my favorite algebra instructor.

The young lady and I hit it off. There were long walks through the Malibu foothills and evening dances under a slowly spinning, glittering ballroom globe. She even made sitting next to her during the breakfast, lunch, and dinner hours special.

I had truly fond memories of doing the Slow Jerk to a particular R & B hit. The song was so popular that, upon returning to TJH, it seemed to permeate the airwaves. The song was "When I Am Gone" by Brenda Holloway.

Comments from several well-intentioned classmates confirmed what I already knew: I had definitely developed a monster gorilla crush on her. After the whirlwind romantic weekend, I began to sketch a draft of a poem in my journal.

First Love

I thought I knew life, as I recall,
But when I met you, I realized,
That I didn't know life at all

Ours was a world of make-believe,
Ours was a world of fantasy,
I was young, and you my first love,
The world became our playground,
Crowned by a halo of blue skies above

The oceans, the forests, naïve bliss,
A constellation of heavenly stars,
A midnight slow dance, your soft dress,
Eternity's gift of a gentle caress

I remember your smile,
So full of warmth and affection,
Your smooth cream-colored complexion,
Your soulful brown eyes,
And gently curling dark-brown hair,
Your loving friendship,
So treasured, so rare

The fireside, and its flickering glow,
The candlelight and lover's row,
The fragrant aroma of soft perfume,
An awkward kiss, at the cabin door to your room,

I recall your gleeful laughter,
Splashing waves, windy fir-lined cliffs,
Your favorite dish,
Grassy slopes, and a lover's wish

That these few days would never end,
That I would somehow become
Something more than, "just a friend"

And I remember my heart's anguished fall,
When we had to part,
For reasons I can never recall,
Except that I was too young to understand,
Why first love, and endless love,
Might never, go hand in hand

I asked the young lady to attend the spring prom, and she graciously declined. Her main reasons for rejecting the invitation were that she had just attended her own Manual Arts Prom in the fall of 1964, and she was taking courses at First City College. She felt like attending a high school prom would be a step backward for her. She ended the conversation by saying, "Well, good luck in finding a date to the prom."

I only made one telephone call to her after returning from Camp Hess Kramer. Perhaps I read too much into her tone and delivery during that conversation. Even though I was raised in a household full of women, I seemed to experience difficulty interpreting the mixed messages they sometimes sent.

After hanging up the telephone, I felt a deep-seated, empty feeling of loss because she really didn't leave the door open for future interactions. It didn't help that the painful feelings of loss seemed to spike every time I heard "When I Am Gone"

That song filled the airwaves everywhere I went. The lyrics streamed from portable radios during the lunch hour in the cafeteria. Like coats of paint on a wall, each time I heard the haunting lyrics, I got multiple layers of the blues. The song sometimes prompted what might be perceived by some as an unmanly desire to cry. As if a bad case of the blues wasn't enough, "Going Out of My Head" by Little Anthony and the Imperials was also trending at the time.

As my mother once said, "you're not the only one who goes through these things, why do you think there are so many love songs?"

I was no stranger to heartache, although I was too young to understand what I was experiencing. Her name was Onnette Henry. The Henry family was temporarily staying with their grandmother next door to me on Forty- Eighth Street. Onnette was slender with a honey-brown complexion, and she sometimes wore her hair pulled back in a tight medium-length ponytail. Even though she was only a month older, Onnette already stood about an inch taller. I often wondered if I would ever catch up with her height. In many ways, interacting with her was a preview of what some star athletes must have experienced when they dated taller supermodels.

When I was around ten years old, Onnette's parents decided to purchase a home on one of the avenues. The new, single-story wood-framed house was located in a picturesque middle-class neighborhood on the Westside of Los Angeles

On the afternoon prior to moving day, I was playing with my plastic soldiers on the front porch. Onnette, wearing a Girl Scout jade green dress with a dark brown vest, walked up to the porch. I felt a little embarrassed, if not annoyed, at being caught with the toy soldiers.

However, she appeared to ignore my rather childish preoccupation. She said, "I guess you heard that we are moving."

I responded, "Yes, I heard."

She said, "Well, since I will be living way across town on the Westside, and you will be here on the Eastside, don't you think we should start seeing other people?"

Her question definitely caught me off guard. I hadn't given much thought to the need to see someone else owing to her pending move. In retrospect, I suspect close girlfriends had been telling her about all the so-called cute boys who resided on the Westside.

In my bewilderment, I didn't respond very well to her unexpected inquiry. I stood up abruptly and said, "I don't care!"

My response mirrored Rhett Butler's famous quote: "Frankly, my dear, I don't give a damn."

From the beginning, falling in love with Onnette just seemed natural. Although words of love were never really spoken, my feelings toward her surged like the magnetic pull of the moon on the ocean's tides—and she reciprocated those emotions with an almost equal force of gravity. Although those passionate feelings never translated into words of commitment, by all accounts, Onnette was my girl. In retrospect, owing to my lack of experience, I believe my relationship-maintenance skills could have been greatly improved.

The sound of Onnette's laughter truly illuminated my world. On top of that, she had the persona of one who was blessed with an abundance of tenderness and affection. It certainly was not my intention to hurt her. However, in reaction to my response, I did notice a look of disappointment on her face.

What transpired that day could simply have been an unfortunate misunderstanding. I couldn't tell if she was asking for a clean break because she was moving to a more upscale neighborhood and wanted to be open to new experiences and new people or if she was testing me for further validation of our existing relationship. I should not have assumed she was asking for the former if there was the slightest hope that we still had a chance.

If my toy soldiers could speak, I suspect one of them would have stepped forward and said, "Permission to speak freely Sir? I believe you just experienced what in the military would be termed a *preemptive dump!*"

If the impromptu inquiry was her way of signaling a desire for a parting of the ways, I should have seized this truly touching moment to give her a proper goodbye kiss. One thing was clear, Onnette may have been only a month older, but she was already leap years ahead of me on the maturity spectrum.

Perhaps there was some truth to a statement made by my future barber. Bill was the owner of the Revolution Barber Shop on East Vernon Avenue near Central Avenue. Addressing a predicament I found myself in with a future girlfriend, Bill once said, "Damn, Joe man, and all this time I thought you was different. But after listening to what you just said you told her, I can see you just like the rest of us. You just a no-good GG!"

With Onnette, I prefer to think I was unknowingly following the lead from a classic expression that some might attribute to the elders: "If you love someone, set them free. If they come back, they're yours."

I soon realized that—from a coulda, woulda, shoulda perspective—I could have done a much better job of providing practical solutions to this rather sensitive dilemma. A one-way visit to Onnette at the new address would have been as simple as a transfer-free, three-mile bus ride on East Vernon Avenue. Frequent telephone calls can also reduce the distance between two parties who have been separated.

As fate would have it, it didn't take long before Onnette was able to secure a commitment from someone else in her new school. According to my sister, he was "really cute."

I only had myself to blame for that unfortunate outcome. In foolishly opening the door and giving her a green light to walk, I inadvertently granted him an all-access pass. That opening enabled him to bust an unopposed move on her. Of course, relationship experts would probably say, "No one can be taken who doesn't want to be."

I thought, perhaps erroneously, that the feelings I had for her but could never find the words to express—were not mutually shared after all. And in the long run, the experience of breaking up was an early lesson in love for me.

It is possible that our relationship could have survived a three-mile separation, but both of us would have needed to be equally committed. And no matter what prompted her to raise that initial question, I had missed a golden opportunity to reassure her of my true feelings.

Once the Henry family was situated in their new setting, my mother drove Bob, Lynette, and me for an afternoon housewarming visit.

At the end of the evening, as we were departing, Lynette asked, "So, how's the new boyfriend, Onnette?"

Onnette, visibly embarrassed, replied, "Oh, he's fine, just fine."

Lynette had a way of bringing up topics that made me feel uncomfortable. On this occasion, she just couldn't pass up a golden opportunity to stir up the pot.

When Onnette asked me that question, it was time to put aside the toy soldiers and man up. In retrospect, perhaps her inquiry that day was my big chance to bypass decades of assorted variations of romantic foreplay. Examples of the latter included playing games, mixed messages, bad-habit dates, long dates, Sugar Daddy dates, and women jungle gymming, hanging ten, burning rubber, performing reverse somersaults in the pike position, and executing emotional dislocates and in-locates on me.

Relationships are like a gigantic game of musical chairs. At some point, in what could turn out as a lifetime quest, the music stops—and someone generally gets left without a partner.

Perhaps the breakup scenario was a preview of what I would experience in spades throughout my life. It goes without saying that relationships can be fragile and are often fluid in nature. Similar to the weather, whenever a status update of my partner's feelings toward me is required, sometimes the best anyone can do is take a snapshot at a particular point in time.

Consider the effect of the moon on the rising and falling of the tides. The moon does have primary responsibility for the ebb and flow of the tides. However, in addition to the moon, the amplitude of the tides and their fluctuations over time are also dependent upon the sun, the shape of the beach, the larger coastline, the angle of the seabed leading up to land, the prevailing ocean currents, and the winds.

It is possible that more than one variable may have prompted Onnette to inquire about a possible breakup. And the sum total of those variables may have simply overwhelmed the innocent passion that had initially drawn us to each other.

In November 1960 I celebrated my thirteenth birthday. Earlier that milestone year I had my first opportunity to witness a fleeting moment in history. The event occurred about six months after my brother and I returned from Galena Park, Texas. It was the beginning of my eight-grade year at Carver Jr. High. That's when I, along with a small gathering of students, pressed up against the wire mesh fence bordering Vernon Avenue and waved at a passing motorcade.

The *entourage* was carrying John F. Kennedy and Jackie Kennedy. They were en route to a speaking engagement at the Elks Auditorium on Central Avenue. It was in the 1960 United States presidential election, that John F. Kennedy defeated incumbent Vice President Richard Nixon to become the 35th President of the United States. John F. Kennedy's assassination occurred in November 1963. At the time he was riding in a motorcade in Dealey Plaza, Dallas, Texas with his wife Jackie.

In 1961, about nine months after my brother and I returned from Galena Park, Texas an event occurred that will be forever etched in my memory. The day started as a routine Saturday morning complete with Quaker Oats, raisin bread toast, and orange juice. There was an unexpected ring at the front door, and through the open mini blinds that draped the glass in the heavy walnut door, I saw that it was one of my neighborhood running buddies. He was also one of my former South Park Little League Baseball teammates. My friend was accompanied by his younger brother and cousin. The trio stayed in a home about halfway down the block on Forty-Eighth Street.

With a sad look on his face, my friend informed me that several members of the Henry family were now deceased. After adding a few brief details, he and his party turned and headed down the front porch steps toward the sidewalk. I was overwhelmed and stunned by the appalling news. The gauntlet of emotions I experienced ranged from shock to panic to utter disbelief. In response to my friend's veiled reference to a survivor, I must have dialed Onnette's telephone number at least ten times. Secretly, if not selfishly, I hoped that she was one of the survivors. However, there was no answer. And as the day progressed, the regrettable saga began to unfold.

Accounts from different news sources provided several variations of the sequence of events during the early morning hours of Friday, February 24, 1961. These sources also set forth contrasting theories regarding factors that may have contributed to the stepfather's apparent psychological meltdown. A few of the headlines from local newspapers that covered this extremely unfortunate tragedy are shown below.

Husband strangles wife, two children
(February 24, 1961), *Los Angeles Mirror*

Jealousy hinted in triple slaying
(March 2, 1961), *Los Angeles Sentinel*

Mother, 2 tots strangled
(February 24, 1961), *Herald Express*

In the past, I noticed quite a few romantic movies that portrayed childhood sweethearts who later married. I am also aware that some Hollywood movies have been released on DVD with alternate endings. Every now and then, I find myself thinking about the tragic ending to Onnette's precious young life. I find a degree of solace in a multiverse theory termed string theory. In accordance with string theory, our universe is not the only one. To the contrary, many universes exist parallel to each other.

These distinct universes within the multiverse are termed parallel universes. We both believed in the concept of heaven and its associated afterlife. However, I understand that there are individuals in the world who do not share in this belief. If so, then perhaps they will find comfort in knowing that string theory could provide a pathway to the door that separates tragedy in one dimension from continued existence in an alternate world.

"If you love someone, set them free. If they come back they're yours." Unfortunately, I never had the opportunity to see if the saying by the elders would come true. I never had a chance to find out whether or not love would lead Onnette home in time for the prom or to experience our undergraduate and/or graduate years together. God willing, perhaps as husband and wife, we could have raised a family and shared our twilight years together.

Not long after the Henry family tragedy, and owing to her pending retirement, the landlord for the Forty-Eighth Street rental property decided to sell. My mother relocated our family to a rental that was just two blocks away on Forty-Sixth Street.

For quite a few years, in what can only be described as a rather immature response to Onnette's sincere inquiry, I experienced my fair share of flirtations and long dates. However, it wasn't until twelve years later, at age twenty-two, that I would be blessed with another true girlfriend.

I met a young lady who seemed destined to be the next big thing in my life. What began as a romantic spark quickly ignited into a passionate flame. Complete with a radiant smile and infectious laughter, she had a natural touch for luring me out of my sometimes-studious cocoon.

During the summer of 1970, I invited a friend, who was enrolled in the University of California at the Blue Pacific (UCBP) Nursing School, for a swim at my seven-bedroom, five-bath home. The friend, who was already engaged at the time, asked if she could bring one of her close girlfriends. And that close girlfriend turned out to be someone I would later come to view as the love of my life.

Actually, the sprawling home did not belong to me or my family. To the contrary, it was left in my care by John's mother. John and I graduated together from the First Private College in the spring of 1969. After graduating, he left the West Coast to pursue graduate studies on the East Coast. His mother decided to take a three-month tour of Europe and perceived me to be a responsible and trustworthy house sitter. So, my romantic interlude with the future love of my life began during the summer that preceded my second year of medical school.

Ironically, the first time I picked her up for a date at a Westside residence, I discovered, to my surprise, that her family's home was on the same street, and only a few blocks south, of the Henry's former residence. When I mentioned the coincidence between her address and the Henry's former location, she acknowledged familiarity with that long-ago tragedy.

She also recalled the Henry's single-story wood-framed home. She remembered how its exterior was once adorned with a fresh coat of white paint, how its well-manicured, expansive green lawn seemed to flow toward the sidewalk, and how it looked after Onnette's stepfather set it ablaze that fateful morning.

At times, Lynette was my in-house sounding board and worst critic. This was a far cry from the nemesis role she sometimes played when I was six years old. Back then, on two different occasions, she became irritated with me for doing what I did best: making an all around nuisance of myself. And so, without warning, her response was to slam a wicked right hook into my gut. Her actions prompted me to drop to the floor, knot up in a ball, and gasp for air. In that moment, it seemed like my entire life flashed before my eyes. It was a short film clip.

And so, while experiencing what felt like a near-death moment I thought, *How cruel. Surely the punishment didn't fit the crime. I mean, she didn't even give me time to put my hands on my hips and flex my stomach muscles in the classic Superman pose.*

I recall Lynette saying, "You better not tell mother!" Then she turned and walked out of the room leaving me there windless and gasping for air.

Following the second episode, I asked my mother for an exception to her long-standing policy that men should never hit women. *Because there was a woman I wanted to send to the moon real bad!* Although the latter policy remained in place, owing to my mother's swift intervention, this particular display of over-the-top behavior from Lynette came to an abrupt end.

During my teenage years and into my early twenties, Lynette assumed the role of my Lipton's orange pekoe tea drinking buddy. So, while sharing a tea bag, I mentioned the young lady from Camp Hess Kramer reasons for declining the invitation to the TJH prom. Man, did I get an earful! Lynette was simply not one to mince words.

"First of all," she said, "when a girl really wants to do something, she will. I mean, some of those other girls you asked said they couldn't go because they didn't have a dress to wear. Well, when a girl really wants to go to the prom, the dress will not be a problem—even if her mother has to make it herself." Our mother had spoiled her by having a Singer sewing machine and proven skills as a seamstress. Our mom also had been trained in furniture upholstery.

The gold satin form-fitting dress that Ava wore on prom night was simply stunning. And the white orchid corsage that Lynette selected definitely complemented and supplemented her attire. In addition to escorting a vision of beauty, the entire evening turned out to be nothing short of magical. And as for not having a driver's license, that problem was easily addressed. A more senior member of the Troop 182 Sea Explorer Unit informed me he was taking one of my classmates to the prom. And given that he had a driver's license, he agreed to pick us up for a two-couple outing.

Despite my inability to properly insert the removable black buttons in the ruffled dress shirt, I somehow managed to clean up a little. So, adorned in a white tuxedo jacket, black patent leather shoes, and tight black dress pants that were slightly on the flood, I made my prom debut. The prom was held in the TJH women's gymnasium.

Following the prom, we drove to the Ambassador Hotel on Wilshire Boulevard near Crenshaw. Entering the hotel we walked down a long hallway towards the Coconut Grove nightclub. We were then seated at a round lounge table that was draped by a white table cloth. Shortly thereafter, a three-course meal was served that included steak and lobster.

The evening's entertainment featured *The Fancy Miss Nancy.* and, it seemed like Nancy Wilson performed all of my favorite hits: "Hello, Young Lovers," "Guess Who I Saw Today," "You Can Have Him," "How Glad I Am," "Our Day Will Come," "The Good Life," "Go Away Little Boy," "Don't Take Your Love From Me," "The Music That Makes Me Dance," and "One-Note Samba."

On a late Sunday afternoon in the early nineties, I encountered Ms. Wilson in the lobby of a Los Angeles area venue. One of her two daughters had just completed a walk down the runway of a fashion show. I shared with Nancy the truly memorable impression her 1965 performance at the Coconut Grove nightclub had on my life. Her only comment was *The Coconut Grove! Ooh! Honey don't tell that to anyone else, you are dating me!*

Of course, I asked her to autograph my program, and she graciously complied. As passer byes began to exit the main forum, they began to navigate towards Ms. Wilson. That's when Nancy asked if she could borrow my pen to accommodate the additional signature requests. Shortly thereafter, I made my way through the growing crowd towards the exit. I paused briefly to glance back at Nancy, surrounded by adoring fans, and signing autographs with my black ink pen.

Following the Coconut Grove, it was on to the after-prom party, which was held across town. Probably related to years of packing items for Boy Scout and Sea Explorer outings, I carried a toothbrush in my tuxedo pocket. However, I later learned that the majority of the crowd relied on Wrigley's and Dentyne chewing gum to power them through the night and into the early morning hours.

Although I was still quite immature at the time, I thought, *Thank Goodness I had enough common sense to not share my feelings for my Camp Hess Kramer companion with Ava.* Over the years, I'd learned that when a woman sort of, kind of likes you, the last thing you want to do is bring up another woman. Especially if you still have a thing for that other woman even though, from your perspective, she done you wrong.

I may have been cycling through the various stages of a major heartbreak, but I wisely accepted the gift that Ava so kindly offered. Overall, we both had a really good time at the prom, the Coconut Grove, and the after-prom party. *Perhaps this might be the way things will happen in the distant future—when it's time for me to propose marriage. Maybe it will be the young lady who actually shatters the impenetrable glass barrier.*

In November 1965 I turned eighteen years old. Malcolm X's assassination occurred earlier that milestone year. I, along with my family, watched the news coverage of his passing. The shooting took place while he was speaking at a rally of the Organization of Afro-American Unity (OAAU). The unfortunate tragedy unfolded at the Audubon Ballroom in New York City. Malcolm X was a charismatic speaker as well as a disciplined leader. He quickly rose to prominence through his affiliation with the Nation of Islam.

In addition to the above, the Voting Rights Act passed in 1965. Less than a week after the Selma-to-Montgomery marchers experienced beatings with many bloodied, by Alabama state troopers, President Lyndon B. Johnson addressed a joint session of Congress. His goal was to enact federal legislation designed to safeguard the voting rights of African-Americans. Coupled with the Civil Rights Act of 1964, the Voting Rights Act represented one of the most expansive pieces of civil rights legislation in American history.

June and July 1965 zipped by in a blur. I took a trigonometry course at First City College. In many ways, that course was a self-imposed make up for the C I received in trigonometry at TJH. At the college level, I earned a final grade of A.

I received a summer internship at the UCBP Medical Center. Ever since I was six years old, my mother had been performing duties in the UCBP Undergraduate Admissions Office. She processed undergraduate applications in that setting for almost fourteen years. Therefore, in addition to stimulating to-and-from travel conversations, I had a guaranteed ride to my internship.

I received a telephone call from Clay, one of my soon-to-be classmates at the First Private College (PC1). During that conversation, my future classmate convinced me to take a brief Evelyn Woods speed reading class. The evening speed reading class was offered in the Wilshire District near Crenshaw.

Once again, music provided a sanctuary from the ongoing pressures of getting ready for my first year of college. Car radios, home hi-fi systems, and storefronts everywhere seemed to fill the airwaves with pulsating, dramatic beats. A unique characteristic of the melodies, were their signature up-tempo, back beat, percussion and Southern-styled soul influence. Of course, to further enhance our listening pleasure, many of us preferred to bump the base. That rhythm often served as my personalized Hollywood-style soundtrack as I made my way to and from the UCBP Medical

Center. In the sweltering heat of the summer of 1965, it seemed like most inner-city residents turned their radio dials to KGFJ.

In the summer of 1965, the KGFJ playlist that seemed to reverberate throughout the very fabric of my persona included "I Can't Help Myself (Sugar Pie, Honey Bunch)" by the Four Tops, "(I Can't Get No) Satisfaction" by the Rolling Stones, "My Girl" by the Temptations, "Shotgun" by Junior Walker and the All-Stars, "Stop in the Name of Love" by the Supremes, "Yes, I'm Ready" by Barbara Mason, "Papa's Got a Brand-New Bag" by James Brown and the Famous Flames, "Nowhere to Run" by Martha and the Vandellas, "The Tracks of My Tears" by The Miracles, "It's the Same Old Song" by the Four Tops, "Ooo Baby" by the Miracles, and "How Sweet It Is (To Be Loved by You)" by Marvin Gaye.

One KGFJ disc jockey seemed to capture the spirit and pride and imagination of inner-city residents both young and old. His name was the Magnificent Montague. Whenever Montague was playing a record that inspired him, his listeners would follow suit. His format allowed listeners to call in and shout, "Burn!" on the air. Characteristically, the emotion in that DJ-versus-listener exchange seemed to reverberate with as much excitement as the array of artists in his playlist. Ironically, when rioters in Willowbrook started shouting "Burn, baby, burn!" during the 1965 uprising, they seemed to be echoing the most popular cry on rhythm-and blues radio.

On Wednesday, August 11, 1965 at 7:19 p.m., a series of events transpired that will be forever etched into local and national history books. The name I retroactively ascribe to those historical events is the Willowbrook Riots. I remember sitting in the living room of the family's upstairs Towne Avenue apartment that evening when the nine o'clock news came on. The telecasts seemed to reinforce information presented in the following *Los Angeles Times* articles:

95

**1000 riot in Los Angeles Routine arrest of 3 sparks
(name of community) melee; 8 blocks sealed off**
(August 12, 1965), *Los Angeles Times*

**McCurdy, J. and Berman, A. Many fires started;
75 reported injured in second violent night**
(August 13, 1965), *Los Angeles Times*

**Berman, A. Scores of fires rage unchecked,
damage exceeds 10 million**
(August 14, 1965), *Los Angeles Times*

**Berman, A. 21,000 troops police rage guerrilla war;
8 p.m. curfew invoked**
(August 15, 1965)*, Los Angeles Times*

**Jackson, B. and Berman, A. Policeman killed as fellow
officer's gun is fired accidently**
(August 16, 1965), *Los Angeles Times*

Jackson, B. and Berman, A. Isolated sniping reported
(August 17, 1965), *Los Angeles Times*

Thanks to the *Los Angeles Times* staff, excerpts from the full text of each of these articles are provided below (copyright 1965, *Los Angeles Times*, reprinted with permission). Following each narrative, the lead stories for mock evening news broadcasts are presented. The mock broadcasts are then followed by examples of comments that may have transpired as the Harris family viewed the various news reports.

**1000 riot in Los Angeles routine arrest of 3 sparks
(name of community) melee; 8 blocks sealed off**
(August 12, 1965) *Los Angeles Times*

An estimated 1,000 persons rioted in the [name of community] district Wednesday night and attacked police and motorists with rocks, bricks and bottles before some 100 officers attempted to quell the 5-hour melee by sealing off an eight-block area.

But the sporadic rioting continued early today as crowds of rock-throwing demonstrators broke through police lines while turning the area around 116th Street and Avalon into a scene of near chaos.

An undetermined number of persons was injured including at least twelve police officers and two newsmen. One officer was knocked from his motorcycle when hit by a brick and another was stabbed. A reporter was beaten in the back by a rioter.

Fifty Cars Damaged

At least ten persons were arrested in the rioting and at least 50 autos were reported damaged. A bus had nearly all of its windows knocked out.

A fire truck that answered a call of a burning auto, a television news unit was damaged by rocks and reportedly was unable to fulfill its mission.

About 9:30 p.m. police threw up barricades at 118th Street, San Pedro Street, Imperial Highway, and Stanford Street to keep motorists out of the area. Police set up a command post at Imperial and Avalon with patrol cars parked in a defensive circle.

But rioters continued to pelt police with flying objects and taunting calls. Several charges into the crowd by police with riot helmets and nightsticks dispersed rioters temporarily.

But shortly after midnight, one charge by about twenty officers touched off a hail of missiles and screams, the most riotous time of the evening.

Avalon Boulevard, which is lined mostly with apartments and homes in the area, was littered with debris. But few buildings were damaged.

Male Coanchor: Good evening all, I would like to update the series of developing events that have occurred since the first breaking news report at the seven o'clock hour. At 7:19 p.m. in Willowbrook, California, a California Highway Patrol motorcycle officer named Lee Minikus pulled over twenty-one-year-old Marquette Frye on suspicion of drunk driving. The officer, Minikus, was White. The suspect, Frye, was Black.

Female Coanchor: Apparently an altercation between the two occurred at Avalon Boulevard and 116th Street. As a result of that altercation, a crowd began to gather.

"'Good grief,' said Charlie Brown!" my mother commented.

"Well," I replied jokingly, "it appears that some people have a strange sense of what constitutes Wednesday night entertainment!"

"I think so," my mother commented in an amused tone. "It looks like these people think it's just another night to throw rocks at the cops!"

Lynette said, "This seems to be a lot more serious than just throwing rocks!"

"Well, I don't know about all that!" my mother replied.

Bob said, "It looks like somebody really pissed off these people!"

Out of curiosity, I picked up the remote and started scanning, the TV channels. It seemed like the coverage of the rioting was everywhere: Channel 2, Channel 4, Channel 7, Channel 9, and Channel 11. After viewing the sense of urgency portrayed by the broadcast journalists, it soon became clear to all of us that the events unfolding that evening would have far-reaching implications for South Central Los Angeles, as well as possible spill-over effects for the rest of the country.

On Thursday morning, August 12, 1965, my family decided to remain in the Towne Avenue apartment. The only outing my mother and I made was a trip to the local Ralphs supermarket for groceries. There was a sense of panic in the crowded store as shoppers scrambled to grab whatever items were left on the shelves. People were frantically stocking up on staples and bottled water as if a major storm was bearing down on South Central Los Angeles.

Store managers all along East Vernon Avenue were starting to board up their windows. Some owners even used cans of black spray-paint to write *Black-owned* on the outsides of their establishments. The heavy plywood boards covering storefront windows reminded me of images I had seen of seaside resorts just before the onslaught of a hurricane. Upon returning to the Towne Avenue apartment, I decided to investigate the various telecasts and L.A. newspapers. I was desperately trying to make sense of what was occurring.

The crowd that my family and I had observed on the news the night before had apparently viewed the altercation between the alleged drunk driver and the police as just another incident of racially motivated abuse by the police. It seemed like the riot was fueled by residents of Willowbrook who were embittered by years of economic and political isolation. They were disillusioned by years of racial injustices and political discrimination, but more specifically, they resented widespread inequalities in housing, education, and employment.

According to reports, the initial tactic employed by police was to seal off an eight-block area. Other reports indicated that stores had been looted and some buildings torched, while some Whites had been beaten. Of foremost concern were reports that shots had been fired by snipers allegedly targeting police, emergency rescue personnel, and firefighters.

And that's when I decided to use the creative approach called *poetic license* to try to climb into the minds of the rioters. My goal was not only to release the stress I felt from viewing the rapidly developing events, but to try to capture what some rioters might have been feeling. I started with drafts of a series of short poems collectively titled *Notes from an Angry Black Man.*

Elementary School

I was only four years old on a city playground

When I painfully scraped my knee against a jagged reality.

While cruelly pointing, Johnny Mosqueta

Viciously shouted, "Negra! Negra!"

My instincts flashed, my pride was offended,

And a triad of learned responses from my hot lungs rendered,

"%$@#!, #$@$%!, @#%@!!! su madre y tu padre!"*

Tightened fists, tensed arms, awaited his attack!

Reflex pounding, cool sweat flowing, couldn't hold him back!

Freestyling in a sea of angry foreign tongues,

I continued cursing and swinging as though my life on victory hung

I was tripped and kicked till the snot drooled from my nose,

And the humiliating tears of a never-to-be-yielded defeat

Unavoidably rolled down my burning black cheek.

Until the blurred vision of day became dearth and I choked,

And until the hot dusty asphalt with my blood and tears was soaked,

I would continue swinging, kicking, cursing, and crying,

For I knew a sacred part of my human soul had shriveled
and lay dying.

Junior High School

Grinning, I crouched low in the movie-house seat,
Ashamed to see my African brothers hurling spears at the
White man's jeep,
Ashamed of their bright white eyes, black shining skin,
Ivory pale teeth, and uncivilized manner,
Embarrassed because my Negro buddy next to me had
Hollered out that their Bantu Chief was my father.

High School

Tan to caramel brown to bright white skin,
Skinny nose, blue, green, or hazel eyes with
Wavy black hair or reddish-blonde tints,
A narrow ass, fine shape, and thin smooth lips—
So, have the White man's values infiltrated
The Black woman's wide-set hips.
So, do we laugh at ash gray to black skin,
At wide noses, bright black eyes, coarse, kinky hair, and thick lips.
Who are we to judge the beauty of a race?
And who are we to conform to the White man's pace?

After dinner, my mother turned on the evening news. The thirty-two- inch color TV perched on a rolling stand in the living room. In order to keep abreast of current events, she decided to leave the TV on to cycle through one depressing news report after another. During the first hour of broadcasts, we all remained riveted to the TV screen. However, after the initial hour— possibly out of a psychological need for some sort of break from wave after wave of depressing images— each of us wandered out of the living room.

The images resembled a war-torn, ravaged country wrought with ceaseless strife. And those nightmarish images only served to trigger within each of us even deeper feelings of hopelessness and powerlessness.

During breaks, some of us migrated to the kitchen and used the wall- mounted phone to check on friends and family members. My mother sometimes chose to drag the main phone, extension cord and all, into the bathroom or her master bedroom. She was probably calling her sisters in Houston to let them know we were okay.

McCurdy, J. and Berman, A. Many fires started; 75 reported injured in second violent night.
(August 13, 1965) *Los Angeles Times*

An estimated 7,000 persons rioted Thursday night in the second day of violence in the (name of community) area as stores were looted and set afire, automobiles were destroyed and 75 persons were injured, including thirteen policemen and two firemen.

The 10,500-member 40th Armored Division of The National Guard was placed on standby alert by Gov. Brown and a 500-man brigade was ready to move in if needed.

Shotgun armed officers moved into a portion of the riot torn district shortly before midnight, dispersing many of the demonstrators.

Rioters were reportedly firing guns at policemen and civilians as bands of Negro youths and adults roamed the turbulent neighborhoods. Hundreds of householders telephoned police seeking protection.

Many Fires Burned Unchecked

Police said fires from markets and liquor stores, overturned cars and, debris were burning unchecked along Avalon Boulevard. between Imperial Highway and 120th Street.

Store windows were being smashed by rocks, and widespread looting was taking place, officers said.

Rifles and machetes were reported stolen from stores at 114th Street and Compton Boulevard. and 108th Street and Avalon Boulevard. There were reports that all stores on 103rd Street near Avalon were looted.

"We saw many people walking out of stores with loot piled high in their arms," one officer said.

Church Reported Fired

There was a confirmed report of a church and numerous buildings on fire at Imperial and Central Avenue.

Police estimated there would be a heavy toll of damage from the looting and fires.

Gas-filled bottles reportedly made into Molotov cocktails were being hurled into cars and crowds. And a number of motorists said they were dragged from their cars and beaten by groups of unruly Negroes.

The rioting spread to the Willowbrook district in county territory shortly before midnight when officers requested tear gas to control a crowd of some 300.

Three cars were reported overturned and police were being fired upon from the apartment houses at Imperial Highway and Parmelee Avenue.

Long-Ranged Tear Gas Guns Sent

Long-range tear gas guns were sent to the area, but permission was not immediately granted for their use.

Numerous automobiles were reported burning throughout the eight-block area and motorists who were beaten by the mobs sought sanctuary in nearby homes.

Fire trucks and ambulances were unable to enter the area to fight the fires and pick up the injured because of the danger from flying rocks, bricks and fire bombs.

The Fire Department and hospitals reported receipt of many false reports designed to lure vehicles into the riot area.

Male Coanchor: Good evening, all. On this Thursday, August 12, we continue with coverage of the series of events that have unfolded in the Willowbrook area of Los Angeles. In the way of a recap, it has been reported that an estimated seven thousand persons engaged in rioting in what is now a second day of violence. Stores in the Willowbrook area were looted and set afire. Also, automobiles were destroyed, and, at last count, seventy-five persons were injured, including thirteen policemen and two firemen.

Female Coanchor: Governor Edmund G. Brown has placed the 10,500-member Armored Division of the National Guard on standby alert. In addition, he has indicated that a five-hundred-man brigade is ready to move in if needed.

"Here we go again," I said.

"I think these people are just generally miserable," my mother replied.

"Looks like somebody gave the wrong answer to the question 'Is you is—or is you ain't my baby!' I replied.

The inappropriate example of subject and verb agreement prompted my mother to burst out in laughter while, almost simultaneously, waiving her right hand in the air.

"Oh, check out brother man!" I exclaimed.

"Looking like who done it? And please don't let it happen again!" my mother commented.

"As you might say, Mom, I think somebody messed around and found his last nerve!" I replied.

Lynette said, "This situation has clearly escalated to an entirely different level."

"Like I said," my mother commented, "when I was in the jury box for a gang-banger murder trial, one of the attorneys asked me if I had any preconceived notions. I replied, 'The way I see it, where there's smoke, there's fire!'"

"That explains why," I added, "the attorney walked up to the judge and whispered something."

"Yeah," my mother responded, "and the judge said the court would like to thank and excuse juror number two."

"You sure got out of that pretty!" I said.

"Let's just say I did my thing!" my mother replied.

We both laughed upon recalling how she managed to sidestep that situation.

"Rifles and machetes?" I said. "This situation has turned into an old-fashioned slave-ship rebellion!"

"I am going to tell you something," my mother said. "And I don't want you to repeat it to anybody."

I nodded, indicating I would be in compliance with her request.

"My mother's mother, Rosie … was the daughter of a slave."

I nodded. I appreciated the profound nature of this newly disclosed information.

Years later, while structuring the Harris Family Tree in ancestry.com, I would learn more about Rosie Burse Edwards. For example, she was born in February 1862 and passed away on December 24, 1919. The first names of her parents were Joseph and Christiann. In addition, her husband (my great-great- grandfather) was named Hector (H.R., Heck) Edwards. Rosie and Hector had the following eight children; Mattie Edwards Jackson, Cora Simone Edwards Wortham, Lula (Louise) Edwards Freeman, Bessie Edwards Barnes, Elma (Elmer, Delmar, Edma) Edwards Pittman (my grandmother), Green "Buddy" Edwards, George Edwards, and Rebecca Edwards Murphy White.

"Oh, stupid ass!" my mother continued. "It looks like somebody got drunk and set a church on fire! I mean how low can you get? Get low!"

I laughed at my mother's reference to a line from *Purlie Victorious*, a Broadway play written by Ossie Davis. In addition to Ossie Davis, the play also starred Ruby Dee (his wife) and Alan Alda.

"This is just too much!" my mother commented. "I mean, all of this is simply for the birds!"

"This is what happens," I said, "when you try to bull shit the bull shitter!"

My comment drew a loud laugh from my mother. The phrase, we believed, had been coined by her older brother Foster, whom we all affectionately referred to as Uncle Brother.

Later that evening, another news reporter stated that rioting had spread to the Willowbrook District. The most recent outburst occurred just before midnight. I grabbed the remote and increased the volume.

My mother shouted from the kitchen, "Too loud! Too damn loud! Luther!" It was a reference to a joke we all heard while listening to my mother's favorite Moms Mabley album.

Upon learning about multiple false alarm reports, my mother said, "Oh, what a tangled web we weave, when at first we do ... portend deceive."

I replied, "Maybe it's just me, because we've been under self-imposed house arrest, but I'd say that female announcer was a bad Mama Jama!"

"You always did like 'em pretty! But, you need to stop grasping at straws. Instead of always pursuing a *show piece*, try going after someone who actually want to be with you for a change," my mother replied.

"Seems to me," I continued, "that when the producers hire news women and weather forecasters, the viewers often get an extra helping of eye candy. No doubt about it—she is definitely the kind of girl I would bring home to meet you!"

My mother put her rarely used over-the-counter reading glasses on to take a closer look. Upon viewing the female announcer's plunging neckline and voluptuous beasts, she emitted a hearty laugh and said, "I'll tell you what, I meant to raise nice daughters, but I didn't mean to raise a nice son!"

On the morning of Friday, August 13, 1965—out of an abundance of caution—my family decided to remain in the apartment. The only outing planned was an afternoon drive to Compton to pick up my eldest sister. Rowena was pregnant with her second child, and she was scheduled to deliver any day now. Her husband had already departed for his 2:00 p.m. to 10:00 p.m. shift at the Mobile Oil Refinery in Torrance. Owing to the ongoing disturbances, and just to be safe, my mother decided to pick up Rowena and bring her to Towne Avenue.

With my mother at the wheel, we traveled south on Avalon Boulevard toward Compton. On Avalon Boulevard, between Imperial Highway and 120th Street, I came up close and personal with the evidence of last night's chaos. I observed burned-out markets and liquor stores, the burnt-out shells of vehicles, and smoldering debris that had been allowed to burn unchecked.

Returning from the Compton location, we headed north on Avalon Boulevard. We got as far as South Park at Fifty-First Street and Avalon. About halfway down the block, our vehicle was ordered to a halt by a small group of young Black men. The presumed leader of the group motioned for my mother to roll down the window. He peered into the car, apparently looking for any White passengers we might be hiding. When he gave the all clear, we were allowed to move on toward Towne Avenue.

With my dark ebony complexion, there was no chance of mistaking me for a White man. However, I had heard rumors that similar groups of men, frustrated because they couldn't locate any White people, resorted to pulling fair-skinned Blacks out of vehicles and beating them.

Upon returning to Towne Avenue, I wandered into the bathroom, removed my glasses, and splashed some cold water on my face. I entered the bedroom I shared with Bob and sat down at my small oak desk. Once again, under the umbrella of the exercise I termed poetic license, I began to sketch a draft of a poem.

Dark Shades

Dark shades shield me,
From a world I no longer wish to see.

A world filled with suffering, death,
And institutionalized poverty

A world that a barefooted boy,
Once naively appraised by propagated American truths

A world that leaves Black men no choice,
But to fight or forever live as youths

A world as empty as a smoke-ringed smile,
Intangible promises in a lily-White vial.

A Black youth dies in Vietnam
Pork and beans and mustard greens,
Mixed with chunks of ham.

As a boy in prayer, I cried,
And could not weep.

Black men chained to White pillars of inhumanity,
Haunted a sleepless sleep.

But I'll never be that barefooted boy again,
Peanut butter and jelly smeared over a defiant black grin.

As a young man, my nightly prayer
Takes on a new thrust.

For it's still in the grace of God
That I am willing to place my trust.

Now I lay me down to sleep,
I pray the Lord my soul to keep.

If I should die before I wake,
I pray the Lord,

That a new dawn in Blackness,
Will break.

In addition to the ongoing disturbances, the past few days had been extremely hot and sweaty. The temperatures were averaging in the high nineties. The Towne Avenue apartment did not have an A/C unit. For that reason, the windows were left open, and at night, the lights were kept as dim as possible. Even the cold tuna and noodle casserole with Ritz crackers dinner was designed to help combat the sweltering heat.

After Rowena and Robin had settled in, my mother turned on the evening news and allowed the ongoing coverage of the riots to cycle through.

Berman, A. Scores of fires rage unchecked, damage exceeds 10 million.
(August 14, 1965), *Los Angeles Times*

A White deputy sheriff and at least seven Negroes were killed by gunfire Friday night and early today and National Guardsmen moved into the area where riots raged for the third straight night.

A huge section of Los Angeles was virtually a city on fire as flames from stores, industrial complexes and homes lit the skies.

Shootings were being reported with increasing rapidity during the hot early morning hours, and rioting outbursts were reported in Pasadena, Compton and Venice.

Several other people reportedly were shot on the hot, muggy night, as Negro mobs fought bloody battles with police, looted stores and set fire to scores of buildings.

Sniper fire and uncontrolled flames were reported over a widening area. It reached almost to City Hall from the South Los Angeles area ten miles away where the violence began.

Well over 200 people were injured in the three days of terror, including more than 30 peace officers.

Dep. Sheriff Ronald Ernest Ludlow, 27, was shot in the stomach at Imperial Highway and Wilmington Avenue and was pronounced dead on arrival at St. Francis Hospital in Lynwood.

Three suspects were arrested in the murder.

Ludlow was the father of two.

Two Negroes died in Oak Park Community Hospital, 369 W. Manchester Boulevard., as Negroes rioted outside its doors.

A hospital official said that one of them might have been saved if the rioters hadn't prevented an anesthesiologist from reaching the hospital.

Three other gunshot victims were being treated in the hospital.

Alleged Looter Shot by Police

One of them, an alleged looter, was shot by police in the 2800 block of South-Central Avenue. And another was shot at 97th and Figueroa Street.

Police made plans to reopen the old Lincoln Heights jail as those arrested passed the 300 mark.

Damage from fires exceeded $10 million.

Fires blazed from 41st Street to 108th Street.

A minor blaze was set at 9th and Main Sts., only nine blocks from City all.

The first of 2,000 National Guardsmen reached the riot area about 9:45 p.m. to bolster the overwhelmed force of 560 police, deputy sheriffs, and highway patrolmen.

Another 3,000 Guardsmen were on standby alert.

Helmeted Guardsmen in jeeps with mounted machine guns established a headquarters at Walter Riis High School and others gathered at Manchester Playground.

By 1:00 a.m. about 200 Guardsmen with fixed bayonets had relieved 200 police officers in an area bounded by Century Boulevard., 104th St.., Grape St., and Compton Boulevard.

Lt. Col. Thomas Haykin of the 1st Battalion called the devastated square "secure." He stationed his troops along streets and at intersections while fires still burned in ruined stores and buildings.

He said there was no immediate plan to expand the perimeter, but he held 250 Guardsmen in reserve at

Manchester Playground.

Male Coanchor: Good evening, all. On this Friday evening, August 13, we continue with our coverage of the series of unfolding events that have occurred on what is now a third day of violence in South Central Los Angeles. According to the latest reports, a White deputy sheriff and at least seven Negroes were killed by gunfire Friday night and into the early morning hours. In addition, National Guardsmen have been moved into the riot torn area.

Female Coanchor: It now appears that a huge section of Los Angeles is virtually a city on fire as flames from stores, industrial complexes, and homes light up the skies.

"Tough titty! I mean all of this is just too Black bad!" my mother commented.

"This situation is just a low-down dirty shame!" I replied.

"Check it out, Mom!" I added. "This mess is even happening in Pasadena and Venice!"

"I'm hip," my mother replied.

Upon hearing this most recent report, I exclaimed, "Oh no! These people are having a field day at the expense of the LAPD."

"As for the snipers," my mother replied, "I am sure the police are saying, 'Where you at, you dirty rat?' Well, it appears that some people take the phrase what you see is what you get way too literally. I mean, just look at them, carrying on like it's nobody's business."

By Saturday, August 14, the entire household had grown weary of the ongoing turmoil. Essentially, we were landlocked because it just wasn't safe to venture out more than a few houses down from our apartment. However, like an epic movie unfolding in wide-screen panoramic vision, we couldn't help but be drawn to every twist and turn in the plot.

And so, under the umbrella of the exercise I termed poetic license, I tried to climb into the minds of the rioters as I began to sketch a draft of a poem.

Frustration

Disappointed in anxiety-ridden,
Ego-deflating, bulletproof, prophylactic, Unequalizing emancipation?
Damn that Lady named Liberty!
Dedicated to the proposition,
That someday, somebody's bound To set me free!

Where does it all end?
At the beginning of the begin?
Why is it always, "GG, GG, run! GG, GG, jump!
GG, GG, snap your finger!
GG, GG, pump?"

Has the world gone berserk,
In the tokenism, numbers game pathos of men?
Frustration, integration,
Neuroticizing, assimilation,
With light-skinned diffusion,
And curly, blue-eyed ... dig ... perfusion!

But that wino there got piss stains
In stiff underwear.
And funky armpits full of musk,
Without deodorant-beautifying soap,
Like a county check evaporating,
In a bursting fart of hope.
And them punks at the set,
Would stick an ice pick in my balls,

113

Grinding on that bitch,
Waiting their turn to rip,
Between sighs and thighs as
Another moans and groans,
Through filter-tit walls.

Walking in the footsteps of a
Shadow you can't see.
"Peace, brother! Where's it at?"
"Groove and freak out in your own bag, chump!"
"But how's it feel to be Black?"

Answering them in grunts and groans,
As you drop your contribution,
Into the pot of air pollution,
And hope you can sanitary flush free,
What you don't want nobody else
To hear, see?

"Put on your guzzling suit, MF!
Time to get some!"
"Hold it steady right now, pig!
Gonna waste one!"
"Bust this licking stick across your red face,
Then gear my ass to stepping
In the wind, right in place!"

"Then you tell me how it felt to be White!

After I done put the hurt to my man!

Done grabbed that greasy pork-chop wallet of yours!

Ripped off your blonde floosy wife!

Stripped your smooth shiny sought!

And then put the flame to that fiendish pad,

That I built—but you bought!"

Berman, A. 21,000 troops police rage guerrilla war; 8 p.m. curfew invoked (August 15, 1965) Los Angeles Times

The guerrilla war of South Los Angeles claimed its 25th victim Saturday night as bands of armed Negro looters took to the streets and snipers defied the efforts of 21,000 National Guardsmen and law officers to bring peace to the area.

With no end in sight, Lt. Gov. Glenn N. Anderson signed a disaster proclamation and invoked an 8 p.m. curfew in the 50-square-mile riot area.

One of the new victims was a 5-year-old Negro boy, Bruce Moore. Police said he was killed by a sniper bullet while he was in the yard of his home at 8800 Mary St. in the Firestone area. He was pronounced dead at St. Francis hospital.

The latest fatalities were a Negro shot and killed by National Guardsmen who said he ignored commands to halt at a blockade. Another Negro was shot, police said, while looting a liquor store.

Firemen trying to control a blaze in a store at 47th Street and Broadway were pinned down by snipers shortly before midnight. Forty guardsmen and police came to their rescue and used tear gas—the first employed during the rioting—to disperse the attackers. Five firemen were hospitalized after inhaling the tear gas.

The Firestone sheriffs' substation at 7901 S. Compton Avenue fell under siege from armed men zipping past in cars taking potshots at the building.

Two more looters were killed just before midnight, and two deputies were wounded in a shootout with looters at Holmes St. and Florence Avenue.

Numerous buildings were set afire from 40th to 49th Street. But firemen, some reportedly wearing bulletproof vests, were prevented from fighting the flames by sniper fire.

Violence also flared in Venice. At 7th St. and Broadway there, a fire truck responding to a false alarm was set afire by a Molotov cocktail and eleven people were arrested for failing to disperse, as heavy crowds began to mass.

Pasadena Also Cocktail Target

The deadly cocktails also were hurled along Fair Oaks Avenue in Pasadena but failed to ignite any major fires.

Bottle-throwing incidents in Compton led to the dispatch of 200 guardsmen to duty there.

In the hitherto peaceful harbor area, there were reports of sniper fire and bottle throwing.

The curfew seemed to be proving effective. Guardsmen behind jeep-mounted machine guns blazed away over the tops of cars and anything else that moved in the curfew area.

Sheriff Peter J. Pitchess, using authority granted under Anderson's proclamation, asked law enforcement agencies in San Diego, Orange, Ventura, Santa Barbara and Riverside Counties to stand by for possible assistance.

The 10,000-man 40th Armored Division of the National Guard was being bolstered by 8,000 troops from the 49th Infantry called in by plane and motor convoy from Camp Roberts as sniping, looting and burning raged.

A huge section of the Negro area was in flames. The casualty figures besides the dead, include 512 civilians, 63 police, 17 firemen and two military personnel injured and wounded.

Male Coanchor: Good evening, and on this Saturday, August 14, we continue with our coverage of the series of unfolding events that have characterized what is now a fourth day of violence in South Central Los Angeles. Tonight, amidst reports of widespread power outages, the life of a twenty-fifth victim has been claimed by what has been described by some as the Guerrilla War of South Los Angeles.

Female Coanchor: There appears to be no end in sight on this fourth night of violence. In addition, there are continued reports of bands of armed Negro looters who have taken to the streets and snipers who seem determined to defy the peace-restoring efforts of 21,000 national guardsmen and law officers.

So, as had become her custom, after dinner and as dusk began to settle, my mother turned on the evening news and allowed the various broadcasts to cycle through. "Looks like these people think they are sitting in the catbird's seat," my mother commented.

I replied. "I'd say that, up until now, they've been living high off the hog, but every dog has his day!"

After a restless night, I woke up the morning of Sunday August 15, 1965 thinking that things would take a turn for the better in the ongoing conflict. My mother had always been our source of strength during troubled times. She had a unique way of staying optimistic and upbeat in the midst of a storm. I did notice that she had quite a few projects going on in the kitchen.

In addition to the traditional Sunday morning breakfast of sausage, eggs, and grits, she was brewing several pots of coffee. Shortly after I arrived and sat down for breakfast, she and Rowena (with my one-and-half-year-old niece Robin in tow) indicated they would be right back and left the apartment. They were armed with a large container of coffee, Styrofoam cups, and several packages of danish rolls.

Approximately twenty minutes later, the group returned. Mymother's spirit seemed to have been dampened a little. In her words, she was "crushed." According to Rowena, they had walked

117

down to the end of the Towne Avenue and East Vernon and offered members of the National Guard hot coffee and danish rolls. My mother was aware that the men had been out on the street all night doing their best to keep the community safe. However, a spokesperson for the group respectfully declined my mother's very generous offer, citing guidelines that had been set forth by his commanding officer.

We all reassured our mother that her act of kindness was thoughtful, considerate, and very sweet. Like the biblical story of Jesus with the loaves of barley bread and a few small fish, my mother was trying to feed the multitudes of National Guardsmen with a couple of pots of coffee and a few packages of danish rolls.

Later that afternoon, under the umbrella of the familiar exercise I termed poetic license, I again tried to climb into the minds of some of the rioters. And so, I began to sketch a draft of a poem.

Times Is Getting Hard

It's like this, brother.
The man cut me loose from my gig
'Cause one of his pigs caught me
Pushing Vanguard pamphlets
After hours, you dig?

Ma wheels are in the pound.
My woman put me down.
"Don't want no no-good GG
Hanging around!"

I'm cold and hungry and tired
Tired of looking at that neon light,
Of thinking about the Mohair Edwardian
That was so out of sight!

Tired of thinking about home
And being alone
About the books I ain't read,
About my old lady's bread

About the shrapnel in my back
"Just trying to be Black!"
About that bitch down under that light,
And whether she's gonna get up off
Some tonight.

About last night just when
Everything was getting so uptight
And that last joint, and how my mind
Got dark, and deep, and mellow,
While brother Wes "Bumpin' on Sunset"
Tuned in on a sunset soft and low.

About tripping on down to the liquor store
And righteously scheming on some
Wholesale Red Mountain
That was hard up yesterday.

Or running it on down to that bitch,
About getting some tail
On the layaway.

And if she says,
"GG, I ain't got time
For no fast-talking jive,"

I'll grin and show her my
Master Charge card.
You hear where I am coming from, baby?
Times is getting hard!

Jackson, B. and Berman, A.
Policeman killed as fellow officer's gun is fired accidently
(August 16, 1965) *Los Angeles Times*

A Long Beach policeman was killed in midst of a mob Sunday night apparently by another officer's shotgun as Negro rioting shifted from a broad area of South Los Angeles where police and National Guardsmen were patrolling.

The dead officer, Richard Le Febre, 23, was one of two policemen believed felled by the shotgun of Officer Stuart C. Gordon, 26. Gordon was jumped from behind by three Negros, police said, and his gun discharged as he turned.

The melee to which eight Long Beach patrol cars responded, started with a mob throwing bricks and rocks at passing autos near Anaheim Street and California Avenue. Sniper fire followed the police shotgun blast and police at first reported that Le Febre had been killed by a sniper.

Le Febre and another officer George Medac, 23, who was wounded in the arm, were shot as they tried to push back the crowd.

A 40-block area was subsequently sealed off with the help of 350 National Guardsmen and 100 Los Angeles officers, who were rushed to the scene.

Meanwhile sniping and fire-bombing continued in a 56-square-mile area of South Los Angeles despite patrolling by 15,000 National Guardsmen and 1,000 law officers. And there were other fires believed started by Molotov cocktails in scattered sections outside the riot zone.

Five fatalities, including the Long Beach officer, raised the riot death toll to 30 since Friday night.

Police stations throughout Los Angeles and Orange Counties received telephone calls threatening further fires and bombings in an apparently organized "campaign of terror," as one official put it.

Blazes started by bottled gasoline raged at a beer warehouse at Van Nuys Boulevard and Dronfield Avenue. Others erupted at a lumber yard and two-story hotel at Kohler and 6th Streets and in a commercial building at Hollywood Boulevard and Wilcox Avenue in Hollywood.

Issues Instructions

There were among 24 major fires Sunday night. All were brought under control without further incident.

Fire stations throughout the riot area were placed under military guard and guardsmen accompanied firefighters to help protect them from snipers.

Governor Brown, in the meantime, acted to alleviate hunger in the ravaged sectors.

Male Coanchor: Good evening, and on this Sunday, August 15, we continue with our coverage of the series of unfolding events that have characterized what is now a fifth day of violence in South Central Los Angeles. Tonight, amidst continued reports of widespread power outages, a Long Beach policeman was killed while attempting to control a mob. Apparently, the fatal shot was fired from another officer's shotgun.

Female Coanchor: The deceased officer, Richard Le Febre, age twenty-three, was one of two policemen who sustained wounds from a shotgun fired by Officer Stuart C. Gordon, age twenty-six. The tragic accident occurred when Officer Gordon was jumped from behind by three Negroes, causing his shotgun to discharge as he turned.

As had become the nightly after dinner custom, once dusk began to settle, my mother turned on the evening news and cycled through the various broadcasts.

My mother said, "I see, said the blind man!"

I replied, "Like you always said, Mom, what's good for the goose is good for the gander!"

Jackson, B. and Berman, A. Isolated sniping reported
(August 17, 1965), *Los Angeles Times*

Violence tapered off throughout the Los Angeles area Monday night under a massive concentration of police and National Guardsmen on the south side.

Isolated hit-and-run sniping, brisk at times, was still being reported but the overall mood of police officials was one of guarded optimism.

"We've got our fingers crossed," a policeman said as the crisis reached the end of its fifth day.

And Captain Donald J. Foley, Information Officer for the guard, added: "It looks a bit quieter, but we intend to remain at strength until all the streets are definitely safe."

Gov. Brown declared the five-day riot was over, although he added: "We must and will continue to deal forcefully with the terrorists, until Los Angeles is safe again."

Outbreaks Monday night included sniping at a sheriff's patrol car at 107th Street and Compton Avenue in the 50-square mile South Los Angeles riot zone, but no officers were hit. The snipers vanished when police and guardsmen set out after them.

Truck Fired On

A newspaper delivery truck was fired upon outside the riot area at Jefferson and Hauser Aves. The windshield was shattered, but the driver was not hurt, police said.

There were few fire bombings. Vroman's Book Depository in a Negro neighborhood of Pasadena at Waverly Drive and Pasadena Avenue suffered $200 damages in a fire that was quickly controlled.

Monday was a day of hit-and-run attacks over a widespread area by Negro snipers and arsonists, most of them outside the zone where nearly 16,000 officers and guardsmen patrolled.

An 8 p.m. curfew was again invoked in the riot zone.

Male Coanchor: Good evening all, and on this Monday, August 16, the Los Angeles area is experiencing what is now a sixth night of turmoil. However, it appears that, largely as a result of a massive concentration of police and National Guardsmen on the south side, violence has indeed tapered off.

Female Coanchor: Although there have been isolated reports of hit-and-run sniping, often brisk at times, the overall mood of the LAPD top brass is one of guarded optimism. This spirit of optimism was also echoed by Captain Donald J. Foley, information officer for the National Guard.

Male Coanchor: To piggyback on what my Coanchor just said, in general, today was characterized by hit-and-run episodes that took place over a widespread area and Negro snipers and arsonists. The majority of these incidents occurred outside the riot zone patrolled by almost sixteen thousand officers and guardsmen. Unlike the events of the last two days, there were no new reports of widespread power outages in South Central L.A. today.

Female Coanchor: Tonight, an eight o'clock curfew was once again enforced in the riot zone. So, after six days of rioting, recent reports show that thirty-four people have died, more than a thousand were injured, and property damage has been estimated to be as high as $40 million.

After hearing the evening news updates, I said, "Hey, Mom. I am glad I win!" My mother seemed especially amused by this quote. According to her, boxing great Joe Louis occasionally spoke these words into a reporter's microphone after he had won a heavy weight fight. My mother also recalled that some of the White ticket holders who had purchased rather expensive seats were often extremely upset. That's because the Champ had a reputation for knocking out opponents while some people were still filing down the aisles looking for their seats.

The next morning, I took a thirty-gallon brown Hefty cinch sack down the stairs and headed toward the dumpsters in the rear of the apartment complex. Each morning when I conducted this particular chore, I noticed a decline in the acrid smell of smoke and soot, from burned-out wood frames and melted plastic. I even noticed a daily decline in the red glowing hues in the skies. Things were indeed changing for the better. Later that afternoon, under the umbrella of poetic license, I attempted to climb into the minds of some of the rioters. I began to sketch a draft of a poem.

Who Am I?

I am the trajectory of a sphere,
Sent flying toward an ancestral foe.

I am the Rock of Ages,
That withstood the shifting sands,
And the foaming seas.

I am the synthetic product of four generations
Of de-educating, emasculating, incorporating.

I am the genetic extension of the sons and daughters of Africa,
Usurped from their rightful homes, as rulers of men.

I am the thankful recipient,
Of the words, and deeds, of
Tubman, Dubois, Medgar, Malcolm and Martin

I am the foreclosed mortgage,
On a race riot, anti-poverty program, welfare check,
And educational system geared to a White-cultured society.

I am the mark of oppression,
And the salvation fire,
That burned the ropes on the hanging tree.

I am the voice of the four winds,
Rustling through the valleys of despair.

And I am the eternal life,

That branded a white-hot message upon the midnight skies:

I am Black—and I am proud!

In keeping with the nightly after-dinner tradition, as dusk began to settle, my mother turned on the evening news and cycled through the broadcasts.

"Now that's boss," my mother replied. "It sounds like the news reporters are trying to wrap up this coverage. I definitely need to get back to work. I mean, sometimes I feel like I've got so much debt I can hardly see straight!"

"Most of the time," I replied, "when you are having a really bad nightmare, you generally wake up in a cold sweat and holler. That has not been the case with these riots. I mean, this all happened while we were wide-awake. Suddenly opening our eyes while abruptly sitting up in bed simply wasn't an option."

By August 16, 1965, and according to most of the news outlets, order had been restored in the fifty-square-mile riot zone. Ironically, two days later, Rowena gave birth to Rachelle, my second niece.

My family decided to pile into the car, and with my mother at the wheel, we retraced the route I used to take from TJH to Towne Avenue. All that was left of my once-familiar visual and auditory landmarks were charred building frames, broken glass, piles of bricks, mounds of rubble, and scattered debris.

Gone were the Taco Bell stand, Thrifty's Drug Store, the barber college, the Central Avenue Pawn Shop, and S.H. Kress & Company five-and-dime department store. Although several Black-owned businesses on Central were burned down, the Dolphins of Hollywood Record Store was spared. Fortunately, the Vernon Branch Library, probably due to its fortress-like construction, was also spared.

However, included among the riot casualties was the liquor store and pharmacy at Forty-Eighth Street and Avalon. All that remained of that two-story brick-and-mortar establishment, including the second-floor living quarters, was a vacant lot. Word of mouth on the streets was that the pharmacist had decided not to rebuild. So, driving through what can best be described as a war-torn area, I couldn't help but recall the almost prophetic daily radio greeting from the Magnificent Montague: "Burn, baby, burn!"

Fifty-seven years later, the 1965 Willowbrook Riots would serve as a precursor to the Black Lives Matter campaigns against violence and systematic racism towards Black people. The international human rights campaign began on social media in 2013 with the #BlackLivesMatter hashtag. The campaign has assumed a leadership role in calling for Black people to be treated fairly by authorities in the United States and worldwide.

Shortly after the news announcements that order had been restored in the riot zone, I received a welcome letter and orientation package from the First Private College (PC1). Included in the orientation package was the college calendar for 1965–66.

During the riots, most of us had learned to live life on a day-by-day basis. Since the riots and turmoil were still fresh in my mind, I felt it best to view the milestone semester dates on a month-by-month basis. Surely, I couldn't possibly experience anything as traumatic as the Willowbrook Riots in the upper-middle-class Clareville college setting.

First Private College (PC1)
Calendar 1965 – 66 (Abbreviated)

	First Semester
September 17 (Friday):	Residence halls open for new students
September 17–24:	Program for new students
September 20 (Monday):	Registration for new students
September 21–22:	Registration for returning students, residence halls open for returning students
September 23 (Thursday):	First semester classes begin 8:00 a.m.

129

Chapter 4

Orientation week arrived, and I was one of five entering Black freshmen in the WASP culture that was in 1965 the First Private College. We were identified by preprinted name tags that provided first and last names. My first week in Clareville was filled with a whirlwind of activities. The events ranged from a steak barbecue dinner with my classmates in the grassy quad between the dorms to a small group dinner at a faculty member's home. During the latter dinner, we discussed *Young Man Luther* by Erik H. Erikson, the administration's assigned summer reading. In addition, we attended orientation dorm meetings conducted by the residence assistant and a Friday night dance at McKenna Auditorium.

Sunday morning even included a visit to selected girls' dorms on the Second Private College campus. Despite intermittent downpours that morning, we proceeded to the assigned locations and serenaded the ladies. The pre- rehearsed song, "The Sacred Seal," was gleefully received by the enthralled recipients. Some of whom tossed panties from upstairs windows and balconies.

Throughout the week, most guys diligently studied the information provided in the *Five College Look Book*. And that was certainly true of the two very unique personalities who were assigned to share my second-floor corner room in Beckett Hall. One of my roommates was on the Stagg football team, the other was on the Stagg water polo team. Included in the look book were photographs of entering freshmen from the First Private College and four other small private colleges. The caption under each image revealed city of residence and former high school.

During my first week at PC1, in terms of the opposite sex, it became clear that there was always more than one side to a story. Some of the incoming male freshmen complained that, when it came to scoring a date, an unspoken pecking order seemed to exist at the colleges. Some of the freshmen girls expressed a preference for the company of upperclassmen. From their perspective, the older men had money—and they could learn a lot more from them. That observation prompted some of the guys to drive over to Clareville High School and hang out. At the high school, they would rank as big men on campus.

At TJH, each leg of the two-mile journey home evoked a wide variety of visual and auditory stimuli, interspersed with assorted memories and sometimes pit-stop reward stations. That journey had certainly been abbreviated at PC1. Everything I needed was within an easy five- to ten-minute walk from my dorm room. There was breakfast, lunch, and dinner at Collins Hall. Honold Library, the main campus library, unlike the Vernon Branch Library back home, was easily accessible.

There was even an on-campus bookstore that also stocked personal hygiene items. And there was an on-campus soda fountain for casual dates and snacks. Similar informal date settings existed on the surrounding campuses. For example, the Pit was on the Fourth Private College campus. In addition, a secluded place for romantic walks and evening talks was the Margaret Fowler Garden at the Second Private College. It was a setting I would later refer to as the "Garden of Green Ivy" in a short story I wrote for a fiction-writing class at the First Private College.

The insomniacs and late-night study people often showed up at Story House, a mansion-styled, three-story building, adjacent to Collins Hall (the First Private College's main cafeteria). Story House was the home for the student mailroom. The majority of the letters I received during my four years at the First Private College came from my mother and Lynette. Story House also provided sleeping quarters for several students on the third floor.

A unique feature of Story House's quaint structure was the green ivy that—except for the windows and main entrance—adorned the exterior of its south-facing façade. Inside the living area of its ivy-covered, gray, rock-faced exterior and supporting front porch pillars, and next to a large open-faced wood-burning fireplace, were two tournament-style pool tables. Owing to the clanking sound of my manual Royal portable typewriter, I spent many all-nighters in the second-floor study room, which faced west. Stacks of the *Clareville Collegian*, the five-college newspaper, were often left at the entrance to the Story House mailroom. Copies were also deposited in front of both entrances to Collins Dining Hall. Before the end of my senior year, several of my poems, including "Notes from an Angry Black Man," "Dark Shades," and "Who Am I?" as well as a short story titled "Soul Set Number 5," were published in the *Collegian*.

In Los Angeles, the traditional means of keeping abreast of current events was the evening television news reports. A television set was mounted to the lounge wall of each dormitory, but most students didn't have time to watch. In fact, the Clareville coursework and day-to-day routines were so intense that the *Collegian* often served as our only source of information regarding local, state, national, and international events.

It didn't take long before my need to adapt and adjust to this entirely new array of auditory and visual stimuli temporarily suppressed recent memories of the Willowbrook Riots. The primary reason for this new perspective was that Clareville represented a completely different culture, environment, and rhythm. For example, my ears were accustomed to Stevie Wonder, the Temptations, and Diana Ross and the Supremes. However, dormitory stereos everywhere seemed to blast the Beatles, the Stones, and the Mamas and the Papas.

I soon learned that one of the unspoken roles in this new environment was to respond to questions related to civil rights and Black pride issues. Sometimes the questions centered on the conditions that led to the Willowbrook Riots. An expressed goal for PC1 administration was to use recruitment as a means of bringing diversity to the Clareville learning experience. An unspoken element in achieving this goal entailed my willingness to address some of the topics that were raised and debated in the larger society.

From a romance perspective, my freshman year at PC1 was basically a bust. There were simply not enough eligible Black women to choose from. The curriculum was also extremely demanding. I had an unsubstantiated concern about possible retaliation from some of the faculty members if they somehow became aware that I was dating White women.

Beginning with my freshman year, I found quite a few of the women to be rather friendly and extremely attractive. Paradoxically, throughout my tour of duty in Clareville, most students had a rather permissive attitude toward interracial dating. However, an interracial relationship outside college boundaries was a horse of a different color.

From a romance perspective, similar statements about the eligible dating pool could be expressed for my sophomore year, including my ongoing attraction to women of any race. In fact, it wasn't until my senior year that the romantic floodgates seemed to open. However, I do recall at least one instance where a Sista accused a brother of talking Black, while sleeping White.

At times, I expressed my true feelings in conversations with coeds, only to have them say things like, "You do realize that my father is paying for all of this, and he would freak if he found out I was associating with you!" or "It's okay to interact with me here in Clareville, but it is not okay for you to call or visit me during the break in Beverly Hills"—or Newport Beach or a similar locale—.

I was fascinated by people who hailed from different parts of the world. One of my best friends in Clareville was from Panama, and my junior-year roommate was from Costa Rica. When I was invited to have breakfast with a group of international students in Collins Hall, I gladly obliged. The small gathering of young people were members of a performing group called Up with People. Urged on by the spokesman for the group, I decided to attend one of their concerts at Big Bridges Auditorium.

I still remember the date I had with a blond-haired, hazel-eyed, Second Private College co-ed. *In addition to a rather alluring personality, she embodied my favorite dimensions, five foot-seven and slender.*

Before the concert started, a White lady behind us abruptly stood up and remained standing. I assume that was her way of expressing some form of silent protest against me and the Second Private College coed. I whispered to my date to just ignore the lady's rather strange behavior, and so we did. The concert started, and prompted by the people sitting behind her, I guess, the alleged protester eventually sat down.

At the conclusion of the concert, and as we exited down the stairs, we encountered a Black Student Union (BSU) Sista from the Fourth Private College. She was clad in an army green fatigue jacket and held a protest sign. Upon seeing me and my date, she shouted "Joseph!" in a surprised voice.

I replied, "I'll talk to you later."

I later discovered that the young singers who comprised the international Up with People group were sponsored by the conservative, Republican John Birch Society. So, exploring the dating world in Clareville was somewhat akin to navigating a multiracial, multicultural, politically charged, and sometimes international minefield.

I set aside my high school background on the swim team because the swim coach required swimmers to play water polo in the fall and the swimming pool was outdoors. During the winter, there was a view of a snowcapped Mount Baldy.

I was admitted to the First Private College on an academic scholarship, but during my first two years, I voluntarily joined the Stagg track team. I had a pretty good initial burst of speed, but I lacked endurance. For this reason, the coach directed me toward the 100-yard dash, the 440-yard dash, and the relays.

Coach Vince Reel had a thick southern drawl and a rather mischievous twinkle in his right eye. In front of others, he would playfully say, "Before I met, Joe Harris, I used to think all Black people could run. Here comes Clay and his shadow!"

I was quite impressed with Coach Reel in spite of his rather dry sense of humor. That was because he spoke favorably of Uncle Jake. From Houston, Coach Reel knew my uncle by his formal name, J. C. Lilly. Coach Reel informed me that Uncle Jake was coaching the Texas Southern women's track team. I departed the track team after my sophomore year to focus on improving my overall GPA. However, whenever my schedule allowed, I woke up early on Sunday mornings and completed a ten-mile run from Clareville to Upland and back.

During my first three years at the First Private College, I never lost my passion for creative writing. In accordance with PC1's academic policies and procedures, I was allowed to take Fiction Writing as an elective. I was also allowed to take an independent study in Creative Writing. The PC1 administration approved my request to submit a creative writing project for my required senior thesis.

I will always be grateful to a very attractive brunette from the Third Private College. She allowed me unlimited use of an IBM Correcting Selectric Typewriter. It was because of her kindness and generosity that I was able to complete my senior thesis in a timely manner.

There were days when I lifted my pen and began to write because I was in a romantic mood. And then there were days when the outpouring of creative expressions seemed to instill in me a sense of ethnic pride and identity. During my senior year, an extremely attractive ebony-toned Third Private College coed inspired a poem.

Somewhere in My Lifetime

Shimmering, glimmering, glowing,
Kaleidoscopic patterns of white, against a dark night,
Silhouettes of streetlamps, searching forever,
Illuminating, young lovers
Vowing to part, never, never,

Bright headlights, red tail signals,
Of cars moving much too slow,
A bitter throbbing in my heart?
Baby you'll never know,

That once upon a midsummer night's dream,
When your lips caressed mine serene,
Two hearts beat as one,
While love blossomed under a midnight sun,

I loved, you loved but weren't in love
As true couples who adore,
Still I secretly promised to be yours, forevermore,
You became my cause for living,
The very essence of my being

I am doing my own thing now sweetheart,
Only the fading shadows of your smile remain,
And warm memories of clinging arms,
Destined someday to part,

The budding wisdom of my broken heart,
Cries out in agony,
As the bus below makes its nightly sojourn,
Toward a scheduled destiny,

You were once the ticket to my every passionate desire,
My headlights and my taillights,
And I boarded a one-way Rapid Transit Flyer,
To a romantic rendezvous permeated
With jasmine-scented delights

But I lived in a dream world,
A sacred garden of evergreen ivy,
When youth and innocence,
Stood beside me,

No longer can I cast my pride away,
I count my blessings with each passing day, and
Somewhere in my lifetime, 'neath the twilight's
Dusky journey, somewhere serenaded by
A rhapsody in blue's celestial symphony,

I tenderly embraced a coed miss,
Who filled my world with meteoric streaks of happiness,
And shared the joyful bliss, of a passionate kiss,
Against this self-same skyline,
Shimmering, glimmering, glowing

In November 1967 I turned twenty years old. Earlier that milestone year in *Loving v. Virginia* the U.S. Supreme Court unanimously struck down Virginia's law prohibiting interracial marriages. The legal basis for the decision was that the anti-miscegenation laws violated the Fourteenth Amendment.

In 1967 sixteen states still had laws prohibiting interracial marriages. As a result of the Supreme Court ruling, those laws were abruptly revised.

During the summer of 1968, I added my high-pitched falsetto to the hook of a rather catchy tune's radio broadcast. The song was a 1966 version of "See You in September" by The Happenings. The contemporary pop release was originally written by Sid Wayne and Joseph Edwards. That's not to say that I had completely crossed over into pop music. To the contrary, "See You in September" seemed to evoke in me a kind of anticipation of Clareville-based relationships that were yet to come.

In November 1968 I turned twenty-one years old. Dr. Martin Luther King's assassination occurred earlier that milestone year. The tragic incident transpired outside of his room at the Lorraine Motel in Memphis, Tennessee. His untimely death led to marches and rallies across America. Largely due to Dr. King's assassination, riots broke out in over 100 cities.

Approximately two months after Martin Luther King's assassination, Robert F. Kennedy (Bobby Kennedy) was fatally shot at the Ambassador Hotel in Los Angeles. The shooting occurred shortly after he won the California presidential primaries in the 1968 election.

Bobby Kennedy (RFK), was a United States Senator and younger brother of assassinated President John F. Kennedy. As previously noted, the Coconut Grove lounge, the setting for the 1965 Jefferson High School Prom dinner, was located in the Ambassador Hotel.

Booker, a volunteer in the RFK presidential campaign, was also present at the Ambassador Hotel the night of the assassination. If prompted, my brother- in-law would occasionally share accounts of the tragic events that unfolded that fateful night.

From an emotional perspective, my senior year started out like a treasure chest that was overflowing with romantic riches. That was also the year I seemed to have naturally migrated to dating women of any race. The policy shift also helped to offset the fact that several of the eligible Black bachelorettes already had boyfriends back in Los Angeles. And owing to the proximity of Clareville to Los Angeles, the young ladies sometimes traveled home on weekends to spend time with those boyfriends.

I am sure Lynette's husband, Booker, probably would have asked, "Joe, why didn't you just bust a bodacious move and bogart the objects of your affection?" The truth was that being outrageous, bold, and daring just didn't seem to be my style.

I was infatuated with a very attractive Third Private College Jewish female who became the creative inspiration for a poem.

This Masquerade

Two worlds as different
As night and day,
Two polar refractions,
Diverging on their way

Two hearts caressing, two lips embracing,
Two lovers challenging, their inherited past,
Too naïve to realize, that it couldn't last

What brought the lovely Miss Ann,
To the Lion's Den of a Black man?
The pulsating stereo? soft blue lights?
Borrowed Mustang? or moonlit nights?

Or was it curiosity challenging sincerity?
Or maybe you were weighing in shame,
Sensual myths against validity,

But I never learned to play that game
Under a velvet cover of darkness,
You had a romantic interlude with Blackness,
The definition of interlude,
Depending on your consciousness

For one precious evening we shared,
The freedom and beauty
Of a world as we had never known,
Yet the distortions of reality,
Sought to force us into abandoning
This world, or risk compromising our own

I dug your personality, your pretty face,
your soft auburn hair, and warm embrace,
Could we have been victims,
Of a masquerade in the guise of historical tragedy?

That today for Blackness and Whiteness,
There can be no sanctity?
That we are all puppets,
In society's production of irony?

That tenderness and caring,
Two hearts sharing,
Could never exist,
Beyond warm memories,
Of a lingering kiss

And when the curtains,
Separating Black and White
Divided that starlit night,

Two worlds stood exposed,
Before an audience without sight,
And acted out their roles,
As fugitives in hopeless plight

Following that episode, I became truly enchanted with a Fourth Private College Hispanic senorita, and she became the inspiration for another poem

For My Race Speaks the Spirit
(Por Mi Raza Habla El Espiritu)

From across the borders of Mexicali,
Over a vast Painted Desert,
Gorged ridges, a jagged valley

Past azure blue stretches of oceans churning,
Upon distant sandy shores,
Bleached and burning

From across the brownish-green waters of the
Rio Grande, came your culture, your tradition,
Your love, your land

And the third world encountered the Black man's fate,
Your sacred Virgin Mary wept tears,
Upon smoldering hate

Copper-toned Senorita, with eyes as quiet, and deep as
The midnight sky, jet-black hair, moist enticing lips,
The warmth and being of complete gentleness

Now your face is forever mirrored in my mind,
And the deep expanse of my longing,
Breaches all barrier of mankind

For your parents may have come,

From across the Rio Grande,

And my ancestors from fertile African land,

And at times you may speak,

In syllables that,

Only my heart can understand

But I know the meaning of your warm embrace,

And I Am held spellbound,

By the burning eyes of a proud race

And two lips caressed in passionate tenderness,

As two lovers embraced under a starry crown,

Two worlds met in Black and Brown

And then there was the Sista from Neighborhood Community Church on the Eastside of Los Angeles. I had been a loyal member of Neighborhood Church since my family moved to the Forty-Eighth Street location from the Rose Hills Projects. She was the kind of girl I had always admired from afar, but it wasn't until one of my teenage-era buddies asked her to be his steady girl that I realized I should have beaten him to the punch. In addition to being very attractive, her academic abilities gained her admission to a prestigious private research university in Northern California. By then, she had long since parted ways with my former teenage buddy. She was the inspiration for a poem.

Ain't No Way

With each passing day,
I know that there "just ain't no way,
For me to love you baby,
If you won't let me"

Will your love always glow,
Like the pot of gold at the end of the rainbow?
Or will it always remain,
Like an impossible dream,
A chest full of jewels,
On a bottomless ocean bound stream?

Though you're constantly on my mind,
And it's difficult to integrate
The collage of warm memories soft and kind,
And though the love I long to give,
Knows no barriers of distance and time

Though you are the girl,
That for the rest of my life,
I'd promise to have and to hold, and
Though your radiant personality,
Strengthens my desire, and makes me bold

Though your smile's heavenly touch,
Captivates my heart much too much,
And though my arms long to embrace you,
My life to surround you

Though the caution signs
Of collected experiences warn,
That I am moving much too fast,
And the rapid pace of my desire exhausts itself,
In a passion that could never last

Still, I know,
That for every little tear, there's a heartache,
For every dream of love, that longing can make,
For every gale of wind, that blows upon a rocky shore,
The message in my heart cries out,
You're all I worship and adore

And though I've walked this way,

And felt this way before,

I stand defenseless at the sound of your voice,

For I know that the tender bliss of your caress,

Is the key to my heart's sacred choice

A red-orange carpet of autumn leaves,

Dampened by a cold wintry freeze,

A barren tree waiting a springtime green,

Beckoning the singing robins, pink apple blossoms,

A warm summer's breeze,

While I await the only answer,

That can set my heart free

For I know, that with each passing day,

For every lover's quest,

For every moonlit night in May,

There "just ain't no way,

For me to love you baby,

If you won't let me."

From an academic perspective, which was the primary reason for my four- year journey at PC1, I was still on target for achieving my goal of admission to medical schools such as the University of California at the Blue Pacific (UCBP), First Southern, and an East Coast HBCU medical school. I was a psychology premed major and had completed a year of biology, a year of chemistry, a year of organic chemistry, a year of physics, and a year of calculus.

The role of the PC1 registrar was to track the forward progress of all enrolled students. However, she seemed to take a particular interest in my premed ambitions. For example, upon receiving an F in Macro Molecular Biology of the Gene, she notified me that I might not have enough credits to graduate in June 1969. Owing to scheduling conflicts, I took the latter course even though I did not have the required biochemistry prerequisites.

I was truly upset by the registrar's revelation. However, she amended her statement after discovering I had taken a college-level trigonometry course the summer before I began my studies at PC1. She said, "Joe, if medical school is what you really want, why don't you stay an extra year and let us make you stronger?" For a variety of reasons, including ongoing Black Student Union (BSU) activities, I was not in favor of the extra year concept.

During my freshman year at PC1, I was aware that fraternities and sororities were conducting active recruiting campaigns throughout the six colleges. In general, the Black students were not solicited to join these groups. When asked if we could import the predominantly Black Los Angeles chapters of the Alphas, Kappas, and Omegas into the Clareville environment, the PC1 dean stated he was not in favor of such a move. From his perspective, our individual dorm assignments were intended to serve in place of traditional fraternities.

The BSU formed during my junior year at PC1. Soon, the BSU became our five-college fraternity and sorority. Overall, the Clareville BSU members got together for Saturday-night parties and other social events. We even attended BSU-sponsored functions at the neighboring colleges.

The political platforms we supported led to strong bonds between the BSU members. However, when the registrar suggested that I consider spending an extra year at PC1, even though I was only twenty-one years old, I felt I should maintain a steady course toward my goals. Reflecting on the South-Central Los Angeles phrase "Straight outta Compton," the time had come for me to get my derriere straight outta Clareville!

The previous example of one of my interactions with the registrar certainly didn't mean that she was partial to me. The registrar had a reputation among many PC1 students for having a no-nonsense persona. She could be quite firm in her decision-making. In the first semester of my freshman year, owing to my premed declaration, she strongly encouraged me to take a Tuesday, Thursday, Saturday Calculus I class at eight o'clock in the morning. According to her, the calculus class was a prerequisite for a PC1 course titled Physics-Chemistry.

At PC1, one semester of Physics-Chemistry, coupled with a semester of physics and a semester of chemistry, was equivalent to a year of each. The Calculus I instructor had a distinctive German accent. He also had a reputation for throwing pop quizzes on Saturday mornings at eight o'clock. The latter policy threw ice water on any plans we might have for Friday night fun.

I received my first D in Calculus I, and I knew that it would probably be viewed as strike one by medical school admissions committees. I skipped taking Calculus II in the spring of 1966 and opted to take it in the evenings at the UCBP Extension during the summer of 1966. I received a grade of B+ in the UCBP Extension Calculus II class.

Throughout my tenure at the First Private College, the decisions I made within the guidelines set by the administration had a major impact on my overall GPA. After completing a year of German in my sophomore year, I took a third semester of German during my junior year, receiving an A. I attempted to test out of the final required semester of German, but my score was too high to warrant placement in a normal second-semester class and too low to have the requirement waived.

Upon learning of my score on the exam, the registrar informed me that I would be required to take an advanced German literature course. I appealed to her to allow me to take the normal second-semester-level course, but my pleas fell on deaf ears. As it turned out, I struggled with writing essays in German. Along with other literary works, the assignments involved analyzing the meters, rhymes, and stanzas of poetry.

My final grade in the advanced German literature course was a

C, and that grade certainly did not help to improve my overall GPA. Later, one of my classmates called me a dummy, because, according to him, "Nobody tests out of the language requirement—that's why everybody trashes the lab test on purpose."

It was definitely against my basic instincts to purposely tank an exam, and I did not receive the underground student body memo about trashing the language lab test.

Despite my best efforts, I made several other costly mistakes during my four-year tour of duty at PC1. Consider the ill-advised Macromolecular Biology of the Gene course I took on the Fourth Private College campus in the fall of 1967. This particular course required the completion of biochemistry, which I had not taken. That decision was made because of a scheduling conflict with the PC1 Introduction to Genetics course, which was only offered in the spring.

From my perspective, looking through the joint colleges course offerings was a lot like perusing the incoming freshmen girls in the look book. As Clay's father used to say, "Everything that looks good ain't good!" Unfortunately, I found out the hard way that his expression was certainly true for two of the science course offerings on the Fourth Private College campus.

I approached a joint college biology instructor to explore the feasibility of allowing me an independent study in genetics. Although she was sympathetic to my request, her reply was that too much effort would be required in setting up the lab component of the proposed independent study. As a result, I received the only F in my entire academic career. I knew it would probably be viewed as strike two by any medical school admissions committee. The failing grade was given to me by a Jewish Fourth Private College professor.

Late in the fall of 1968, a PC1 academic advisor persuaded me to take a Third Private College physiological psychology course in the spring. My preference was to take a Fourth Private College course that focused on Rogerian therapy. Among other things, it would have allowed me an opportunity to capitalize on my research and writing skills.

The academic advisor seemed unimpressed by the fact that I had Earned an A in a First Private College experimental psychology course during the spring semester of my junior year. Experimental psychology was a very rigorous course, and it was PC1's equivalent to a statistics course.

There have been times in my life when I simply didn't do a very good job of speaking up for myself. The counseling session with the academic advisor certainly qualified as one of those times. I probably didn't explain that I was experiencing symptoms of stress as a result of three years of intensive coursework, two summers spent riveting airplanes at Lockheed Aircraft, one summer spent working evenings at McDonald's (so that I could take a daytime physics class at First City College), and Christmas of my senior year spent delivering USPS holiday packages.

Additional campus-related jobs held during my tenure at PC1 that I didn't mention to the advisor included carrying furniture at the Third Private College, working in the campus soda fountain, working in the campus library, and helping with registration. In retrospect, I suspect that I was so intent on pushing forward that I probably didn't pause to assess the cumulative impact of these various activities.

I more than likely didn't inform the academic advisor that I took a trigonometry course at First City College in the summer of 1965, a Calculus II course at the UCBP Extension the summer of 1966, and a physics course at First City College in the summer of 1968. However, I did inform the advisor that all I wanted to do was enjoy the last semester of my senior year and cruise to the finish line.

I told the advisor that I had been actively attending BSU meetings and was a participant in the rallies and the BSU's ongoing struggle with the administration for increased minority enrollment and funding.

The advisor's response was that he didn't think I was one of the leaders of the BSU group. Therefore, in his opinion, I should not have been adversely impacted by the BSU activities. He also told me that if I didn't take the physiological psychology course, I should consider selecting someone else to serve as my academic advisor.

The advisor was operating from the premise that the medical school path I had selected was not my true strength. Instead, he was of the opinion that my demonstrated talent was in the field of creative writing. However, from his perspective, if I truly desired to go to medical school, then the physiological psychology course would certainly assist me in that endeavor.

In conjunction with the physiological psychology course recommended by the academic advisor, it was important that I also enroll in Vertebrate Embryology on the Fourth Private College campus. Vertebrate Embryology was a prerequisite for admission to the UCBP Medical School. If taken, the latter course would constitute a second spring 1969 lab course.

My final requirement to earn a B.A. in psychology from PC1 was a single psychology course. However, the final psychology course could easily have been something less rigorous than physiological psychology. Knowledge of physiology could prove helpful to my medical school pursuits, but if the immediate goal was to enhance my understanding of physiology, the PC1 bookstore carried a variety of publications with titles like *Physiology the Easy Way*.

Unfortunately, and against my better judgment, I took the Third Private College physiological psychology course. I was the only male enrolled in the class, and my overall impression was that the White faculty member appeared to view herself as a mentor for my female classmates. However, I did not perceive that to be a major obstacle for me. Over the years, I had been blessed with my fair share of effective role models. Each one of those individuals provided an abundance of inspiration and guidance for me.

I had an uneasy feeling that I was not competing on a level playing field in the course. I noticed that several PC1 science faculty members occasionally posted copies of old exams (minus the answers). These postings were mounted inside a locked hallway display in the science building. I had an unverified suspicion that some of my classmates had formed their own private study groups. I barely received a D in the physiological psychology course, which I knew would probably be viewed as strike three by any medical school admissions committee.

That grade was essentially my bad. I should have had enough self-confidence to follow my instincts and walk away from the academic advisor's recommendation. I am sure I could have found another staff member to serve as my advisor for my last semester at PC1. A good candidate to replace the PC1 academic advisor would have been the faculty member who awarded me an A in a spring 1968 experimental psychology (statistics) class.

There was an unintended consequence of the multiple labs recommended by the PC1 advisor. The multiple lab hours conflicted with the only hours available for my selected senior thesis chair. The chair was a Black male who was recruited by the BSU to serve on the Third Private College staff. During the summer after my graduation from Carver Junior High, I shared a music appreciation classroom with him at Thomas Jefferson High. His sister also graduated with me from TJH in June 1965. The senior thesis chair was talented from a creative writing perspective and a kindred spirit. Besides, there was a rumored tradition at PC1, that barring a total meltdown on the part of the student, faculty generally awarded graduating seniors at least a B- on their dissertations.

Unfortunately, the BSU-recruited faculty member was unaware of the rumored B- senior thesis grade tradition. Since I was unable to meet with him to receive feedback, he awarded me a C. However, based upon my previous performances in creative writing, I knew I had submitted an above-average senior thesis.

By the time I received the PC1 grade card via the US Postal Service, I had returned home to my family's Los Angeles residence. When I called to discuss my final grade concerns with the chair, he said he thought the manuscript I submitted was a rough draft.

He later informed me that he had visited the registrar's office and requested that she change the grade from a C to an A.

The next day, I drove to Clareville and paid the registrar a personal visit. The registrar said, "Joe, please, you need to let this go. You got what you wanted. You have been admitted into several medical schools. Your transcripts have already been sent to the medical schools you selected. Sending amended transcripts to these colleges will reflect poorly on PC1. And your dissertation is on a topic that is completely unrelated to medicine."

However, changing the grade from a C to an A would have improved my overall GPA. During my sophomore year at the First Private College, I received an A in fiction writing. During my junior year at PC1, I received another A in an independent study in creative writing from that same PC1 faculty member. I was upset because the C I received from the visiting BSU faculty member was completely out of sync with my demonstrated performance in the PC1 creative writing courses.

On the other hand, there was a great deal of relevance to the position set forth by the registrar. Overall, Clareville had been a very rewarding experience for me. Tuition and room and board for my four-year journey had been paid for by a PC1-based trust fund. In fact, the anonymous donor's only request was that I write him or her a letter once a year. And so, out of respect for the four years of financial support and academic guidance, I complied with the registrar's recommendation and dropped my request for a grade change.

I often wondered why was I so upset by that assessment of my sixty-four-page collection of poetry, a short story, and an essay? First, if I could have looked into a crystal ball, I would have seen that six of the thirteen poems would later be included in a collection of romance poetry titled *Wine Me, Dine Me, Dance Me, Romance Me* (Author House, 2012). Next, the crystal ball would have revealed that three of the thirteen poems would be included in a future novel. In addition, the short story would become the foundation for chapter 2 of that future novel. Finally, the primary focus of the dissertation's five-page essay, "General Hospital," was about why I wanted to become a doctor.

Surely, I couldn't possibly experience anything as traumatic as the Willowbrook Riots in upper middle-class Clareville. Over the years, administrators for the six-college complex had been moving forward with a wide variety of minority-recruitment programs. Still, by fall 1968, my senior year, Black students represented only forty of the five thousand students enrolled in the six-college system.

The BSU was very active during my junior year. The BSU agenda translated into very specific demands for the administrators of the Clareville Colleges. Similar to what was stated about my freshman year at PC1, the ongoing PC1 curriculum and day-to-day routines were very intense.

By the start of my senior year, the Willowbrook Riots and subsequent turmoil had long since been placed on the back burners of my mind. And because the June 8, 1969 graduation date was almost within reach, I no longer felt the need to view milestone semester dates on a monthly basis. An abbreviated summary of the first semester and second semester target dates is shown below.

First Private College (PC1) Calendar 1968–69 (Abbreviated)

	First Semester
September 24–25:	Registration for returning students (residence halls open for returning students
September 26 (Thursday):	First semester classes begin 8:00 a.m.
November 27 (Wednesday)	Thanksgiving recess begins after last
December 2 (Monday):	Thanksgiving recess ends at 8:00 a.m
December 21 (Saturday):	Christmas vacation begins after last
January 6 (Monday):	Christmas vacation ends at 8:00 a.m.
January 23 (Thursday):	Last day of classes, first semester
January 25 (Saturday):	Final examinations begin
February 3 (Monday):	Final examinations end
February 8 (Saturday):	First semester ends
	Second Semester
February 10 (Monday):	Registration for all students (second semester classes begin)
April 5 (Saturday):	Spring vacation begins at noon
April 6 (Sunday):	Easter Sunday
April 14 (Monday):	Spring vacation ends at 8:00 a.m.
May 28 (Wednesday):	Last day of classes
May 30 (Friday):	Final examinations begin
June 7 (Saturday):	Final examinations end
June 8 (Sunday):	Commencement

Shortly after February 10, 1969, the beginning of the second semester, the unthinkable occurred. The tragic events of Tuesday February 25, 1969, were best presented in the *Los Angeles Times* article shown below. The text of the article provides a rather vivid description of this unfortunate, yet historical day. Thanks to the *Los Angeles Times* staff, excerpts from the full text of this article are provided below (Copyright 1969, *Los Angeles Times*, reprinted with permission).

Greenwood, Leonard. Bomb victim may lose sight; school helps Negros hide out. (February 27, 1969), *Los Angeles Times*

Members of the Black Students Union at the (name of colleges) have gone into hiding—with the assistance of the school's administration—after a bombing that may leave a young woman blinded, *The Times* learned Wednesday.

However, Dr. Mark H. Curtis, president of (name of college) and this year's provost of the six-college (name of city) system, said, "I don't believe anyone from the Black Students Union had anything to do with this."

The Tuesday explosions came at a time of high emotion on campus over student demands for Black and Mexican-American studies programs, Curtis said.

The Black students went into hiding "with our assistance," Curtis said, because it was feared they might be blamed for the bombings and become targets for retaliation.

Mrs. Mary Ann Keatley, 20, a bride of five months, lost part of her right hand and was in danger of losing her sight as a result of the first blast, which struck the Carnegie Building where she worked as a secretary.

Mrs. Keatley was reported in good condition Wednesday at (name of city) Valley Community Hospital. She lost two fingers on her right hand and suffered severe damage to the other fingers.

Because the bomb exploded virtually in her face, injury to her eyes "is severe and she is in danger of losing the sight of both eyes," her physicians said.

Mrs. Keatley picked up a package from a pigeonhole mail delivery slot about 4:15 p.m. Tuesday. A bomb in the package exploded seconds later.

Mrs. Keatley is a secretary in the political science department of (insert name of college). Her husband Robert is a student at (name of city).

The college faculty and administration, said Curtis, have been having "critical discussions, some of them fairly emotional" over student demands.

Curtis said he had spoken with BSU leaders since the bombing, and they were astounded by what had happened. "But they have already been—without foundation—accusations that they (members of the BSU) were responsible," he said. "It was feared there might be retaliation. They have been given police protection."

The BSU members reportedly dropped from sight a few hours after the explosions.

"If there is any connection between the dispute over the introduction of a Black studies program and these bombings, I cannot see it," Curtis said, "and I refuse to speculate on this point."

Within minutes of the explosion that injured Mrs. Keatley, another bomb exploded in a women's restroom next to the auditorium at (name of college) on the other side of the campus.

Second Blast

No one was injured in the second explosion, but the force of it splintered and blew out a heavy wooden door, shattered marble partitions, tore tiles and plaster from the walls and ceiling and blew out the windows.

Experts of the sheriff's bomb squad said both bombs were apparently home-made, put in shoe boxes and wrapped with paper. Police said first examinations indicated the bombs were made from lengths of pipe with timer devices.

Several accounts from the *Los Angeles Times* provided additional details regarding the events that transpired in Clareville on February 25, 1969. A series of articles published in the
Los Angeles Times presented alternative perspectives regarding the factors that addressed this extremely unfortunate turn of events are shown below.

Two bombs rock (name of city) colleges
(February 26, 1969), *Los Angeles Times*

Two colleges tighten security after bombings and shootings
(February 28, 1969), *Los Angeles Times*

Additional articles were published in the *Collegian*. The titles of two of these articles are shown below.

Two bomb blasts, secretary injured
(February 26, 1969), (name of city) *College Collegian*

BSU in seclusion, rally postponed
(February 26, 1969), (name of city) *College Collegian*

Owing to the bombings, appropriate security measures were taken by members of the Clareville Colleges BSU. The concern was that some individuals might mistakenly conclude that the BSU was in some way responsible for the tragic acts. As a result, the handful of Black students enrolled in the six-college system departed the campuses and were housed in various undisclosed locations.

I cannot speak for all of the locations, but in my setting, the male students formed our own security system. The rumor mill was in high gear that evening. And a threat that many of us felt was specific and credible was that a vigilante group had been formed. Of foremost concern was that the group allegedly intended to seek revenge upon Clareville's Black students.

In our security plan, two-at-a-time night-watch shifts were

assigned to each male student at my location. Did I fear for my personal safety that evening? All I can say is that there was a strong possibility that, if attacked, the two parties assigned to a particular night-watch shift would be fired upon first. However, when you are in survival mode, your focus is not on personal injury. Instead, your focus is on staying alert, staying vigilant, and staying alive. The possibility of injury definitely applied to those on watch outside the location, but the majority of the group who remained inside the location were also at risk of experiencing grave bodily harm.

I was unaware of the procedures followed at the other five colleges, but the next day, two male students and I conducted a main corridor sweep of the Third Private College campus. I was concerned that there was a 33.3 percent chance that I could be the recipient of a sniper bullet as we walked three abreast down the exterior corridors of the Third Private College. However, in survival mode, the primary focus of your concentration is on staying alert, staying vigilant, and staying alive. Since we were not armed, my plan was simple. If sniper fire erupted, I was prepared to drop, roll, and seek cover behind the nearest trash can.

After the bombings, a high priority for the majority of the students was to reset and refocus on academic studies. As a result, a kind of unspoken code of silence regarding the incident emerged. I am unaware of the existence of a final law enforcement report addressing the Clareville bombings.

Along with other requests, negotiations for a Black Studies Center continued after the tragic bombing. The negotiations were conducted between the Clareville BSU appointed leaders and six college administration representatives. When negotiations broke down, the BSU voted to pack up and depart from the college. At least one of the underclassmen approached me and said, "Look, I know you are premed, so if you decide not to stand with us, we'll understand." I strongly supported many of the concerns set forth in the BSU demand letter.

With the other members of the BSU, I packed up my belongings and prepared to depart. However, leaving my single room on the top floor of the newly constructed eight-story tower would have been bittersweet for me.

I truly enjoyed taking in the spectacular views of the campus. And those breathtaking views were complemented by the colorful hues of the evening sunsets. That was the inspiration behind the first poem and cover page title for my senior dissertation: "A Room with a View."

My affinity to the room was also due, in part, to the fact that I had spent the majority of my life sharing sleeping quarters with at least one other party. I am sure many would say my loyalty to the BSU was rather naïve or even a bit foolish. However, all the multiple personalities that comprised the BSU had found a way to bond together for a common cause. Unfortunately, my medical school ambitions ended up in second place behind the emotionally charged demands of the BSU. The six college administration representatives agreed to a few of the demands set forth by the BSU.

In the fall of 1968, I had an opportunity to visit the First Southern Medical School. The campus was immediately adjacent to General Hospital in Los Angeles. A First Southern medical student was kind enough to pick me up from my dorm in Clareville and take me on a tour of the Health Sciences Center campus. On another day, I had an opportunity to visit the University of California at the Blue Pacific Medical School campus. A Black medical doctor in Clareville suggested that, if possible, I should arrange for a meeting with Dr. Thomas L. Kennon. Dr. Kennon had an office on the A Level of the UCBP Neuropsychiatric Institute.

Dr. Kennon was very cordial and informative, and at the conclusion of the meeting, I asked if I should go to UCBP.

He said, "I am certainly pleased that your hard work has provided you with a wealth of opportunities to explore; however, whatever you decide, don't come here." Dr. Kennon did not elaborate on the rationale behind his recommendation, but I probably should have paid closer attention to his advice.

During my twenty-first birthday weekend in November 1968, I had an opportunity to visit the Second UC Medical School campus. I spent the weekend with a group of medical students who strongly encouraged me to Attend. I was truly impressed by the attention and encouragement from the Group. So much so, that the Second UC moved to the top of my list. An added bonus to the Second UC decision was the fact that Keith, one of my oldest friends had migrated to the Oakland-San Francisco Bay area.

Throughout my journey—from elementary through graduate school and beyond—I always felt Keith's presence through a telephone call, a birthday card, a Christmas card, or an impromptu visit, usually accompanied by one of his brothers, whenever he was in town. His friendship was a positive force during the majestic heights of my greatest victories and the deepest valleysof my lowest defeats. Sometimes he encouraged me, and at other times, he laughed with me—or *at* me.

Keith was an effective listener. He often assumed the role of best friend/ advisor without passing judgment on my sometimes-impulsive decision- making. Ironically, when things didn't work out for the best in medical school, I ended up following in his academic footsteps. He obtained a B.A. in public administration from First Southern University.

Years later, I would be admitted to the Ph.D. program in Public Administration at First Southern University. After graduating from First Southern, Keith matriculated to a San Francisco Bay area college where he obtained a Masters in Industrial Psychology. He then continued graduate studies at the Third UC campus where he obtained an M.B.A. degree.

I began teaching college-level courses on a part-time basis in the fall of 1988. For the next eighteen years, I served in various full-time, permanent positions while teaching evening and weekend courses. I taught statistics to M.B.A. students. I sometimes reflect upon "The Road Not Taken" by Robert Frost and wonder how different my career path might have been if I had followed my desire to obtain an M.B.A.

On March 19, 1969, during my final semester at PC1, I received a message that Dr. Granville Coggs had called. When I returned the call, he informed me that I had been accepted into UCBP's special five-year program for disadvantaged students. I would be receiving a second acceptance notice from the First Southern School of Medicine soon. On March 21, I received the acceptance letter.

On April 23, 1969, I received an acceptance letter from an East Coast HBCU medical school. I was supported in the latter effort by Dr. Ernest Everett Just, a prominent Los Angeles-based obstetrician. I first met Dr. Just during a career fair at TJH in 1964. I was beginning my senior year of studies at TJH that year. Those medical school goals were achieved despite having what I perceived to be three strikes against me. In reference to my acceptance to UCBP, First Southern, and the East Coast HBCU medical schools, I suspect the elders would say, "Sometimes it's not always about what you know, but who you know."

Unfortunately, the Second UC admissions committee decided to delay sending me an acceptance letter. I was under a great deal of pressure because each of the acceptance offers came with a firm deadline. I wrote to the Second UC and underscored my desire to attend their medical school. They replied, "We are pleased to learn that you have been admitted to a Southern California regional college. The University of California at the Blue Pacific School of

Medicine is a very distinguished and prestigious institution. We therefore recommend that you give serious consideration to their invitation."

As a result of a prioritized list of criteria, I selected the special five-year program for disadvantaged students at UCBP. At First Southern Medical School, I was asked to declare an area of specialty. I was definitely interested in becoming a psychiatrist. However, owing to undergraduate courses such as Child Development and Adolescent Development, there was a possibility that I might have been interested in pursuing a career in pediatrics. The goal of the First Southern program was to condense the traditional fifth-year internship into the four-year curriculum. The First Southern School of Medicine was affiliated with Los Angeles County General Hospital, and I made multiple trips to General Hospital for routine childhood health-related matters.

During the fall of 1968, I visited the Clareville Colleges' Student Counseling Center and completed the Kuder Occupation Test and the Strong Vocational Interest Test. The highest scores achieved on the Kuder were a seventy-one for psychologist-professor and a sixty-seven for psychiatrist. On the Strong Vocational Interest Test, I scored in the A range as a math-science teacher and the B+ range as a physician.

The Strong Vocational Interest Test revealed an academic achievement score of seventy. The psychologist who assisted in interpreting the results said that people who score at that level often fall in the same category as those who aspire to be president of the United States. Since, in his opinion, that would never happen for me, it could lead to depression. The depression would result from the fact that, although others may perceive my accomplishments as being outstanding, from my perspective, I could always have done better. I also scored in the B+ range as a minister.

The attraction that the First Southern Medical School held for me was that I already knew I wanted to specialize in psychiatry. As a psychiatrist, one of my goals was to write books about the Black experience. I wanted to emulate *Black Skin, White Masks: The Experiences of a Black Man in a White World* by Frantz Fanon, *Wretched of the Earth* by Frantz Fanon, and *Black Rage* by Grier and Cobbs.

As previously noted, I had taken a child development course at the Third Private College and an adolescent development course at the Second Private College. The information in both courses was fascinating, and there was always a possibility that I might consider specializing in pediatric medicine.

I had taken the bare minimum number of required courses for admission to medical school. For a variety of reasons, I experienced difficulties with Clareville College-based math/science courses, especially in the two science-related courses I took at the Fourth Private College. So, the five-year program at UCBP seemed to be the best fit for me.

Starting when I was eight years old, I often accompanied my Mother to the UCBP campus during the summers. I didn't stay with her during the day while she performed her duties in the UCBP Undergraduate Admissions Office. My brother and I were allowed to roam the entire campus. The hard and fast agreement was that we were to meet her on the front steps of Murphy Hall (the main administration building) at the end of the day.

The East Coast HBCU medical school, a well-respected institution, was also a very good fit for me, but the medical school did not offer a financial aid package. I found it difficult to consider relocating to the East Coast without some form of financial aid.

On Tuesday, February 25, 1969, one of two bombing incidents occurred at Carnegie Hall on the Fourth Private College campus. The other incident occurred at Balch Hall on the Second Private College campus. After the unfortunate incidents, I did my best to refocus on the remaining sequence of courses at PC1: Vertebrate Embryology, Physiological Psychology, Abnormal Psychology, and my senior thesis.

Vertebrate Embryology was an elective that I was allowed to complete in a pass/fail format. At the conclusion of the course, the faculty member informed me that "he couldn't, in all good conscience, award me a passing grade."

My experiences at the Fourth Private College and the Third Private College appeared to be consistent. I was usually the only Black student in the classroom, and I often had the feeling that I was not competing on a level playing field. I suspected that some of my classmates formed their own private study groups.

I informed my professor that I had already been accepted into three medical schools and that I had agreed to accept the UCBP offer to enroll in the special five-year program for disadvantaged students. He seemed especially pleased to hear of my final decision and offered what he felt was an equitable gentleman's agreement. He would award me a passing grade if, during the summer months, I would agree to make several seventy-mile round-trip visits to Clareville. The purpose of the trips was to demonstrate successful progress during the makeup sessions. I did not own a car at the time. In order to hold up my end of the bargain, I took several round-trip bus rides to Clareville for the Vertebrate Embryology appointments.

That was how I allocated my time during the summer between my graduation from PC1 and the start of my first year at the UCBP Medical

School. In retrospect, a more effective use of time that summer would have been to focus on the fast-approaching year of medical school and gross anatomy studies. I had to earn income during the summer of 1969 and worked forty hours a week as a laboratory assistant in a special chemistry lab at General Hospital in Southern California.

At General Hospital, I often spent my lunch breaks viewing vertebrate embryology slides. The slides were observed using one of the microscopes in the hospital's cytology lab. The stress of all that I had experienced at PC1 must have shown on my face because the female director of the lab looked at me one day and said, "You look deep cesspool!"

The two lab workers in hearing range of the comment got a big laugh from her sarcastic observation.

I successfully completed a year of biology, a year of chemistry, a year of physics, a year of organic chemistry, and a year of calculus. In addition, the UCBP Medical School required genetics (one semester) and vertebrate embryology (one semester).

I thought, *I can't possibly experience anything as traumatic as the destructive nature of the Clareville bombings in the hallowed hallways of the Southern California-based UCBP Medical Center.*

Chapter 5

In the fall of 1969, I was walking down a path that was just a few hundred yards from the entrance to the UCBP School of Medicine. The botanical gardens was my go-to getaway destination for peace and tranquility. Entering the gated oasis was one way of immersing myself in an environment that was totally different from the fast-paced medical center. Sprinkled throughout the garden's lush green landscape were colorful botanical collections. Each of the specialized flora and native fauna underscored the garden's historical significance and rare natural beauty. I thought, *How truly peaceful it is, here in this place, where the clouds seem to play peekaboo with the sun.*

At twenty-one, I was beginning my journey as one of four participants in UCBP's special five-year program for disadvantaged students. As I walked along the garden's winding pathways, shadows from the overhanging trees appeared to dance at my feet, as if choreographed by a breeze, that rustled through skyward-reaching leaves. I knew that when I emerged from the botanical gardens, the continuation of that journey awaited. As Dr. Thomas L. Kennon—my first mentor—would say, "I was prepared to do battle."

If I thought my premed semester system studies were intense, the medical school quarter system studies were even more demanding. However, from a potential date perspective, there was no shortage of attractive, intelligent, upwardly mobile Black female candidates throughout the UCBP community. In fact, if companionship was on the menu, I needed to look no further than the nursing students in the medical center.

The nursing program rotations and ongoing course requirements were quite demanding. For that reason, the majority of the nursing students adhered to a form of self-imposed discipline when it came to the dating world. Quite a few of the eligible bachelorettes were already spoken for, but I managed to spend quality time with three of them. For at least one of them, that statement would hold true for the two-year period during and several years after my tenure in the medical school.

I smiled as I thought about my preteen idea that *relationships were like a gigantic game of musical chairs. At some point, in what could turn out as a lifetime quest, the music stops—and someone generally gets left without a partner.*

During my senior year at PC1, one of my classmates introduced me to his former high school girlfriend. We met on a double date while attending a New Year's Eve party in Pasadena, California.

The party host was another *PC1* classmate. My date to the affair was an ebony-toned Third Private College coed. As previously noted, she inspired the poem titled *Somewhere in My Lifetime.* After the affair, the four of us made our way down from the Pasadena foothills to the Rose Bowl Parade route.

The display on the bank's clock tower indicated that the overnight temperature had dipped to around fifty-three degrees Farenheit. By Southern California standards, it was quite chilly. We staked out a sleeping area on someone's front lawn. Prior to departing for the party, John indicated that he would take care of the sleeping bag arrangements. However, when he popped open the trunk, I only saw two sleeping bags. He said, "Okay, people, all I could find were two sleeping bags, and I tell you what, I am not sleeping with Joe!"

To my surprise, John's ex-girlfriend was later accepted into UCBP as a first-year nursing student. While pursuing her studies in the School of Nursing, she became engaged to an enlisted member of the military. Her fiancé was later deployed to South Korea. She later introduced me to one of her girlfriends, and that girlfriend turned out to be someone I would later view as the love of my life. The introduction occurred during the summer prior to my second year of medical school.

Once the medical school courses were underway, I found that there wasn't much leeway for watching television. I did, however, find the time to occasionally browse through the *Los Angeles Times*. The following article highlighted many of the issues encountered by medical students enrolled in a similar program at a crosstown medical school. The topics raised in the article seemed to mirror my experience at UCBP. Thanks to the *Los Angeles Times* staff, excerpts from the full text of this article are provided below (Copyright 1970, *Los Angeles Times*, reprinted with permission).

Dreyfuss, J. Black medical students to get aid from (initials of college): Financial and academic plan told in response to protest by minorities (May 15, 1970) *Los Angeles Times*

"(Initials of college) Thursday announced a broad new financial support program for minority students in the school of medicine.

Full financial aid and special academic preparation will be offered all minority students who need them next fall, said (dean's first and last name), dean of the medical school.

The announcement followed condemnation of the school's admission policies by Black medical students.

(Dean's last name) said every minority student who qualifies for a scholarship will receive up to $4,000 for tuition, fees and living subsidy, plus $1,200 if he is married. An additional $300 will be granted for each child.

Satisfies Demand

Established guidelines will be used to determine financial needs, he added.

The unusual scholarship program satisfied a demand made March 9 by Black medical students who said that (initials of college) must give minority students "adequate financial support."

(Dean's last name) satisfied a second demand in announcing a new program for minority students accepted for medical school although they lack prerequisite courses.

Students had argued that an existing program in the medical school for premedical students without certain prerequisites caused those students to be singled out as inferior by some students, faculty and administrators.

Dean Reveals Plan

To replace that program, the dean revealed a plan to give financial support for minority students who need to take prerequisite courses. Arrangements will be made to enroll in the courses at a state or community college of the student's choice.

Such courses would be taken after acceptance to Medical school, during the spring or summer before enrollment.

However, the principal demand of the Black students remains unsatisfied. They want 30% of next year's freshman class to be minority students.

They reiterated that demand in a campus press conference Thursday, and said about 100 medical students supported it. Twenty White medical students attended the conference to support the Blacks.

(Dean's last name) said in an interview that despite recruitment of minority students, there have not been enough qualified applicants to comprise 30% of next year's approximately 130 freshmen.

He insists on admitting to (initials of college) only students who qualify under present standards, arguing that otherwise he would be accepting students who would not have the potential to be as good doctors as other applicants.

(Initials of college) has 448 medical students, including five Blacks, four of them freshmen and two of them foreign students. Since 1961, (initials of college) has had but two Blacks among its 804 medical school graduates.

I remember the start of my first gross anatomy class and the overwhelming smell of formaldehyde and thirty-two silver containers, each housing a cadaver. A classmate, who already had a Ph.D. in anatomy was assigned by the Anatomy Department as my personal facilitator. He asked some rather uncomfortable questions during our initial meeting. For example, he asked, "What was your undergrad GPA? What were your scores on the MCAT?" He came across as being more concerned with passing judgment than assisting me. Shortly thereafter, and as diplomatically as I could, I asked if I could join the other three special program students in their anatomy study session.

A kind of us-against-them mentality had developed among the special program students. We had reason to believe that, even though a pass/fail system was in place for all UCBP medical students, the test results for the special program students were compared to those of regular admit students.

The anatomy faculty member who conducted the special program students study session had a rather distinct German accent. He was encouraging, supportive, and compassionate toward us. As a result of his assistance, we all successfully completed the gross anatomy course. Future faculty-assisted study group sessions for the remaining medical school courses were not made available to us.

At some point during the first year of the special five-year program for disadvantaged minorities, the medical school administration must have realized that there were some major flaws in the program's design and structure. A female consultant was asked to conduct individual interviews with each member of the special program.

When it was my turn, I emphasized that special program participants needed to be treated with courtesy and respect. Sending us down campus to audit undergraduate courses, and then requiring us to take the final exams for those courses, was counterproductive. It would be very useful if we could audit the lecture components of certain second-year medical school courses: Microbiology and Immunology, Patho-Physiology of Disease, and Pharmacology. Structured study groups, when conducted by a culturally sensitive facilitator, would improve the overall learning experience. Unfortunately, the topic of textbook-specific student study guides was not raised or discussed during the interview.

At the beginning of the gross anatomy course in 1969, as we gathered around the cadaver with our dissection manuals, my three lab partners took turns asking me questions about my undergrad GPA and scores on the MCAT. However, and to their credit, the preliminary questions soon subsided as the focus shifted to the instructions in the dissection manual. In fact, we often met for after-hour dissections and study sessions. At the end of the first quarter, we celebrated together at a popular restaurant near UCBP. We ordered our usual pastrami sandwiches, french fries, and beer.

During my first year at UCBP, I was working on George, the cadaver, with my lab partners. The lead anatomy surgeon stopped by our lab station and asked me to name the cranial nerves that arise from the brain or brain stem. My answer was Olfactory, (2) Optic, (3) Oculomotor, (4) Trochlear, (5) Trigeminal, (6) Abducens, (7) Facial, (8) Vestibulocochlear, (9) Glossopharyngeal, (10) Vagus, (11) Accessory, and (12) Hypoglossal. Well, apparently, my response was not at a pace that was fast enough for him. Essentially, I was clicking through a rather crude *mnemonic* that my lab partners had shared with me. And that probably explained why I was slightly distracted by their beet red faces and snickering. The surgeon said, "You are going to kill a patient someday!"

The demands of the first year of medical school left little, if any, time for dating. However, if by chance you were a medical student who was gifted with a football player's physique and exceptional good looks like Carter, my first-year roommate, then you probably would have no problem attracting the opposite sex. I recall one Saturday night when I decided to spend the evening with my Gross Anatomy textbook.

There I was, deeply engrossed in chapter 10, "The Muscular System," when I heard a knock on the apartment door. Carter answered the door and two well-dressed young ladies walked in. I'll never forget his parting words as he smiled and pimped out the door with a girl on each arm: "What can I say, Joe, man life is tough! It ain't cutting nobody no breaks!"

Carter hailed from the East Coast and was twenty-four years old. The former football player from a Northern California college was six foot-two. In general, I would describe him as a rather handsome, fair-skinned brother. At least one of the thirty-something Student Affairs Office secretaries made a point of saying in a rather flirtatious tone, "Hello, Carter," whenever he entered their area to retrieve his mail.

That is not to say that the secretaries didn't also pay attention to me. They did—but in a different way. They played an instrumental role in matching me with Carter and Phil (my second-year roommate). One of them was kind enough to show me how to set up a personal budget that adhered to the parameters of my monthly medical school stipend. A fundamental understanding of that real-life concept would later prove invaluable in terms of balancing future on-the-average living expenses with projected income.

Carter was self-confident and self-assured, and he appeared to be doing a good job of juggling his medical school studies and his personal life. There were days when I felt like I was his polar opposite. It didn't take long for me to grow tired of covering for him while answering incoming telephone calls from various not-so-secret female admirers.

At Carter's suggestion, we both attended a 1969 viewing of *Midnight Cowboy*. We drove to the Village Theatre, which was located in the downtown area adjacent to UCBP. After departing the theater, I couldn't help but reflect that if Carter and I were starring in the movie, I would probably be cast in the role of Dustin Hoffman's character.

Margaret Wolfe Hungerford's 1878 novel *In Molly Bawn* is often credited with coining the expression "Beauty is in the eyes of the beholder." When I looked in the mirror, I thought my appearance was just okay. However, over the years, quite a few of my dates, my mom, and even several rather mean- spirited supervisors, have commented that, from their perspective, I was indeed handsome.

George received an honorable discharge from the military, was married, had a four-year-old young daughter, and was twenty-eight years old. Van had also been honorably discharged from the military, and he was single and thirty years old. Unfortunately, George lost his wife during the first year at UCBP and was left to raise a daughter on his own.

The first trial program was designed to strengthen the participants' scientific backgrounds. The goal was to improve our ability to cope with the medical curriculum. Of the initial four Black students enrolled in the special five-year program, Van was the only one who successfully graduated from the UCBP Medical School. Carter was released from the program one year after my departure. George voluntarily withdrew from the program about a year after my departure. According to the grapevine, Carter was able to gain admission to a medical school on the East Coast.

George enrolled in a master's degree program in neuroanatomy and neurophysiology at another East Coast college.

Carter successfully completed his medical studies on the East Coast, and George completed a master's degree program in neuroanatomy and neurophysiology. George was later awarded a Ph.D. in nutritional science and brain development from an East Coast college.

According to the grapevine, the UCBP assistant dean may have played a role in assisting Carter in transferring to the East Coast. That particular medical school would have been a good move for him because Carter grew up on the East Coast and probably still had family members in the area.

At the time of his dismissal, Carter allegedly told the second assistant dean, "You are not going to send me down to the School of Public Health, like you did Joe!" The relationship between Carter and the second assistant dean was more than a faculty-to-student interaction; they were close friends.

Van was the only member of the special program group to walk out of the minority admissions- and funding-strategy meeting I chaired during my second year at UCBP. Prior to exiting the room, Van stood up and provided the approximately twenty medical, dental, public health, and nursing students with a brief explanation for his decision to not stand with us.

At the conclusion of the meeting, Ell's, one of the Black UCBP first-year regular admits, approached me and said, "You need to focus on your studies. It's time to let someone else lead!" I definitely took his words to heart. From that point forward, I greatly reduced the level of my involvement in future minority admissions- and funding-related activities.

Early in my tenure at UCBP, Dr. Granville Coggs, my second mentor, cautioned me not to participate in challenging the medical school administration. He said, "We are in the process of building a teaching hospital in Willowbrook. Let us fight for you now, and once you've reached your goal, then, if you so choose, you can continue to fight."

I first met Dr. Coggs at age sixteen when Walter Pittman (Uncle Abbey) introduced us. Uncle Abbey and Aunt Helen had two sons, Wally and Bernard, and a daughter, Elaine. I have always had a great deal of admiration and respect for my aunt, uncle, and first cousins.

On November 25, 1980, Dr. Coggs sent a letter of recommendation to several medical schools:

I had the pleasure of making Joseph Harris's acquaintance in 1964 when he was introduced to me by a coworker as a young man with aspirations of becoming a physician. I was impressed with both the sincerity of his ambitions and his academic potential. Since that time, I have acted on his behalf in an advisory role. My early recognition of academic potential was soon proven well founded when he graduated valedictorian from both George Washington Carver Jr. High and Thomas Jefferson High (in the predominantly Black Eastside of Los Angeles).

In April 1966, Dr. Coggs was one of a group of seven who formed a committee to develop a plan for establishing a teaching hospital in the Willowbrook community. Five months later, the Hale Williams Postgraduate Medical School became a legal entity. He served as one of the original members of its board of trustees, and he also served as interim president of the university from 1989 to 1991.

As a member of the special five-year program, Van's professed goal was to become a pathologist. It is my understanding that he has successfully accomplished that goal. As a member of the special five-year program, Carter's initial goal was to become an orthopedic surgeon. However, similar to the UCBP assistant dean who befriended him, and my second mentor Dr. Granville Coggs, it is my understanding that Carter specialized in the field of radiology. Unfortunately, after assessing the overall performance of the initial group of four Black students, UCBP's special five-year program for disadvantaged students was essentially disbanded.

During the first year at the UCBP Medical School I successfully completed Math (audited), Chemistry 1A, 1B, and 1C (audited), and Clinical Diagnosis (Pass). I also passed Gross Anatomy 105 (two quarters).

Courses I successfully passed during the second year included Biochemistry (three quarters), Physiology Part 2 (third quarter), Psychiatry (second quarter), Group Dynamics (first and second quarters), and Fundamentals of Clinical Medicine (second quarter).

The UCBP Medical School courses I failed during the second year included Micro Anatomy 101 (first quarter), Physiology Part 1 (second quarter), and Basic Neurology (third quarter).

The young lady I had once viewed as the love of my life and I went our separate ways immediately after our 1971 spring break trip to Yosemite. That was not the way I wanted things to go, and I sometimes find myself wistfully looking back on those few days in the national park.

We shared a three-room cabin with Hudson and his fiancé and another UCBP first-year medical school couple. It was located in the lower montane forests, along the western boundary of the park. My girlfriend and I hitched a ride to Yosemite with Hudson. According to the trail guides, the surroundings included California black oaks, ponderosa pines, incense cedars, and white firs. Yosemite's giant sequoias, including the Mariposa, Merced, and Tuolumne Groves also flourished there.

We were surrounded by the sheer beauty of Mother Nature's specialized flora and native fauna and held spellbound by panoramic vistas of majestic rocky peaks. Each morning, we were awakened by yellow-gold sunrises. And as twilight painted the rugged terrain's canvas in dusky hues, we became enchanted by a coral-veiled sunset. Embraced daily by the intoxicating scent of pine in the flowing breeze, it all seemed quite awe-inspiring and mystical.

We even had an opportunity to watch a Monday night broadcast of the NCAA Championship basketball game. The Southern California-based UCBP college earned another national championship title that evening. After a few days, our group departed the serene beauty of the Yosemite landscape and returned to Los Angeles.

And just like that, as she had preordained, our relationship was over. It was as though an impermeable curtain had been lowered from the rafters between us. Ironically, Carole King's "It's Too Late," was released as a single in April 1971. After the breakup, it seemed as though "It's Too Late" permeated the airwaves everywhere. It eventually reached number one on the Billboard Hot 100 and Adult Contemporary charts. After the breakup, I focused on my studies.

After my departure from the medical school, I received a great deal of emotional support and understanding from those who were close to me. Conversely, it seemed like no matter what walk of life, regardless of the critics' race—and irrespective of the number of additional degrees acquired—I was judged by my inability to complete the medical school program.

The negative comments often came from people who had never attempted the sequence of premed courses I completed. In addition, those same critics probably would not have performed as well in the medical school courses I passed. From the perspective of the elders, "Those self-appointed critics needed to walk a mile in my shoes."

Following my release from the UCBP Medical School, I attempted to explore reentry possibilities at the East Coast HBCU medical school and the First Southern School of Medicine. However, both institutions turned down my requests for a transfer of credits earned and/or a fresh start. Paradoxically, prior to selecting UCBP, I had been accepted as a first-year regular admit by both the East Coast HBCU medical school and First Southern Medical School.

And so, the second year, third quarter pattern of final grades noted above placed the matter squarely in the hands of the department chairs. Ironically, throughout my two-year tenure in the medical school, unless I asked a question during one of the classroom lectures, I rarely interacted directly with the department chairs. For a variety of reasons, I refrained from asking questions during the full-class lecture sessions. In general, the majority of my one-on- one communications transpired between lower-level staff members.

Looking back over my two years at the UCBP Medical School, I know I did the best I could at age twenty-one and twenty-two given the problems with special program course structuring and confusing performance expectations in audited versus graded courses. We were asked to audit specific undergraduate chemistry courses, and we were expected to take the final examinations for those courses.

In retrospect, extenuating circumstances affected my overall performance in the medical school. In the first year, I felt a moral obligation to become involved—along with the seven other Black medical students, a handful of Black nursing students, and the one Black dental student—in efforts to increase minority enrollment and funding.

During those two years, I also served on a committee to facilitate Minority students' grasp of medical knowledge through changes in study techniques and curriculum presentation, helped initiate efforts for a joint minority recruitment program for medicine, dentistry, nursing and public health, set up a UCBP Alumni Foundation Fund, ran the fund-raising campaign for the 1971 Student National Medical Association Convention in Chicago, and addressed local community bodies, such as the Daniel Hale Williams Medical Society, in the hopes of generating support for our efforts.

These activities might be viewed as noble or impractical, and they could very well account for grades such as a pass in Physiology Part 2 (third quarter) as opposed to a fail in Physiology Part 1 (second quarter). I did the best I could with the skills I brought with me. My scientific abilities were enhanced by the two years of exposure to the rigorous medical school curriculum.

After the first year, the four of us were left in limbo as to whether we would be invited back for a second year. The Black medical students had a strategy meeting and Harold, a first-year regular admit and the spokesperson for the Black medical students, said,

"Joe, because of your close relationship to Dr. Kennon (a Black psychiatrist on staff in the UCBP Neuro Psychiatric Institute), some members of the faculty are gunning for you. Several East Coast HBCU university medical students have been following our struggle. I was contacted by an East Coast HBCU university medical school representative who indicated that they are holding a slot for you there if you want to transfer out."

I certainly took Harold's comments to heart.

Dr. Kennon once talked to me about his image at UCBP. He said, "Big Tom Kennon, Mafia Tom Kennon, that's what they think of me! I tell you what, we are in the process of building our own hospital in Willowbrook, and when that occurs, I plan to throw my hat into the ring to become chair of the Department of Psychiatry!"

Dr. Thomas L. Kennon was a College of Physicians and Surgeons graduate of a prestigious East Coast university. Throughout the UCBP Medical Center and the inner-city community, he had a reputation for being a visionary and a quintessential transformational leader. In a lecture he gave to my first-year class, he said, "I've never failed at anything in my life." Some of the UCBP faculty may have viewed his outstanding achievements with some degree of envy.

In April 1966, Dr. Kennon formed a committee to develop a plan for establishing a teaching hospital in the Willowbrook community. Five months later, the Daniel Hale Williams Postgraduate Medical School became a legal entity. He served as one of the original members of its board of trustees. In July 1970, he was appointed as the first chairman and professor of the Department of Psychiatry. Dr. Kennon founded and helped build the Central City Community Mental Health Center, the Mafundi Institute, the Inner City Cultural Center, the Frederick Douglass Child Development Center, Ujima Village, Willowbrook Extended Health, and the Willowbrook Writers' Workshop.

I shared the East Coast HBCU medical school information I received from Harold, and Dr. Kennon replied, "Joe, I am not saying that you couldn't go somewhere else and successfully complete your medical school studies. It does appear that you struggled with a few courses here. So, in my opinion, if you can't go to the best and compete with the best, what's the point. If I had it to do all over again, I am not even sure I would go into medicine. I can't tell you what career I would have pursued, but it probably would not have been medicine."

Dr. Kennon's comments seemed to be in sync with those made by my second mentor. Dr. Coggs said, "Joe, the rewards of medicine just aren't what they used to be."

Over the years I observed a wide variation in the career patterns and choices of professionals from all races. For example, a Black psychiatrist employed by the Los Angeles County Department of Mental Health enrolled in law school, and a First Southern faculty member with a Ph.D. later decided to attend law school. I concluded that people could soar as high as their wings could take them.

The uncertainty regarding future enrollment expressed by the members of the special five-year program was echoed by a letter dated June 8, 1970. The letter was written by Dr. Thomas L. Kennon to the dean of the UCBP School of Medicine. A brief summary of the concerns Dr. Kennon raised in the letter is provided below:

- There are a number of rumors and expressed concerns in the community about the UCBP School of Medicine being engaged in harassing and retaliatory acts against the Black medical students who protested about our School of Medicine's discriminatory history.

- Rumors, and some say they are substantiated, have it that none of the four students in the special minority program have been admitted into the first-year medical class.

- Some say the four students are seriously considering transferring to other medical schools.

- I would like to know what the status of the four Black medical students is (he provided the full first and last names of each member of the program).

- Have they been accepted into the first-year medical class? Will they be notified prior to summer vacation?

- Will they receive adequate financial assistance as part of the minority assistance program described in the *Los Angeles Times?*

- These Black medical students are literally heroes in our community, and I fear any delay in clarifying their status will further jeopardize the relationship of the UCBP School of Medicine in the Black community – locally, statewide, and nationally.

- I feel that the best possible solution to this situation would be to give these men written notice of their status, and if acceptance into the first year is the case, then as part of the written acceptance, some statement related to financial assistance.

If there was one silver lining to my second year at the UCBP Medical School, it was the blossoming of my relationship with someone I would later come to view as the love of my life. In addition to having a fun-loving personality, she was a constant source of inspiration and encouragement. As a member of the Willowbrook Writer's Workshop, memories of the spring break spent with her in Yosemite became the cornerstones for two poems.

It's Gonna Take a Miracle

I remember the brightly printed scarf,
Gently caressing your Afro,
An inviting smile, a brown-eyed spell,
That held me so and seemed to know

I remember your smooth, honey-brown complexion,
Joyfully radiant laughter,
Softly sensitive expression,
And tender lips of affection

I remember Levi's,
Hugging you snug and tight,
My pullover sweatshirt,
That for you could only be right

I remember stealthy escapades—away,
Moist lingering kisses, warm embraces,
Lying close, breathing hard in soft places,
Concealed by nature-made hideaway places

I remember trying to forget,
That it was just a weekend thing,
A mutually agreed arrangement,
A climatic end to an autumn-winter fling

That to part was the way it had to be,
For in reality, your plans took you to,
Distantly traced places—an African Sun,
A career with room only for one

You wanted to be free,
To come and go,
To do what you wanted to do,
When you wanted to

Yes, "It's Gonna Take a Miracle," girl for me to forget you,
Because you gave a love, tender and true,
Now your face is forever mirrored in my mind,
And your love enshrined in my heart,
Through endless time

The Last Time I Saw Spring

The last time I saw spring, I knew happiness,
I met towering trees, lime-green acres
Of budding leaves
Redwood-lined mountains, a gentle breeze,
Engulfing shallow brooks, and jagged cliffs

Raindrops fell glistening,
And as the world stilled, listening,
A nakedly damp earth
Rolled in moss-laden mounds

I knew glowing cinders,
Housed in scattered log taverns,
Connected by salt and pepper,
Bicycle-trail patterns

And cotton clouds rolled by,
Revealing an ice-blue sky,
A coral-veiled sunset falling,
A yellow-gold sunrise rising

So you see,
The last time I saw spring,
It was crowned by a halo of
Clear skies above,
Riding high on windblown clouds
Like a dove

It was running away,

In sparkling blue streams,

Evaporating, like misty distant dreams,

Chasing rainbow-laden hopes,

Hidden amid mountainous, rocky schemes

I'll never forget

The last time I saw spring,

The seasons changed, and I stayed behind,

To go to the places we used to find

To lie in cool shade, and toss smooth stones,

Into a stream that churned and foamed,

And tauntingly seemed to murmur,

"Gaze upon the face of your new love,

Her name is summer."

When I returned to the UCBP Medical School in the fall of 1970, I noticed a change in the support system provided by the administration. In the fall of 1969, members of the special five-year program were provided with the services of an effective gross anatomy study group facilitator. In the fall of 1970, I was informed that the latter facilitator had accepted a position with an out-of-state medical college.

Unfortunately, a replacement facilitator was not made available to us. From a sink-or-swim perspective, it appeared that the four members of the special five-year program were essentially on their own. In addition, many of the Black medical students suspected that comparisons were being drawn between the performance of the special five-year students and the regular admits.

In retrospect, I should have at least asked for a study group facilitator. Instead, I resorted to studying on my own. After all, that was the approach I had used in junior high school, high school, and in Clareville. I should have been more aggressive in asking possibly sympathetic classmates if I could join their study groups, but I was too proud to initiate any of those inquiries.

The only Black upperclassman in the group was Wil. Although he did interact with us as often as he could, the demands of his course work often prompted unusual sleeping hours. If I called him at what I perceived to be a normal hour, more than likely, I would wake him up from a deep sleep.

I wish Wil had said, "Joe, you need to purchase the anatomy, physiology, and neuroanatomy sets of the Medical Board Review Series. In addition, once you know which textbooks will be used, contact the appropriate publisher to obtain a copy of the corresponding student study guide."

As the elders might have said, "Joe you are in the big leagues now. This is for all the marbles and all the tea in China."

I purchased several backup references at the medical school, but I suspect that the sample examinations provided in the Medical Board Review Series may have offset the advantages of my nonparticipation in private study groups, and given me a fighting chance of achieving my goal of an M.D. degree. In retrospect, I think subject-specific study guides such as Schaum's Outlines and Barron's Educational Series would have been very helpful. Those resources would have assisted in condensing and summarizing the class notes and assigned readings.

At the end of the spring 1971, I was summoned to appear before a committee. The role of the committee was to come to a consensus about whether I would be retained or released from the program. Prior to my appearance before the committee, I did not seek—nor was I provided—coaching that could have helped me state my case.

In retrospect, I probably should have recommended removal of future funding, pending demonstration of satisfactory performance, and an opportunity to take summer makeup exams in Micro Anatomy 101, Physiology Part 1 (second quarter), and Basic Neurology. According to rumors, the committee's vote was close. However, the final decision was that I would be released from the medical school.

Harold's warning from almost a year prior had come true.

I'll never forget the exit interview with the UCBP School of Medicine assistant dean. Unfortunately, he raised some rather disparaging issues during that meeting. The issues were vastly different from the very supportive entry- level discussions I experienced at the beginning of my UCBP Medical School journey.

During one of the UCBP Medical School entry-level interviews I was informed by the second and third assistant deans that out of the four students enrolled in the special program, I was the one they felt would have the least difficulty navigating the medical school curriculum—and the dean's office had even given serious consideration to enrolling me as a regular admit. The irony of the latter statement was that I had already been admitted as a first- year regular admit to both the East Coast HBCU medical school and First Southern Medical School.

Also, during an entry-level interview, the second assistant dean clearly acknowledged that I should not have taken the advanced-level genetics course at the Fourth Private College. At the beginning of my journey at UCBP, several key decision-makers were aware of and willing to overlook the F I received in Macromolecular Biology of the Gene.

When I walked into the first assistant dean's office for the exit interview, I was depressed and demoralized by the decision to release me from my medical school studies. I had never really gotten over losing someone I had come to view as the love of my life after spring break. Prior to spring break, she asked "How are your studies coming along?" In a confessional moment, I probably admitted that I had struggled with a few courses.

Based upon the information I provided—and a confidential follow-up inquiry to someone close to me—she probably concluded that there was a possibility that I might not make it. As a condition for accepting my invitation to travel to Yosemite, she decided it was best to go our separate ways after the break. It was clear to her that I had some changes to go through, and she didn't want to be the one to get in the way.

During the exit interview, the first assistant dean told me I was in over my head. If I were allowed to move forward, the workload would only get harder. My performance was not at the same level as my second-year roommate, who like me, was a psychology major. He also referenced the outstanding performance of Hank, another Black first-year regular admit. The F I received in the genetics course was not very encouraging. He also mentioned the name of the Vertebrate embryology professor.

In retrospect, at the time of the meeting, I suspected that the first assistant dean had received several letters that were written on my behalf. If so, the letters were probably written by Black medical students at UCBP. Prior to the exit interview, several of my classmates informed me that they intended to write letters of support. It was my understanding that the goal of each letter was to request that I be allowed to continue in the medical school. Wil, Hudson, Ell's, Phil, and Hank planned to write letters of support.

Although the various attempts by the UCBP Black medical students to set up ongoing study groups seemed to consistently flounder, each member of the group had gone out of his way to befriend me. My former classmates had unique math/science strengths and backgrounds that they brought to UCBP, and they had personalized action plans for success in medical school.

For each Black student enrolled in the UCBP Medical School, there was a story within a story. Hank lived with his aunt for many years, and then he started the UCBP Medical School program at twenty-seven. Hank's initial goal in college was to concentrate in engineering. Medical school was not on the horizon during his early collegiate years. He attended a Southern HBCU college, First City College, and obtained a B.S. in engineering from the UCBP. While working on his graduate degree in engineering, he realized that becoming a physician was more in sync with his lifetime goals. Hank discovered that there was a great degree of overlap between the engineering courses he had already taken and the prerequisites for medical school. The only additional courses he needed to qualify for admission to medical school were quantitative analysis and embryology.

From a compatibility perspective, Phil definitely ranked among the all- time best. Prior to attending UCBP, he tutored students at an East Coast college in various science courses. In addition, at the start of the medical school program, he actively participated in an ongoing study group with his gross anatomy lab partners. If asked, I probably would have welcomed assistance from the group. However, I was never invited to participate in those private study group sessions. I should have been more aggressive in setting up my own core study group.

The exit interview was not the only time I experienced a less than optimal meeting with the first assistant dean. In the summer of 1970, I had a $2,000 fellowship from the UCBP Medical School to work with Willowbrook Extended Health Family Planning. Although I did not interact directly with Dr. Kennon, Willowbrook Extended Health was part of his rather extensive empire. In the summer of 1971, I was offered another $2,000 fellowship from the UCBP Medical School. However, that particular dean strongly objected to my request to work for Dr. Kennon for a second summer in a row.

Shortly after my exit meeting with the first assistant dean, a student affairs office secretary contacted me and indicated that the dean of the UCBP Medical School wanted to talk to me. I called the dean, and the conversation was very brief. Essentially, he asked if I thought the department chairs had made a fair decision. I responded, "No, sir! I do not believe that the decision to release me from my studies was fair!"

The dean said, "Oh, well."

Hollywood scripts sometimes portray good-cop, bad-cop scenarios. At the UCBP Medical School, the first assistant dean was the bad cop. A second assistant dean was kind and professional in his mannerisms and always spoke to me with heartfelt compassion and understanding.

Following my telephone conversation with the dean of the medical school, the secretary informed me that a follow-up exit interview had been scheduled with the second assistant dean.

During the follow-up interview, the overall message conveyed was very clear: "I just don't think that the field of medicine is for you. However, rather than have you leave medical school with nothing to show for your efforts, I'd like to provide you with another option."

I was offered an opportunity to scan the entire UCBP graduate school curriculum and select an alternative program. However, it was apparent to me that an offer of that magnitude must have been sanctioned by a very high-level authority within the UCBP educational community.

If I had called the Reverend Cecil Murray of First AME Church shortly after my meeting with the second dean, he probably would have said, "Isn't God good! Sometimes even in your deepest, darkest hour, someone knocks on your door, or the phone rings, and you soon discover, that when one door closes, another one opens."

At the conclusion of my meeting with the second assistant dean, I was allowed an opportunity to share the options provided with my mentors (Granville Coggs, M.D., and Thomas L. Kennon, M.D.). In conjunction with their advice and guidance, I explored alternative UCBP graduate school opportunities in the Graduate School of Clinical Psychology, the M.B.A. Program, and the Graduate School of Public Health, Hospital Administration Program.

The deadlines for applications and qualifying exams for the identified UCBP programs had passed, but it was my understanding that the requirements would be waived for me. It was determined that the admissions policies for the first and third options were simply too restrictive. Only a handful of applicants were admitted to the Graduate School of Clinical Psychology and the Hospital Administration programs each year. Since the M.B.A. program involved a two-year journey, I decided on the one-year M.P.H. Degree program in health administration. The latter program was offered through UCBP's Graduate School of Public Health.

My mentors agreed that I was definitely in need of a quick victory, and the M.P.H. program offered that opportunity. Upon completion of the M.P.H. program, I would have an opportunity to go to work. During that employment phase, there would be ample time for me to chart my future. The deadlines for applications and the Graduate Records Examination had passed for the health administration program, but with the assistance of the dean of UCBP's Graduate School of Public Health, I was granted admission and provided a one-year stipend.

Sista Sojourn was from the South, and she was a first-year regular admit to UCBP. She had been released from the UCBP Medical School at the same time I was. During a brief conversation, she reaffirmed her desire to someday become a medical doctor. I have no knowledge of her record of performance at the UCBP Medical School.

After the offer of admissions and funding to the graduate school of public health had been made to me, I received an unexpected telephone call from Sista Sojourn. I was surprised by the call because, although we sometimes exchanged friendly hellos in the hallways and classrooms, our brief encounters didn't translate into an actual sharing of telephone numbers. During that conversation, she emphasized her desire to receive the same benefit that had been made available to me. I directed her to the second assistant dean, but I have no knowledge of what transpired. Throughout the year-round public health curriculum, Sista Sojourn was enrolled in the majority of my classes. I have no knowledge of any funding arrangements that were made available to her, but either during or upon completion of the M.P.H. program, she applied and was admitted to a Midwestern medical school. Sista Sojourn successfully completed the M.D. degree program at that Midwestern medical school.

I was extremely pleased with my performance in the UCBP Graduate School of Public Health. I began the year-round M.P.H. program in 1971 and completed my studies in 1972. As the elders might say, "It truly is a small world." I had an opportunity to share several public health classes with Edward, a close friend from the TJH swim team. In my public health studies, I rediscovered a great deal of creative enthusiasm for researching projects and writing reports. I was one of ten students (out of a class of forty-five) who scored with distinction on UCBP's M.P.H. Divisional Comprehensive Examination in Health Services Administration. Biology-related courses completed in the M.P.H. program included Principles of

Epidemiology (final grade of B) and Bio-Statistics (final grade of A).

In November 1972 I turned twenty-five years. The infamous Tuskegee Syphilis Experiment ended earlier that milestone year. This study began in 1932 and, as a result of growing public concerns, concluded in 1972. The U.S. Public Health Service sponsored the Tuskegee Syphilis clinical study. The subjects included 399 rural Black men in Alabama who had syphilis and 201 who did not. In 1945 penicillin became the preferred treatment for syphilis. However, the treatment was withheld from the afflicted subjects. Implementation of the latter policy stemmed from a need to adhere to the study's original purpose. That purpose being to continue to view the natural progression of untreated syphilis in the selected subjects.

The UCBP Medical School and the UCBP Graduate School of Public Health shared common hallways and classrooms. During my M.P.H. studies, I was approached by Carter, my first-year roommate as I was walking to the library.

He caught up with me from behind and said, "Wait a minute! Are you just going to put up with this? I mean, how can you live with this!" He paused, and I could tell he hadn't intended for me to take his words literally.

Suicide? Now why would I let a decision that arguably could have gone either way prompt me to take my own life? I glared at him for a moment, and said, "One day at a time!" With that, I turned and walked away. After that brief encounter, our lives took on different trajectories, and our paths never crossed again. With the exception of bits and pieces of information relayed through the grapevine, Carter basically fell off my radar.

Primarily for financial reasons, I decided to complete my M.P.H. studies while living at home in Los Angeles. I did my best to explain the academic and political realities of my UCBP experience to my family. My mother never stopped believing in me, and she always seemed to have my back. Over the years, my sisters sometimes complained that my mother bestowed upon me an abundance of unconditional love. Since unconditional love is often defined as a type of love that has no bounds and is unchanging, my sisters' assessment was quite valid.

At her request, I had the privilege of giving my sister Lynette away in marriage. I will always be grateful to her for bestowing that special honor upon me. However, upon learning that my aspirations of becoming a doctor had come to an abrupt end, she couldn't help but say, "I always knew you weren't going to be a doctor because you don't like blood! You don't even like your own blood!"

As part of my journey to gain entrance to medical schools, in the Summer of 1966, I took a Calculus II class at the UCBP Extension. At the time, I had a day time job in Burbank, riveting airplanes at Lockheed Aircrafts. Lynette agreed to drop me off and pick me up from the evening lectures. While heading west on the 405 for the final exam, Lynette initiated a seriously annoying argument with me. I had my index cards and was doing my best to focus on the topics related to the final exam. She was agitating me by bringing up some totally irrelevant issue. After hearing her comments regarding my medical school setback, I thought, *Lynette may have been my biological sister, but she can also be my worst home-grown critic.*

Over the years, Lynette and I often took turns looking out for each other. I sometimes attended Black College Night functions with her at John Daniels Maverick's Flat on the Crenshaw Strip. Prior to purchasing her first car, she had to take an evening class at First City College. I overheard her telling my mother that one of the men outside the grocery/liquor store facing the bus stop had a habit of greeting her by saying, "Hey, baby. Can I walk you home?"

That was all I needed to hear. From that point forward, I started timing my study breaks so that I could walk down to the bus stop and wait for her arrival. I brought Duchess, my dog, along as backup. I also took a walking stick I found in the Angeles National Forest during a weekend high school retreat. I always received a warm smile of appreciation from Lynette when she saw me standing at that dimly lit bus stop.

After graduating from the UCBP Grad School of Public Health, and in keeping with the advice and guidance provided by my mentors, I decided to join the working world. What followed over the next four years was a series of health science-related jobs: assistant marketing director for Compre Care Health Plan, associate director of finances,

Westland Health Services Family Health Division, research associate consultant, Neighborhood Emergency Treatment and Transportation Services, and research analyst, County of Los Angeles, Department of Health Services, Drug Abuse Program Director's Office.

Biology and math-related courses completed while working forty hours a week during this period included (winter quarter 1974) Intermediate Statistics (final grade of B), (spring quarter 1975) Analysis of Variance (final grade of B), and (winter quarter 1976) General Genetics (final grade of C+). The latter course was taken in response to an August 12, 1975, letter from the former first assistant dean who conducted my exit interview.

The final grade in General Genetics of C+ probably was due to the fact that I was working forty hours a week for the Drug Abuse Program Director's Office. To complicate matters even further, the genetics course had a required lab that prompted the need for special work hour adjustments and extra trips up and down the San Bernardino Freeway to the First Cal State University.

The Drug Abuse Program Director's Office was housed in the old Hospital Administration Building on the grounds of the General Hospital Medical Center. The office was just a stone's throw from the Los Angeles County Coroner's administrative offices on Mission Road (now Cesar Chavez Avenue). Fortunately, the First Cal State University was only a few miles to the east.

The First Cal State University genetics course was the last course I took that was not a part of a traditional degree program. Owing to various promotional opportunities within the County of Los Angeles, I was starting to second-guess my decision not to take accounting as a First Private College undergraduate elective. I did, however, take one year of economics as required by PC1. For this reason, I chose to audit several courses in accounting and finance at the UCBP Extension.

A two-week summer vacation in 1973 laid the foundation for a long-term relationship with a southern beauty from Houston. She also happened to be a former seventh-grade classmate from Fidelity Manor High School in Galena Park, Texas. That relationship provided the inspiration for four poems.

Stoned Out of My Mind

I see your face mirrored a thousand times,
As I pass from day to day,
Along life's passageway,
Along a crowded, yet empty street,
Dodging misguided feet,
Sleeping alone, under an ice-cold sheet

I am disappointed because the shapely Sista,
In the halter top,
Who momentarily made my heart stop,
In the powder-blue Fred Astaire's
With sunlight reflecting gently,
From her dark-brown hair,
And who in the distance, looked so much like you,
False alarmed up close,
And failed to do, what only you know how to

She didn't have your radiant smile,
Softly glowing complexion,
Ebony-dark face, or warm embrace
She didn't smother me with tender lips of affection,
Tease me with an invitingly sensitive expression,
Or gently command my uncompromising direction

I am not everything I could ever wish to be,
But you made me feel comfortable just being me
Dionne Warwick would say I got caught
"Just Being Myself,"
With you I found an abundance of emotional wealth
Ronnie Dyson said you
"Loved, needed, and depended on me,"
And Then had the courage to set me free

The Chi-Lites predicted you'd have me going,
"Stoned out of My Mind,"
I wanted to breach the barriers of reality and time,
To run the race between distance, time, and space,
Now only lingering memories are mirrored on my face,
As a lovestruck heart wanders aimlessly,
In a once-familiar place

Marvin Gaye said, "Let's Git It On!"
But the sincerity is missing now that you're gone,
Curtis Mayfield said, "Future Shock!"
And on my past, present, and future heart,
You placed a lock
The Spinners would say that you're "One of a Kind,"
Because you gave a love so rare, so pure, so hard to find

I awoke suddenly,

To a golden-yellow sunrise,

Only to realize, in my surprise,

That I could no longer reach out and touch your hand,

Distance, time, and space just wouldn't understand,

And my super-cool pride just couldn't hide,

The burning tears that overflowed inside

And my hands reached out in empty space,

Wanting only to caress your delicate face,

In my dreams my arms surround,

An image they futilely try to abound,

In my heart I miss, your moist lingering kiss,

And I'm deeply laden with memories of passionate bliss,

And of heavyweight discussions,

With a sophisticated Southern Miss

LA was a big Hustler-Player Convention,

In too many cases,

The emotionally expensive women's minds,

Seemed to be hung up in suspension,

On money, games, long shiny rides,

And plastic, showpiece dimensions,

On slick bodacious raps, and Afro-blown naps

They came from too many strange bags,
And glanced your way,
Only if you wore funky, elegant rags,
And too much emphasis was given,
To name-dropping places,
And celebrity faces

So I drove to Houston for a warm August vacation,
Foolishly thinking I was headed for another game place,
Hoping to run wild with my fast city trace,
Scorecards ready to discern,
The Sistas I could burn, but not earn,
Knowing nothing could possibly last,
Smiling in anticipation of a lightweight blast

But my smile faded when I met you,
My wrong-Brother scorekeeper quit,
And my heart just didn't know what to do,
I didn't bargain on your warm sweet lips,
Intoxicating perfume, and firm shapely hips,
Or on your flirtatious lashes,
Gentle kisses, and soft caresses

Barry White, "Found Someone," and
"Had So Much to Give,"
As we in our youth had so much to live,
He said he was, "Gonna Love Her Just a Little More,"
But I Forgot how to quantify love
Once I met you at the door,
In Time you had me doing and saying things,
I wasn't quite sure I wanted to
And soon my world, my dreams, my everything,
Became centered around you

Now I feel so painfully all alone, after hearing your
Soft soothing voice on the telephone, Gladys Knight
Knows I'll be taking that "Midnight Train" to Houston,
Dionne Warwick knows "I'll Come Back,"
And the shortest distance to you, will be my track
'Cause the Delphonics know,
"I Don't Want to Make You Wait,"
But with you happiness and joy have never been late

We silently pretended it would last for days, forever,
And inwardly dreaded the final moment we'd part,
Vowing never, never
In two weeks I must have advanced ten years
In stages of personality awareness,
All to become worthy
Of your wisdom and matured gentleness,
We must have gone a thousand places,
Laughed a million laughs in a billion spaces,
And joined sacred ribbons to our hearts
With forget-me-not laces

I remember midnight drives
Along Galveston's sandy stretches,
Imagining soft daylight sketches,
Of dream castles in the sky,
Among windblown clouds on high,
Exchanging passionate kisses in Herman Park,
Witnessed only by the dark,

Dancing closely to in-crowd sounds,
Swaying gently with the deep mellow beats,
Ordering mai tais and daiquiris, upon returning to our seats,
And holding hands in the dimly lit room,
Visibly proud of a budding love's bloom

At the Sports-Page Discotheque,

Hundreds of people were around,

But your deep brown eyes seemed to hold mine spellbound,

I had long since surrendered my ice-cold blue,

Every morning, noon, and night, my thoughts were of you

Your love, your warmth,

And sincere affection,

Were all I knew,

And I found myself whispering,

Secret words of love,

As if on cue,

From a manuscript written above

I trust the future to continue to bless,

And lead us safely through life's wilderness,

For even through bad weather there'll be tenderness,

For as long as it lasts, you are my present,

My future, my past

And even though miles apart,

An eternal place is held for you in my heart,

As together we'll forge our way,

Guided by a brilliantly glowing love,

From day to day

I await the day when our lips will again touch,

For I know distance, time, and space,

Will never hinder us much,

Your unselfish love must have been sent from above,

Because it proved to be a priceless find,

Blew away my game, enraptured my heart,

And drove me, "Stoned Out of My Mind!"

You Make Me Feel Brand New

Empty rooms, soundless laughter,
Gloomy hangover, like the morning after,
Half-restrained tears upon your plane's departure,
Memories of passionate love and burning rapture,
Of your tactically surrounding charm, and my heart's
Unconditional capture

I go to the places we used to be,
And pretend you are there snuggled close to me,
Ebony-dark complexion, slender, embraceable waist,
Full loving lips, gently glowing face,
Your favorite perfume's enticing trace

Packages wrapped with love for my heart to keep,
Surprise phone calls at night while I sleep,
Tender letters saying, "I miss you too,"
Your precious pictures on my walls,
Ever-resounding memories, like a symphony of waterfalls

I miss your presence and warmth and tenderness,
Your soothing laughter and breathtaking kiss,
Your kindness and sincere understanding,
The inner peace of mind assuring our,
Heart to heart's smooth landing

I was once insecure, unsure, adrift directionless,
Profoundly lost in loneliness,
You helped restore my pride, soothed the
Burning pain inside, and though I tried,
From your depth probing eyes I couldn't hide

You helped me find hope and strength
And faith in a brighter day,
We shared promises of a home and children,
And joys that would never fade away,
Considered navigating toward unchartered ports,
Or staying safely moored at bay

You helped rebuild my world anew,
Gave meaning to each glistening blade of dew,
Provided a windblown caress of completeness,
The sun's radiant embrace upon my face,
And the earth's bountiful harvest, from the seeds of
Courage, time, and place

You gave me a starlit night's sparkling delight,
Twinkling messages of love,
Flowing down in streams of moonlight,
Unbound seagulls in airborne flight,
And foaming white oceans of wisdom,
Beckoning me to come

You repainted my gray-clouded skies
Clear and blue,
Gave birth to a golden-yellow sunrise
And the fresh morning dew,
And conquered my world,
As no one else, could ever do

Only your return can make my every dream come true,
Bring back my wonder world of love,
And a heavenly chorus from above,
A chorus singing in tranquil harmony,
A song of timeless hew,
"God Bless You, You Make Me Feel, Brand New."

You're the Best Thing That Ever Happened to Me

Love was like the pot of gold at the end of a rainbow,
An unharnessed moonlit night's glittering glow,
Ever-distant mountainous peaks,
Abundant with snow

It was like the gentle autumn breeze,
Rustling through towering eucalyptus trees,
Fresh morning dew, glistening upon fallen leaves,
Slowly shifting shade, beneath a lakeside shanty's eves

And then you came into my life, my ebony-toned beauty,
Dark-brown eyes, sweetness and sincerity personified,
Straight brown hair, golden earrings hanging near,
Delicate lips, firm shapely hips, slender waist, soft embrace

And I immersed myself in your love's soothing stream,
And found the answer to a long-searched dream,
You held the key that set me free, brought warmth
To my winter-chilled world and loved me, for me

Like a spring-green sapling from Mother Nature's seed,
You became my joy, my strength,
The fulfillment of my every need,
As face-to-face my arms embraced, warmth and tenderness,
Beyond limits of passionate bliss

You're my heart's every desire,
The spark that rekindled my blazing fire,
And like ever-surging waves,
Pounding upon a sandy summer shore,
You provided a rhapsody of infinite love,
Each pitch resounding higher than before

I once stumbled through life, struggling in useless strife,
Trying to make be, what wasn't meant for me,
My heart once bore, the scars of half-healed mistakes,
My face the weariness of
Disappointment and unlucky breaks

It was as though I had vision, but couldn't see,
Beyond camouflaged spaces and perfumed traces,
Beyond mascara-lined eyes,
Beckoning to nowhere places, heartaches, and disgraces,
And I've known the backstabbing pain
Behind smiling faces

I was once alone, adrift on a merciless sea,
Your love provided a chain,
Each link leading me away from pain,
You rescued my heart, and set me free,
And in my life you'll always be,
The best thing that ever happened to me

Traces Of Love

Traces of love, will always linger on,
Long after you're gone,
Long after the photographs and souvenirs,
Have been neatly placed away,
Long after the patent answers to curious inquiries,
Lose their necessity from day to day

I'll remember your smooth ebony skin,
Dimpled cheeks, and long brown hair,
The silken yellow evening gown,
You used to wear,
Your dark-brown eyes,
So full of tenderness and trust,
Your slender, embraceable waist, and enticing bust

You're gone now, and I share the blame,
Forgive me if I caused you anguish or pain,
I fell in love with love,
And ignored the vital signs,
Sensuous pleasures, confidences shared together,
Now left far behind

I thought I knew you, thought I knew you well,
But distance and time often camouflage,
What only sharing day by day can tell,
We had a fly-in, fly-out, fantasy affair,
When you left only echoes of emptiness,
And heartbreaking memories lingered here

I foolishly ignored where each of us,
Was coming from, too busy I guess,
Making romantic vows in the sun,
We never seemed to have time to sort out,
How our hopes and dreams,
And plans for future things, could become one

Instead, I blindly sought,
To shoot the raging rapids of love,
Inner words of caution, held in vain,
And forced myself upon the jagged rocks,
Of reality, loneliness, and pain

There will be another, but none such as you,
There will be another,
To help make my every dream come true,
To share long strolls in shady-lane parks,
Tossing coins and wishes in bubbling white streams,
Exchanging passionate kisses in the dark

I wish you understanding and
Companionship on moonlit nights,
Promises of hope and peace and
Sun showers of brighter days,
Shooting stars of happiness to guide your gentle ways,
And when the chilling storms of winter, hover above,
I wish your paths, to be warmed with love

And after all the loves of my life,

After all the joys, tears, and strife,

I'll remember watching you walk away,

Long after the pain had fled my heart,

Long after the Miracle Worker,

Of hopes, and fantasies, had torn us apart

Chapter 6

In 1975, while working forty-hours a week as a research analyst with the Los Angeles County Drug Abuse Program Director's Office, I decided to apply to graduate schools in medicine, clinical psychology, and public administration. I received rejection letters from all eight of the medical colleges I applied to.

In addition to the medical colleges, I applied to the Clinical Psychology Program at the First California School of Professional Psychology in Los Angeles and was accepted. I also applied to the First Southern University Graduate School of Public Administration and was accepted. Dr. Granville Coggs was instrumental in crafting letters of recommendation to all of the institutions of higher learning.

In addition to applications submitted to the eight medical colleges in 1975, I attempted, on two different occasions, to seek readmission to the UCBP Medical School. The first reapplication to the UCBP Medical School was made in 1975, and the other was in 1981. As the elders might say, "Fool me once, shame on you. Fool me twice, shame on me."

The following series of letters assist in highlighting my UCBP Medical School reentry efforts. On June 12, 1975, I sent a letter to the first assistant dean of admission, who conducted my 1971 exit interview from the medical school.

I attended the UCBP Medical School from 1969 to 1971, obtained a master's degree in health services administration in 1972, and entered the working world. I can't say that it was easy to accept the fact that the goal I had worked so hard to obtain had been extinguished. To the contrary, the same question emerged over and over again in my mind and in the minds of others: "How could you get so close and not follow through?"

I've been through the whole gamut of mental gymnastics from the initial ego-crushing loss of self-esteem to the numbness of ambivalence to the adamant denial of any interest in the medical profession. The truth is I've always maintained a deep respect and admiration for medicine. The job settings I chose to work in reinforced my hidden thoughts of a second try at medical school. I started off as an assistant marketing director for a prepaid health plan, moved on to become associate director of finances for a family planning clinic, did some consulting work as a research analyst in emergency medical care, and am currently employed as a research analyst for the Los Angeles County Drug Abuse Program Director's Office.

The sincerity of my interest in the health field is evident. I explored alternative educational fields (clinical psychology, educational psychology, public health, and public administration) and found that they were only successive approximations (compromises, if you wish) to my original goal.

I still feel I can make significant contributions to the field of medicine in the areas of research, patient care, and educational training.

The past four years were necessary for growth and maturity. I am no longer the starry-eyed twenty-one-year- old full of noble yet impractical ideologies and enamored with the glamor and prestige of a medical degree. I am not the punch-drunk individual from 1971 who wanted to return to medical school immediately to prove (to whom and for what?) that I could do the work.

The advantages on my side include two years of inside experience in the mechanics behind the making of a doctor, one year of academic experience in theoretical concepts of health care administration, three years of on-the-job experience out "where the rubber meets the road," and countless years of close relationships with friends who have successfully passed through your doors (and community doctors) and constantly shared their wisdom and knowledge with me.

In the M.P.H. program, I was not content to just "feel the pulse" of the people through monthly incidence and prevalence reports prepared by the Los Angeles County Health Department. I proceeded to immerse myself in the needs of my community. I believe I can do more for that community by returning to medical school. The medical degree will allow me the flexibility to work toward more positive changes in community health care delivery. If anyone should ever write my life's story, I don't want the chapter on medical school to end with a 1971 board decision that I've never learned to accept or to live with.

I am formally requesting a second try at medical school. I would like to see this initiated in the fall of 1975 as a first- year medical student (course load negotiable). The pluses on my side are obvious. The only major minus is the inner fear of reopening old wounds by possibly making myself vulnerable to further emotional turmoil, public embarrassment, and excessive explanations. That's just something I'll have to learn to live with and overcome via positive progress through the medical curriculum. I've had too much of an orientation to try to fool myself into thinking it will be easy. I know it won't. My spirit may have been hurt deeply in 1971, but it was never broken. At twenty-seven, I am still willing to try if you and your colleagues are willing to allow me the opportunity.

On August 12, 1975, I received a response from the former first assistant dean that essentially denied my request. A brief summary of the reasons given for the denial are shown below.

Firstly, your credentials, including grades in premedical subjects, lack of recent course work, various test scores, and your poor performance in medical school courses do not make you competitive with those disadvantaged or minority students who are presently being offered places in the first-year class.

Secondly, it should be noted that the level of this competition has risen in recent years, making minority applicants a much more competitive group in relation to all other applicants.

Thirdly, although you have a number of noteworthy job experiences since leaving school, in our judgment, you have done little to show that you can now successfully master the hard science courses.

If you are seriously interested in demonstrating that you are prepared for readmission to medical school, I suggest spending the next year preparing to apply for 1976.

I would personally suggest that you retake the Medical College Admission Test during the next academic year and enroll in some difficult science courses such as genetics, where you received an F as an undergraduate.

It appeared that the assistant dean inadvertently failed to recall information I had already provided regarding the F in that ill-advised Macromolecular Biology of the Gene course. I reached this conclusion because the genetics course had already been discussed with two other UCBP Office of Student Affairs assistant deans in 1969 (one of them was the second assistant dean, and the other was a third assistant dean in charge of student financial aid).

I tried to view the first assistant dean's recommendations through the eyes of a former twenty-one-year-old first-year admit. From the perspective of most premed students, once you have achieved the status of a medical student, you have been accepted into the ranks of the major leagues. Referring me back to an undergraduate college setting to repeat an unspecified number of courses was equivalent to sending me back down to the minors for an indefinite tour of duty.

Similar to quite a few Black men, both young and old, Muhammad

Ali was one of my idols. Although my skill level in medical studies was in no way comparable to Ali's mastery of the ring, the dean's recommendations reminded me of the irony linked to Ali's suspension. Between 1967 and 1970, Ali was suspended from boxing for refusing to be drafted for Vietnam. Some alleged that his status was changed so he would be picked.

When Ali finally returned to the ring, there appeared to be a decline in his performance. In many ways, that's exactly what happened to me. I had been removed from medical studies for a rather lengthy period of time and then attempted to reapply. My sense of timing was out of sync, and my self- discipline was a little rusty.

In November 1978 I turned thirty-one years old. Earlier that milestone year Booker, my brother-in-law, provided a third opportunity to witness a fleeting moment in history. Booker's outstanding lifetime credits included; community activist, talk show host on KGFJ radio, a publicist for Motown Records, a volunteer in Robert F. Kennedy's presidential campaign, a columnist for the Los Angeles Sentinel, and a publicist for a former Cleveland Browns running back/fullback and NFL legend's Black Economic Union. Thanks to Booker's assistance, the former NFL star agreed to speak at a BSU sponsored Conference on Urban Unrest. The event was held in February 1968 on the campus of the First Private College in Clareville, CA.

In 1970 and 1972 Booker mounted two unsuccessful campaigns to unseat a former California Assemblyman. The female campaign manager for his 1970 election bid joined the California Assembly in 1976. In November 2018 she achieved a fifteenth term in the U.S. House of Representatives. Her outstanding accomplishments include; member of the Congressional Progressive Caucus, and member and past chair of the Congressional Black Caucus.

Booker also worked as a boxing publicist. The famed *Rumble in the Jungle* boxing promoter hired him to handle the 1974 Muhammad Ali versus George Foreman fight in Zaire. In 1978, Booker called and invited me to an informal reception for Muhammed Ali in Los Angeles. The gathering was held in the lobby of a hotel immediately across the street from the First Southern University. During the event

I was close enough to make eye contact with Ali, as well as his third ex-wife. However, I recall being a little disappointed because I didn't have an opportunity to shake his hand. That's because, when I arrived, he was actively engaged in a back-and forth poetry fight with the Willowbrook Prophets.

First Ali recited a poem, then the Willowbrook Prophets responded with a melody of poems. The latter poems provided further emphasis to the Prophets' improvisational word riffs. Music historians often cite the Willowbrook Prophet's style as a forerunner to hip-hop. I later found out that Ali's presence was a result of a challenge he received from one of the Willowbrook Prophets. The former lead facilitator for the Willowbrook Writer's Workshop also participated in the lively exchange. He was one of the three founding members of the group.

Booker, my brother-in-law, provided still another opportunity to witness a fleeting moment in history. In this particular instance he, and my sister Lynette, were scheduled to attend a business meeting with Whitney Houston. Whitney was on tour and staying at a Beverly Hills, California hotel. Owing to the nature of the meeting, my request to *tag along* was not granted. However, Booker and Lynette agreed to ask Whitney for an autograph on my behalf.

I was aware that Whitney graced the cover of the August 26, 1985 edition of JET Magazine. So, prior to the meeting, I gave Lynette my subscription copy to be used for the autograph. Miss Houston, graciously complied with the request and wrote the following words, suggested by me, on the cover, *To Joe, Always, Whitney Houston.*

In 1982 I purchased Season Seats Memberships to the Universal Studios Amphitheatre (Los Angeles, California within Universal City) and the Greek Theatre (Los Angeles, California within Griffith Park). I recall inviting Booker, Lynette and my mother Florence, to a December 1, 1985 performance by Whitney Houston at the Universal Amphitheatre.

Whitney was an American singer, actress, model, and producer. She was also one of the world's most successful female entertainers. The debut album titled *Whitney Houston*, catapulted her into Grammy and super-pop-stardom. What followed was a string of Hollywood film features and production efforts. In her lifetime she released seven studio albums and three movie soundtrack albums resulting in numerous awards.

In addition to the above, Whitney Houston was the creative inspiration for the following poems titled; *Hold You, The Greatest Love of All, I Will Always Love You, and When You Believe.* (Gene Hewett, Ph.D., Wine Me, Dine Me, Dance Me, Romance Me, Author House, 2002, 2012, 2022).

Finally, in regards to the recommendations from the *first Assistant Dean*, I was no longer a teenager living rent-free in a room that was shared with my brother in my mother's house. My mother used to say, "Children are for the young." With the hectic lifestyles that newborns often bring, young couples may be better equipped to raise them than older couples. A similar analogy can be applied to taking multiple biology-related courses and corresponding labs. A teenage college student living in a dorm or at home is probably best suited for that kind of lifestyle. The first assistant dean was asking for something that could be difficult for an adult with an apartment and a forty-hour-a-week job.

While enrolled in the UCBP Medical School, I often viewed in a favorable light a fellow classmate who already had a master's degree in biochemistry. Several members of the first-year class also viewed with envy another classmate who already had a Ph.D. in anatomy. In addition, at least two of my classmates in the UCBP Health Administration program already had M.D. and Doctor of Dental Science degrees (D.D.S.).

From my perspective, it appeared that the first assistant dean was attempting to disregard and/or ignore the fact that I already had a master's degree in health administration. And years later, at age thirty-two, I would again ask to be enrolled as a first-year admit—with an "All But Doctorate" (ABD) and an M.P.H. degree behind my name.

In a sincere attempt to comply with the first assistant dean's request, I took the appropriate steps to adjust my forty-hour workweek. The adjustment allowed me to travel the San Bernardino Freeway to the First Cal State University and complete an Introduction to Genetics class. I approached the teacher near the end of the first class and informed him that I was a former UCBP medical student. I also mentioned that a UCBP Medical School dean had given some rather specific instructions regarding what I needed to do if I wished to be reinstated. I told him it would certainly help my cause if I were to receive at least a B- in his course. My final grade in his class was a C+. The Jewish faculty member shrugged and said, "Oh, well. Everybody can't be a doctor."

Similar to my experience in the UCBP Health Administration program, I was extremely pleased with my performance in the First Southern University School of Public Administration. I started that program in the fall of 1976 and I reaffirmed that I had a great deal of talent for researching projects and writing reports. At the First Southern University, I found the majority of the faculty to be encouraging and supportive of my efforts. From an office politics perspective, I knew I had to be careful when it came to who I placed on my dissertation-level committees. As part of the admissions process, I acknowledged my previous medical school experience. That declaration was made in an essay that was one of the required elements of admission.

In November 1978 I turned thirty-one years old. Earlier that milestone year the U.S. Supreme Court ruled on *Regents of the University of California v. Bakke*. Essentially, the Supreme Court upheld the constitutionality of affirmative action. However, the Supreme Court also invalidated the use of racial quotas. The expressed purpose of the removal of racial quotas, was to make sure that providing greater opportunities for minorities did not come at the cost of the rights of the majority.

As previously noted, I began my public administration studies at First Southern University in the Fall of 1976. Later, in the spring semester of 1977, I enrolled in an advanced level *First Southern* course titled *Seminar in Public Administration*. Once the First Southern University program started, one of my favorite faculty members looked at me during class and said, with a distinctive Brazilian accent, "It is a fine thing that this university can allow a man a chance to redeem himself." Admission to—and successful performance in the First Southern program—helped to restore my feelings of personal dignity and self- worth.

Often viewed as being both charismatic and brash, the Brazilian-born faculty had formal training as an attorney. His frequent use of verbal judo assisted in defusing arguments between parties with opposing views.

During the presentation of my weekly essay, he noticed that my initial selection of a Ph.D. dissertation topic was related to the medical school admission process. More specifically, the preliminary topic focused on the Bakke reverse discrimination decision. In front of the entire class, he said, "Joe, do you want to be a martyr?"

I slowly shook my head.

He said, "You should read *Persecution and the Art of Writing* by Leo Strauss."

I am grateful that he didn't refer to my written submission as a violation of the natural order of things in the universe. In general, he reserved the latter comment for submissions he truly disliked. He had an almost magical way of encouraging dynamic discussions in the classroom. He often gazed at my classmates in the semicircle and invited them to "come to the symposium. Plato will be there. Aristotle will be there." He discouraged students from bringing multiple books to the classroom. From his perspective, knowledge should be internalized. Therefore, proper adherence to this basic tenet should offset the need for book bags and backpacks. In fact, he often referred to them as scaffolds.

Between the fall of 1976 and the spring of 1982, I successfully navigated the rigorous Graduate School of Public Administration curriculum and dissertation requirements. For the 1976–77 academic year, I was awarded a teaching assistant (TA) position with full tuition remission and a monthly stipend. However, due to budgetary constraints, only half of the award was offered to me for the 1977–78 academic year.

The six faculty members in the First Southern Graduate Programs in Health Administration took turns dividing up my twenty-hour TA commitment. The majority of the TA workload consisted of Xeroxing journal articles in the Doheny Library instead of actual teaching assignments.

Due to financial concerns, I elected to return to full-time employment with the County of Los Angeles, Department of Health Services. And my half of the First Southern teaching assistant award was given to a very attractive Hispanic classmate. She was quite appreciative of the gesture. I completed the required course work in two years, and I spent four years working on the dissertation. At the time, I thought, *Occasionally, in life, there is symmetry.* My first job out of the UCBP M.P.H. program in 1972 was with a prepaid health plan. Ten years later, I completed my First Southern dissertation: "The Participatory Polling Technique and the Prepaid Health Plan Rate-Setting Process: A Policy Analysis."

From a romance perspective, I met a former member of Lynette's East Sixtieth Street Charm School Class. At the time, she had already made the decision to drop out of an L.A. area private liberal arts college and join the air force. That young lady would later become the inspiration for another poem.

Firefly

May love and beauty,
Always be your guide,
Radiant sweetness, and personality,
Your innermost pride,
Blossoming womanhood understood

Today an unlimited horizon,
The beckoning warmth of a glowing sun
Tomorrow flying high,
Navigating distant dreams,
By a starlit sky

Soon the runway will clear, flashing
Takeoff beams, will appear,
But I'll never say goodbye,
You've touched my heart,
"Firefly."

While I was working forty hours a week for the County of Los Angeles and commuting back and forth to First Southern evening classes, I met an attractive First Southern senior who became the inspiration for a new poem.

My Forbidden Lover

I once outstretched my arms to embrace,
A stream of glowing sunrays,
Tried to cradle their warmth to my body,
And became imprisoned in the morning haze,
Sunrays as elusive as your radiance, and charm,
Like your "Infini" perfumed trail which never lingers,
Slipping away as so many grains of sand through my fingers

I once pressed my lips against yours, tenderly,
Exploring every soft curvature, gingerly,
Hoping to permanently enrapture,
My teasingly resistant capture,
Foolishly seeking to control,
Tidal waves of emotion flowing from my soul,
Unharnessed desire generating,
Passionate crescendos of raging fire

I close my eyes and envision your slender, shapely body,
Your smooth copper-toned complexion,
Flirtatious hazel-green eyes of affection,
Your sandy-brown hair, gently caressing a delicate face,
Nefertiti's precious gift to the Black man's race,
Full lips, firm breasts, thighs and hips,
An embraceable narrow waist,
And soft, silk-like shoulders upon which hungry kisses taste

And yet, you are my forbidden lover,
And as long as I feel as I do, I know there can be no other,
Despite the lighthouse flare, and the warning buoys there,
I navigate my heart toward this unpredictable affair,
Blindly yet boldly daring to dare

Your closeness has provided me,
A constellation of heavenly memories,
Upon which to chart my course,
Memories of soul-searching sharing,
In late-evening discourse
Memories of you combining your magnetism,
To a George Benson "Unchained Melody" serenade

To the gracefully choreographed movements,
Of the Los Angeles Ballet,
Memories of warm summer nights,
And musically colorful fantasia in Griffith Park,
You and I, in a crowd, and yet alone, in the dark,
Under a cosmos of ever-changing, and infinitely stretching
Midnight skies, that seemed to sparkle
With a thousand brilliant fireflies,

Memories of you responding
With the warmth of your laughter,
To the playwright-scripted humor of a Hollywood Actor,
Of you casting your alluring spell upon the soft lights,
And evening delights of a towering seashore diner,
Of a candlelit table for two at home, alone, and later,
Listening to a soulful rendition of "Ooh Baby, Baby,"
By Smokey Robinson and the Miracles,
While relaxing on a living room recliner.

Memories of us slow dancing to the sensual vocal styling,
Of Peabo Bryson singing, "I'm So into You,"
And of you pressing your body close to mine,
Gently encircling your arms divine,
Our heart-to-heart embrace,
Forever entwined

Perhaps the sanctuary of your love,
Was meant for another to share,
Perhaps I am asking much too much,
To always want you near,
Today your freedom is a priceless possession,
You are not willing to spare,
Outwardly I try to make no demands,
While inwardly you know that I care

I sail my heart toward a truce and alliance,
With a youth and wanderlust you have yet to explore,
While time sways in breathless suspense,
Awaiting the welcoming torches at your harbor's door,
Despite words of caution, I trust in you, I believe in you,
And have faith that the guidance from our closeness,
Will someday steer me true

Let me be the one you choose to engulf,
In your seemingly vast expanse of insatiable longing,
When your heart needs a friend, a lover, a brother,
When the world seems lonely and cold,
The feelings I try so futilely to hide,
Will never drift afar or grow old

There comes a time in everyone's life,
Of forking paths to choose,
Of faraway shores, unknown depths to explore,
Of rainbows arching, where distant seagulls soar,
A time of laughter and crying, of quiet reclining,
And reflective sighing

And in times of restless desire,
When the melodic lyrics of Peabo's "Feel the Fire,"
Are lapping at your shores, My forbidden lover,
For me there can be no other, and in your heart,
You know, I am yours

In November 1980, I turned thirty-two years old. And in anticipation of my pending graduation from First Southern, I decided to mount another round of efforts to reapply to medical schools. This time, Dr. Coggs assisted in crafting letters of recommendation to ten medical colleges. Included in this group of applications was the UCBP Medical School and the Willowbrook-based Hale Williams/UCBP Medical School. Perhaps the advice of Dr. Kennon prevented me from considering medical schools in Grenada, Cuba, and Mexico.

I was invited to interview for one of the hundred slots available at the Hale Williams/UCBP Medical School. The interview was conducted by Dr. Garrett Morgan, a Black physician who was based at Martin Luther King Jr. Memorial Hospital in Willowbrook. I was referred to him by the Reverend Cecil (Chip) Murray of the First AME Church (FAME). Dr. Morgan and I were both members of FAME.

At the conclusion of the interview, Dr. Morgan said, "I am hesitant to recommend you for admission."

I replied, "But you have a hundred slots!"

"I know," Dr. Morgan replied. "The main reason I am adopting this position is that many of the people who did this to you are probably still at UCBP. Daniel Hale Williams is a new medical school, and it is dependent upon UCBP for the first two years of classroom instruction. Hale Williams now has its own hospital for the clinical instruction phase. I would, however, like to thank you for all you have done to improve minority admissions and funding at UCBP."

Just like that, what might have been the final door to readmission to medical school had been closed. It didn't seem to matter that I already had an M.P.H. degree in health administration from UCBP, was a dissertation short of a Ph.D. in public administration at First Southern, or that I had successfully completed the undergraduate introductory course on genetics.

Following the interview with Dr. Morgan, I reflected upon the following words by Kunta Kinte in Alex Haley's *Roots*: "My name is Toby."

After medical school, among several noteworthy courses, I completed epidemiology and biostatistics while enrolled in the UCBP M.P.H. program. In addition to the master's degree-level biostatistics course at UCBP, I completed two additional statistics courses in the First Cal State University master's degree program in psychology.

The operational word for my meeting with Dr. Morgan was *mercy*. First, the Northwestern-based medical school demonstrated *mercy* in allowing Harold to transfer credits and complete his medical studies. Next, the Midwestern-based medical school showed *mercy* to Sista Sojourn. In addition, the East Coast-based medical school demonstrated *mercy* in allowing Carter an opportunity to transfer credits and continue his journey. However, it appeared that the Hale Williams/UCBP Medical School chose to not extend a similar hand of compassion to me. This decision was made despite the fact that the Hale Williams/UCBP Medical School had one hundred slots available in its first-year class.

Carter, George, and their immediate families were forced to uproot, relocate, and reorient to new and unchartered settings. Sista Sojourn was single at the time. Carter had recently married, and his wife had a young son. George's wife passed away during the first year at the UCBP Medical School, and he was left to raise a four-year-old daughter on his own.

The direct and indirect power and influence of the UCBP Medical school center was extensive. After completing the M.P.H. program in health administration at UCBP and the Ph.D. program in public administration at First Southern, I was turned down for at least two UCBP campus-wide employment opportunities. The primary reason for the denials may have been because I self-disclosed that I was a former UCBP medical student.

The first office to reject my application was located in a UCBP campus-wide grant proposal-writing unit, and the second was in a UCBP campus-wide research unit. Both work settings were responsible for responding to requests from throughout the UCBP undergraduate, graduate, and administrative sectors. However, during the interview phase, each key decision-maker overseeing the open positions stated, in so many words, "We receive quite a few assignments from the UCBP medical center, and we don't want any problems."

The Hale Williams/UCBP Medical School recommendation to deny my request for admission was probably made to Dr. J. McCune Smith, dean of the Hale Williams/UCBP Medical School. It is important to note that Dr. Smith was the dean of the Hale Williams/ UCBP Medical School. I first met Dr. Smith in 1969 during my first-year tenure in the UCBP program for disadvantaged students.

I did not know much about Dr. Smith's background. For some reason, Harold labeled him a puppet (to put it mildly) for John Harrington, dean at UCBP. However, other community leaders in the Willowbrook area shared a similar impression of Dr. Smith. Sometime in the fall of 1969, Dr. Smith sent an invitation to the UCBP Black medical students to join him for dinner at his family home in Compton. Most of us accepted.

I was very impressed by the fact that Dr. Smith chose to establish residency in a rather upscale part of Compton. Black professionals of similar means generally chose to live in Brentwood, Beverly Hills, Westwood, Baldwin Hills, Windsor Hills, Ladera, or View Park. Since this was an invitation to dine with Dr. Smith and his family, his wife, and nephew, who was premed at the time, were also present at the dinner.

Six Black medical students were present that evening, including three of the four members of the special five-year program for disadvantaged minorities. After a brief roundtable introduction, Dr. Smith began to speak in a rather soft, mild-mannered tone.

The general message he conveyed that evening was a request for us to curtail our efforts toward improving admissions and funding opportunities for minorities at the UCBP Medical School.

We respectfully indicated that we did not agree with the position he was advocating.

I had no way of knowing that three of the four special program members would eventually be forced to depart from the UCBP Medical School. Harold, our spokesperson, was married at the time, and he had a four-year-old daughter. However, because of the leadership role he played in challenging the UCBP Medical School administration, he had already notified the group that, prior to the fall 1970 quarter, he planned to voluntarily exit his studies at UCBP. Owing to a safety net with family ties, Harold was able to transfer to a Northwestern- based medical school.

After my departure from the UCBP Medical School, I discovered a little more information about Dr. Smith's rather extensive accomplishments. Similar to two of my three mentors, in April 1966, he was one of a group of seven who formed a committee to develop a plan for establishing a teaching hospital in Willowbrook. Five months later, in August 1966, the Hale Williams Postgraduate Medical School became a legal entity.

In 1981, in addition to the rejection from the Hale Williams/UCBP Medical School, I was also rejected by nine other medical colleges. The six years spent working on my Ph.D. had definitely taken a toll on me. From a stress-reduction perspective, perhaps the across-the-board rejections were a blessing in disguise.

En route to the Ph.D. I completed the required course work at First Southern in two years. I spent an additional four years working on the dissertation. Understandably, after almost five years of working forty-hour-a-week jobs, attending evening courses at First Southern, and working on the dissertation, I was long overdue for a break from academia. In addition, completing my dissertation took a year longer than expected. If I had been accepted to one of the medical schools, I would have more than likely accepted the challenge.

As the elders might say, it was "half past the monkey's ass and a quarter to his balls."

For many years, I frequented the Revolution Barbershop near Central Avenue and East Vernon in South-Central Los Angeles. Bill, my former barber, said, "Well, Joe, man you had your shot."

I had a Ph.D. an M.P.A., and an M.P.H. I was thirty-two years old, I had never been married, and I had no children. I decided it was time to end my quest for readmission to medical school and concentrate on other aspects of my life.

A more reasonable career-related effort, at that stage of my lifetime journey, would have been to apply to an M.B.A. program that was tailored to students with full-time jobs. M.B.A. programs that fit that model were offered by the Second Cal State University and the First Southern University School of Business. Completion of an M.B.A. degree would have been in keeping with the achievement score I received on the Strong Vocational Interest Test at PC1. In addition, the latter program would have allowed me to participate in evening as well as weekend classes while maintaining a forty-hour-a-week job.

I mentioned to the young lady who was the inspiration for "My Forbidden Lover" that I was considering making a run for an M.B.A. She expressed concern about my desire to pursue another degree. I didn't tell her that I had also applied for readmission to medical school.

For five of my six years in the First Southern program, she served as my creative muse. She was the wellspring of my artistic expression, and she provided the spark that ignited the flame that powered me to the finish line. With a single comment, she had the ability to prompt me to pause and reevaluate my career aspirations.

Referring to my thirteen-year career as a research analyst with the County of Los Angeles, she once described me as someone who was essentially at the mercy of the county when it came to possible layoffs. Ironically, steady, full- time employment with the County of Los Angeles afforded me an opportunity to pay my own way through the First Southern Ph.D. program.

County employment also allowed me to qualify as a joint tenant for my mother's purchase of a first home. Shortly thereafter, she asked if I would assist in purchasing a second home next door. I gladly agreed. A few years later, the dual-joint-tenant status greatly assisted in my ability to qualify for the home I would reside in for the next thirty-five plus years.

Other friends made similar M.B.A.-related comments. Many of them had already achieved their educational goals. An attorney who had M.B.A. and CPA credentials talked to me about what I wanted to do with an M.B.A. degree. If my goal was to start my own business, then he felt it would be a good move.

Starting my own business might not have been a bad idea.

Over the years, I've certainly had more than my fair share of mean-spirited, nasty supervisors of all races. Some of them were envious of the fact that I had attended institutions such as the First Private College, UCBP, and First Southern University. Little did they know that successful navigation of those settings did not come with a free pass from discriminatory behavior. As my nieces, Robin and Rachelle, might have said, "Those supervisors were simply first-class player haters."

Another close friend who already had a Ph.D. in clinical psychology told me an M.B.A. degree might prove to be a very expensive venture. At that stage of my life, it might not be advisable to accumulate new student loan debt.

Dr. Granville Coggs provided his support for my readmission efforts in letters dated November 25, 1980. The letters were written to John Harrington, dean of the University of California at the Blue Pacific School of Medicine, and to J. McCune Smith, dean of the Hale Williams/UCBP Medical School.

Dr. Ernest Everett Just also wrote a letter to Dr. J. McCune Smith in support for my readmission. The date of the correspondence from Dr. Just was December 10, 1980. Dr. Just, was chairman of the board of directors for the Daniel Hale Williams Postgraduate Medical School.

Forty-two years later, on Tuesday, October 18, 2022 Daniel Hale Williams University, in the Willowbrook area, would become the first historically Black university west of the Mississippi to offer a 4-year medical degree.

I graduated from the First Southern University Graduate School of Public Administration in the spring of 1982 and decided to continue to work forty hours a week throughout various areas of the County of Los Angeles Department of Health Services. During that period, I made the acquaintance of a young lady in San Diego at a convention for the American Public Health Association. She became the inspiration for another poem.

Hold You

I wasn't really sure, what to expect that day,

And then I felt a force, a tug, a beckoning call,

An eerie, yet gentle sway

I turned and met your brown-eyed gaze,

Trusting, sensitive, and warm

One glance, one breathtaking view, and I knew,

I was enraptured by the spirit of future romance

A mirage, a secretly veiled promise of unharnessed emotion,

Camouflaging fathomless depths of unchartered devotion,

Perchance? never again would I wander alone,

Through this world of random circumstance,

For I had been rendered spellbound,

Entwined by the silken ribbons of your impending advance

A mysteriously woven web, spun tenderly

By a lover's dance

A five-foot-seven, slender, sexy, frame,

An ebony-eyed princess destined to rival Nefertiti's fame,

Shoulder-length brown curly hair, embracing your face

In a wind-tasseled caress,

Accentuated by a white chiffon blouse,

And knee-length gray woolen dress

High cheekbones complimenting

A lightly bronzed complexion,

Full rich lips, and dark-brown eyes of affection

I had a thousand questions,

But couldn't find the words to express,

The pure and simple honesty I sensed,

As our eyes tenderly caressed,

In a quandary, I chose to ask nothing at all,

Choosing merely to let my instincts and your actions,

steer me clear of an emotional fall,

And like a synchronized swimmer, gliding through

A watery ballet, cast aside all doubts and fears,

And let the rhythmic tides of passion, choreograph my way

In time, I came to understand, the rare essence of that day,
To know the cling of your arms about my neck,
The warmth of your body as we lay,
To learn the joy of exploring firm breasts, thighs, and hips,
Of tasting moist kisses of plum-pink, on gently parted lips,
Lulled by the soft murmur
Of the New York taint in your voice,
Your teasing ways, and half-hearted resistance,
Perhaps by design, perhaps by choice,
Positivity personified, and the heavens rejoiced

But like the ominous gray and black clouds, that hovered
Above, in time I also learned of impending danger,
Felt the threat of pain from a far-off stranger,
A silent torch you once carried,
That flickered but still burned,
A smoldering ember of emotion,
Rekindled by an undampened yearn,
I held you close, and listened to your confession,
Yet felt powerless anew, only time and caring,
Tenderness and sharing could undo,
The years of memories, held hostage inside you

And when the pervasive clouds of reality, finally engulf our
World, in a seemingly relentless downpour of wet and wind,
They'll bring a drenching message of future hope,
In anticipation of the morning sun, a dawn inspiring new
Passion, rendering old romance undone,
And may the tears of a thousand lovers past,
Flow down upon your face and breasts, may they moisten
Your sandy parched memories of yesterdays, and nurture
Tomorrow's fertile-green promise of completeness

May you envision a chorus of Angels,
Reciting this sacred vow,
"Build another life in his world,
Find another dream, as your fantasies unfurl,
Embrace another hope in his arms,
Feel the warmth of a mightier fire,
As you brave the glowing coals of his charms

"Share his world of love and laughter,
Navigating distant shores, beneath windblown sails,
In search of exotic adventure,
Under a constellation of dazzling planetary stars,
Arrayed like cosmic diamonds, on a black-velvet drop cloth,
And shimmering in the night in amorous rapture,
Fill his home with sunlight flowing, through thinly veiled
Curtain doors, casting intermittent, shadowy patterns,
Upon a glistening kitchen floor, silhouetting the study,
Where you'll pen beautiful imagery,
Upon the memories of modern folklore

"Walk beside him as you greet the changing of the season,
Among autumn leaves of
Pastel orange, red-brown, and gold,
Nature's kaleidoscopic gift to man's reason,
Slowly making your way,
Along a fir-lined mountainous trail,
Exploring a Lake Arrowhead Village Resort,
Patiently awaiting its wintry-white veil"

And tonight, beneath windblown and stormy skies,
Emitting a cascade of showers upon my frosty pane,
I will kneel in prayer, and gently whisper your name,
May I dream the dreams of a thousand kisses,
Of fiery passion, and tearful caresses,
Of blissful suspense in the midst of heavenly thunder,
Of unheralded rapture, casting caution asunder,

Of agony and ecstasy, hopelessly
Entangled in a turbulent fight,
Of a hero and heroine clinging desperately,
To the precipice of a heartache's plight,
"And I will hold you, and touch you,
And make you my woman, tonight."

Still another former member of Lynette's East Sixtieth Street Charm School Class caught my attention. As a graduate of an L.A. area, top-ranked Catholic university, she became the inspiration for five poems.

Stardust

I tried to remember
When you weren't there,
It seems as though
I've always cared

From the day I reached for your number,
With a trembling hand,
Through changing seasons—I knew of another,
But chose to simply understand

I close my eyes and envision
Your smooth copper-toned skin,
The gentle press of your breasts next to me,
The dimple in your chin

The unforgettable soft, moist, feel
Of your gently parted lips,
The beckoning lure
Of shapely French Jean-framed hips

Your dark-brown hair, shoulder-length style,
Gingerly caressing a delicate profile,
And I bask in the glow,
Of your soulful brown eyes, and radiant smile

In defense, I tried pursuing women of fortune and FAME,
The ending to my infatuated rendezvous always the same,
Drawn again to your intoxicating perfume-scented trail,
Like a moth to a flame

Smothered in my dreams by an avalanche of
Coral melon lip-gloss kisses, as I murmured your name,
A series of interwoven memories,
Comprising the unbreakable links in your chain

Memories of you at the '84 Olympic Finals,
Looking World Class in French-cut Levi,
And later appearing even more elegant, at
An evening gown sequined—Black Tie

Of the tender touch of your hand in mine,
Your embraceable narrow waist, and unknowingly
Sexy recline, your independent, yet dependable command,
The seemingly boundless depths
Of your wisdom to understand

Memories of you doing the wave,
At Laker-Raider, Forum-Coliseum Arenas,
Of your sophisticated admiration of Firebird,
Performed by Dance Theater of Harlem Ballerinas,

Of candlelit sandwiches for two on a VCR tray,
And wine and roses birthday dinners in Marina del Rey,
Of you by my fireplace, on a stardust wintry night,
And of me, under the jasmine-scented spell of
Summer Greek-Amphitheater skies, softly whispering,
"Starlight, Star Bright."

Lead Me into Love

Spellbound, I gazed out my window for a garden view,
And there among a kaleidoscope of morning rays,
I saw a Mariah-like vision of you,
A crown made of white Lily of the Nile, and
Soft pink Queen Elizabeth rose petals, adorned your hair

I saw a five-foot-five, shapely,
Brown-eyed image of you,
Envisioned your smooth, silk-like, copper-toned
Complexion, felt the unknowingly inviting lure
Of your tease-me affection

Saw your gently curling sandy-brown hair,
Accentuating the lightly blushed rouge on your cheeks,
With wind-tasseled respect,
And gingerly woven in French braid, down the nape,
Of your sun-caressed neck

A bright red Tuxedo rose was behind your ear,
A trail peppered with pink Duet, white trimmed in
Lime-green JFK, and burgundy-red Mr. Lincoln rose petals
Beckoned me there,
To your star jasmine-scented throne - easy chair

A bouquet of Bewitched pink and white Honor roses
In your hand, a torch handle woven from
African violet stems and topped with,
Fiery-red Ole' and JFK roses at your left's command,
A gown of white, lined with pastel-pink azalea bells,
Rested on your nightstand

And, as if on cue, a chorus of hummingbirds,
Perched high in flowering white oleander trees,
Seemed to harmonize in the morning breeze,
As the heavens rejoiced above towering
Avocado-green leaves

Emitting softly, sweet lyrics,
As if sent from above,
Anita Baker's soulful rendition of,
"Lead Me into Love"

And now, as our new passions overflow,
My heartbeat desperately struggles for control,
If our love based on friendship, is destined to be so strong,
Then something truly magical is coming on

"Let your love light the way for me,
For without your touch I cannot see,"
Humbled, I fell to one knee before this miracle
Sent from above, and breathlessly whispered,
"Honey take my heart, and lead me into love."

The Power of Love

Have you ever felt the force of a summer's gale,
Behind a towering red-white-and-blue catamaran sail,
As you glided through gently rolling, foaming blue seas,
Tasted briny spray on your lips, in the windblown breeze,
Felt the might of ever-surging waves against your bow and
Stern, crashing across your deck in random unconcern

Been rendered breathless,
By the beauty of freshly fallen autumn leaves,
Draped in red-orange, and tan-yellow mounds,
Around the base of,
Nakedly ascending brown maple trees

Felt the wet and weight,
Of a stormy winter's wrath,
Or the chilled rush of a brisk wind across your path,
As you struggled to maintain balance,
Through your thunder shower impeded advance

Been rendered spellbound,
By the magnificence of lime-green leaves,
Adorning budding pink apple blossoms,
Serenaded in the springtide breeze,
By bamboo chimes, hanging from
Neighboring townhouse eaves

Have you ever laid down to rest, under
A constellation of dazzling stars,
Been lulled to a dream-laden sleep,
By the peace of the evening's midnight,
Only to be awakened gently,
By flowing steams, of golden-yellow sunlight,

Or paused to admire, a brilliantly glowing, red fireball sun,
Setting over an ever churning, blue-green Pacific ocean,
Contrasted against, a coral-pink sky,
Speckled with soaring, white seagulls which fly,
In seemingly suspended motion

Have you ever tasted the sweetness,
Of a passionate kiss,
And felt flushed and warmed,
As though you had just consumed,
Vintage wine squeezed from grapes,
Left longer on the vine,
Or felt yourself whirling, seemingly twirling,
In time and tenderness,
Mysteriously captivated, by an overpowering bliss

Have you ever closed your eyes,
And envisioned her gentle face,
Become engulfed by the fragrance,
Of her intoxicating lures,
Or felt the soft, warm touch of her hand in yours,
Known the press of her breasts, against your chest,
Or the cling of her arms, about your neck

Have you ever felt the radiance, of her smile,
Seen the sparkle, in her dark-brown eyes,
Or known the splendor, of her sighs,
Wanted To share Nature's bountiful harvest,
From season to season,
To be by her side, under shimmering skies,
Enticing rapture, beyond reason

And, have you ever wanted to awaken to her kiss,
Between each golden sunrise,
And coral sunset's precious abyss,
To hold her tight,
And become lovingly entangled,
In the twilight's solace

Then you've been blessed, with awesome wonderment,
Known the myth and majesty,
Breathtaking emotions and spectacular pageantry,
That can only be sent from above,
And you've truly experienced the excitement,
And timeless enchantment, of
"The Power of Love."

Vision of Love

Have you ever been asked, "what character, personality, and
Physical traits in a woman, are you really looking for?"
Only to find yourself rendering a terse but polite response,
As you cautiously headed toward the door

Diplomatically electing not to reveal,
The labyrinth of passages,
Leading to your most precious ideal,
As though it were a sapphire diamond held suspended
In place, by alternating patterns of black onyx and blue-gold,
Lapis lazuli in a glittering necklace

Have you ever paused at the summit,
Of a sandy windblown cliff, overlooking a surging blue sea,
And watched the turbulent waves merge and diverge,
Upon slick and jagged rocks, made velvet in texture,
By layers of brownish-green algae?

Gazed upward, in search of wisdom and understanding,
Toward the afternoon's,
Patchy-gray and powder blue azure?
And in response to your query, about this elusive allure,
Deciphered only that, she must be in love with you,
And you with her,

Perhaps she'll be like a favorite,
Well formed, and time-softened shoe,
You'll just feel more comfortable with her,
Than with someone new

In solitaire moments of *déjà vu*, have you ever,
Reflected back, on the road maps of your life,
Reassessed camouflaged hints and flashes,
Fragments and slashes, hoping that they would somehow,
Guide you to your future wife?

And like the distant lighthouse beacon, signaling
Safe mooring, in a fog-thickened landing,
Seen images of sweetness, a homemaker,
Kindness and understanding?

Images of one who is not overly demanding,
And who graciously shares,
Who has Nefertiti's touch, with lip gloss and fragrant
Perfume, and adorns garments, which show
How much she really cares?

She's irrepressibly sentimental,
Looks up to you, a sports enthusiast, yet tenderly gentle,
She's ever-charming, with a youthful flair,
And the sound of her voice, is like music to your ear

She's someone who draws her strength in Godliness, and is
Culturally aware, of your destiny in Blackness,
She's ardently independent, and yet, not overly defensive,
She shares your long-ranged goals, and objectives,
And is not overly sensitive

She's intelligent, practical,
And blessed with creative desires,
Is attractive, affectionate,
And can kindle your passionate fires
She looks good in a pair of Levi's,
And is outrageously stunning,
In sequined after-five

Alone, in the coral-pink sunset,
With high tide drawing near,
Have you ever peered down,
Upon the foaming white ocean,
Assailing and spraying your twilight dimmed,
And ruggedly towering fortress,
With seemingly wanton obsession

And whispered Mariah's message
To your woman-to-be,
"I have a vision of love,
And it was all that you've given to me,
I have a vision of love,
And it was all, that you turned out to be."

The Greatest Love of All

The foaming white Pacific tumbled and roared,
Awakening a shrill cry, from scrambling flocks of
Hungry white seagulls, which lifted and soared,
Into coral-pink and wind-chilled skies,
As the golden-yellow Sol emerged from its murky depths,
To complete the morning's sunrise

Casting its mirror-image glow,
Across a choppy, blue-green canvas,
Of seemingly perpetual ebb and flow,
Creeping and spreading its warming reach,
Over a jaggedly rocky, and reddish-brown sandy beach

Embracing a brisk, and salty breeze,
Which scattered the dimming flames,
Of a fire that warmed you through the eve,
As you struggled to come to reason,
With what you truly believe,
Pondered through the moonlit, and starry night,
In search of wisdom, which can only be unveiled,
By a lover's hindsight

Reflecting back on the sweetness and innocence of first
Love, surely Nefertiti's descendent sent from above,
On the sometimes emotionally turbulent,
And anxiety-filled plight, of early interracial romance,
Recalling how you desperately tried,
To shelter your inner fires from extinction,
By the random, and misguided forces of outer chance

On your lifetime voyage of discovery, into the beauty,
And depth, and charm, of Black Womanhood,
Navigating their many spectrums of eye shades,
Shapely frames, skin tones, and spellbinding charades,
Reflecting on your forbidden romantic affair,
With a sultry and bewitching Sista, who
Seemed to only half-heartedly care

On a once-passionate and burning, cliff-hanging plight,
That left you tossing and turning, with seemingly endless,
Heartache through the night,
Or the surprise evolution of a friendship, that blossomed,
And flourished, through patience, time, and tenderness,
And to this date, has the power to hold you in check,
With a kiss, only an arm's length away from passionate bliss

Sometimes it seems as though you've,
Scanned the entire world from above,
In search of your ideal vision of love,
Occasionally clutching at a straw,
Hopelessly attempting to outdraw,
A Mariah Carey-like challenge to "Make It Happen!"
Then seeking a quick fix in someone new again

Someone who would help you feel
More complete, and secure,
Inevitably finding yourself wandering,
Aimlessly, from enticing lure to lure,
As though being in the right place, at the wrong time,
Was destiny's twilight zone punishment,
To be reaped upon mankind

Like the charcoal-gray and black stones,
Which encircle the now dying embers,
That once warmed you during your rendezvous with *déjà vu*,
It seems that with the passage
Of the glimmering starlit night,
you too, have come full cycle,
In the radiant haze of the morning's first light

Reaching for a nearby brown-and-white speckled,

Semi-dome-shaped, conch shell,

You explore its sharp, briny texture to reveal,

The cream and pink smoothness of its hollow inner core,

And recalling years of myth, and ancient folklore,

Lift it to your ear, to hear the majestic ocean's roar

However, what you detect, ever so faintly, ever so small,

Are timeless words of wisdom, from

"The Greatest Love of All," first sung

By George Benson and later made even more

Popular by Whitney Houston,

"And if by chance that special place,

That you've been dreaming of,

Leads you to a lonely space,

Find your strength in love."

In the fall of 1988, I was invited by Dr. David Lopez-Lee, the chairperson of my doctoral dissertation committee, to begin teaching courses at First Southern University's School of Public Administration. In that setting, I had an opportunity to teach statistics and various research methods courses. The invitation from Dr. David Lopez-Lee was significant because it signaled the beginning of a thirty-four plus year career teaching part-time courses at the collegiate level.

In the fall of 1990, I was invited by a graduate of the UCBP Doctoral Program in Epidemiology to teach courses at the second Cal State University. In the second Cal State University setting, I taught a research methods course and various health education courses. In the latter setting, I met an attractive coed senior who later became the inspiration for a poem.

Following "A House Is Not a Home," the graduate from an L.A. area, top-ranked Catholic university was the primary source of inspiration for four poems.

A House Is Not a Home

As though overcome by a fast-moving summer storm,
The peaceful star glimmering early evening veil,
Became suddenly engulfed in a semi-permeable hail,
Of resonating booms of sound,
And radiating bursts of colors,
As accelerating mini-rockets arched and tapered
Into rainbow towers,
Which exploded and fell to the earth,
In incandescent showers,
Leaving grayish-white clouds to trail in the dusky sky,
Creating a scintillating fireworks salute
To the Fourth of July

And I closed my eyes
And pretended you were there with me,
Envisioned your joyfully inviting smile,
Tender lips of affection,
Your sparkling brown eyes,
And silky-smooth light-tan complexion,
Your gingerly curling dark-brown hair,
With crafted earrings hanging near,
The moist, glowing, purple-violet lipstick you used to wear,
The scent of aromatic perfume,
Intoxicating beyond compare,
Your unselfish offer of a friendship, so priceless, so rare

Spellbinding memories interwoven by the threads
At your command, of you in Levi's and pullover sweat top,
On the Cal State Dominguez campus, textbooks clutched,
Fleeting glances during a midterm week's rush,
Thinking of you while parked on the hilltop under the light,
A panoramic view of the sprawling campus,
Unfurling in the night,
Scattered with diamonds which glimmered,
And vanished from sight,
Of you and me enjoying a concert,
Or an intriguing movie plight,

Of you dressed in graduation after-five, and me without an
RSVP, at the bottom of a crowded, Redondo Beach
Cheesecake Factory's waiting list, stealing away into a
Dimly lit empty room, reserved for 150 guests, sharing
A tequila-yellow sunset, as the waning twilight danced,
Over rows of moored sailing vessels, and a yacht dubbed
Affianced, of you in the Crenshaw Christian Sanctuary
Choir, on the "Night of Jubilee," of me in the Faith Dome
Audience harmonizing with ten thousand voices, which
Seemed to ebb and flow, like a gentle sea which rejoices

Of me beneath the starburst finale to
The "Rockets' Red Glare,"
Thinking of you, with the moonlight glistening
Softly from your hair,
Of you thinking of me, living alone,
And of me thinking of you, whenever I hear,
"A House Is Not a Home,"

"A chair is not a chair,
Even when there's no one sitting there,
But a chair is not a house, and a house is not a home,
When there's no one there, to hold you tight,
And no one there, you can kiss good night."

Finder of Lost Loves

Radiating waves of moonbeams,
Flowed down to the earth creating a bridge,
To a steeped and rugged windblown ridge,
Rippling across its jaggedly towering height,
In diffused spectrums of incandescent light

Beckoning to an ever-surging and churning Pacific flow,
Which collided and ricocheted
Off dark and rocky formations below,
Catapulting sea drifts of foaming white spray,
Into turbulently swirling crescendos,
Which pounded against the sheer wall of the bay

And a translucent Blue Moon,
Seemed to focus a twinkling beam of light,
Upon this soliloquy rendered at midnight,
Orbiting the globe as a natural satellite,
Spreading its luminous glow,
Throughout a west to east rotation,
Permeating stellular skies,
With a sun-harnessed reflection

Searching and scanning,
From its heavenly perch above,
Zealously pursuing its destiny,
As nature's finder of lost love,
Signaling an exclusive invitation,
To this symposium by moonlight sensation

Persuading us to pause,
And gaze longingly from afar,
Enticing us to once again,
Wish romantically,
Upon a shimmering, glimmering star

Illuminating silhouettes of a first kiss,
An interracial Miss, an autumn-spring affair,
A vacation-sparked amour which was far from cavalier,
An Air Force firefly who took my heart to the sky,
Forbidden love, passionate bliss sent from above,
Friendship perchance? and campus romance

Calling upon us to again revel
In the seductive ambience of the moonlight,
To untie the hostage ribbons, which bind us to our plight,
Releasing them to soar into the rapture,
Of the windswept and starry night,

To experience a last-chance slow dance,
To sensuous vocal stylings, in the full moon's glow,
To understand that with the passage of time,
Knowledge and wisdom will surely grow,
And, like celestial music,
Flowing from an angelic choir above,
Inviting us to heed the timeless, and tender lyrics of
Dionne Warwick as she sang of lost love

"Finder of lost love,
It's never too late to find love,
Put the past behind you,
Keep your heart open,"

Here and Now

The Saturday afternoon sun cast its warming glows,
Upon First AME Church's immense stained glass windows,
Illuminating their mosaic patterns,
Of colorfully detailed artistry,
Bringing substance and form,
To elegantly crafted figures, of historical personality

Highlighting in rainbow shades of pastel hues,
A spectacular collage of religious imagery,
Radiating in alternating light and dark spectrums,
Which seemed to leap, over the three
Parallel aisles, in crisscross patterns

Immersing the plush wall-to-wall,
Camel-beige carpet, in waves of flowing sunrays,
Ascending upward, toward a towering balcony,
Now engulfed in a quicksilver-like haze,
Cascading down upon empty rows of walnut-stained pews,
Which faced an elevated podium, and were arranged in
Jury style, to enhance the congregation's multiple views

I looked toward the alter in my solitary affair,
Seeking to follow the lead, of generations of parishioners,
Who once paused to kneel,
And lay their burdens down in prayer,
I glanced toward the choir loft, arranged in a
Semicircle formation, behind the pastor's stately chair

And marveled at the intricately portrayed mural,
On the oval-shaped wall,
Which depicted the historic passage,
Of the Black experience, from Africa,
To slavery's bondage, to modern day's freedom call

Mesmerized, I gazed toward the podium,
In this blessed house of prayer,
And centered among a kaleidoscope,
Of converging noontide glare
I saw a Mariah-like vision,
Of my future bride standing there

The delicate features of her beautiful countenance,
Slightly obscured, beneath a sheer nylon net veil,
Her low-cut gown of silken-white tulle,
Was accompanied by a twelve-foot,
Flowing white rayon trail

It was embroidered about her slender waist and firm bust,
With iridescent clusters, of studded white pearls,
Which blossomed in design like spring-budding leaves,
Her naked and smooth light-tan shoulders and chest,
Were gingerly embraced, by large puffy white sleeves,

Each sprinkled, with opalescent drops of pearl, and
Adorned with a single, alabaster-toned chiffon rose swirl,
She carried a bouquet of peach and yellow roses,
Embellished with, white orchids,
And green leather ferns, in her right hand,
With a gentle, yet teasing command

And, a chorus of FAME's Brookinaires, as if rehearsed,
Permeated the sanctuary, with tranquil yet melodic verse,
Emitting soulful lyrics, in ever-resounding symphony,
Which echoed, and reverberated, from the main hall,
And throughout the overhanging balcony

It was a harmoniously romantic interpretation,
Composed especially for this precious moment,
Of God's most sacred vow,
A distinctly timeless and tender rendition,
Of Luther Vandross' "Here and Now,"

"Here and now,
I promise to love faithfully,
You're all I need,
Here and now,
I vow to be one with thee,
Your love is all I need."

I Will Always Love You

Honeymoon with me in the land where,
Tropical sunsets set the sky on fire,
Where trade winds carry the sweet scent,
Of ginger, frangi pani, and passionate desire,
Where lush palms sway, in rhythmic illusion,
And majestic orchids bloom, in unbridled profusion

We will watch a master lei maker,
Create colorful garlands, fashioned in a flowery weave,
Go snorkeling in a world, embellished with iridescent
Sea creatures, and an intricate coral reef,
Exchange caresses, in vast fields
Of pineapple and sugar cane,
Join hands, while strolling through,
A macadamia nut farm's sweet refrain

Share a golden-yellow sunrise,
From atop a crater named Haleakala,
Romp in the black sand beach of Kamoamoa,
And later, traverse a rope bridge over a sparkling lagoon,
In quest of the coral-pink sunset,
Which seems to gently cradle our room

Spend our days relaxing,
Behind a thundering waterfall,
Enchanted by a lava rock oasis's beckoning call,
And witness a concert performed by
A mystical wind and wave band,
Surrounded by a sheltered amphitheater, of coral and sand

Vacation with me, in a world of endless splendor,
Breathtaking wildlife, timeless crafts, and historic culture,
We will tour the open plains of Tanzania's sweeping
Serengeti, to Mt. Kilimanjaro's towering majesty,
From the ancient island of Lamu in Kenya,
To the volcanic shores of Lake Turkana

We will sojourn through Africa's vast wilderness,
At first enamored, then held spellbound in scenic bliss,
Beneath an orange-gold tainted sunrise,
And pastel-pink sunsets that illuminate vast blue skies,
And immerse the rugged territory
In swirling patterns of kaleidoscopic dyes

In Tanzania, we will marvel at the sound,
Of an emerald-spotted wood dove,
Feel the warm evening breeze,
Rising above the plains, to embrace our love,
Experience prismatic heat, in successive waves,
Which engulf the landscape and bordering village enclaves

We will toast to our aspiring future,
Against the backdrop of,
A distant horizon's beckoning allure,
Observe a hang glider off Mount Kenya,
And a skin diver securing his rubber raft float,
Then tour through East Africa,
On the Catalina Flying Boat

On the Serengeti, we will experience anonymity,
On a more infinite plain, molded from volcanic ash,
Uniquely adapted to the grassy terrain,
And realize the freedom, of being on a great frozen ocean,
Which yields breathtaking views, richly endowed,
With showers of nature's love portion

Where every *kopje*, beckons an encore curtain call,
And provides panoramic vistas, of great herds of,
Wildebeest, and zebra in the fall,
Traveling in a massive dust storm,
Impaling a sense of hypnotic dizziness,
And mortal forlorn

You and I, alone together
Under a dazzling star-laden sky,
Testing the breadth and depth of our romance,
Against the supranatural power
Of the Serengeti's vast expanse,
Sharing exotic explorations in a domain where,
Sleep seems to be held in suspended animation,
While we listen to a continent,
Filled with ever stirring sensation

In Zimbabwe, we will greet the Hwange sunset,
Gingerly unfurling from on high,
And marvel at the land where, the lone acacia tree,
Defines the infinite sky,
We will navigate the Pungoe River, on a one-car ferry boat,
Poled by chanting villagers,
Through a crocodile-populated moat

We will traverse a plain, scattered with acacia trees,
Past giraffes nibbling thorns, and lofty leaves,
And herds of elephants, bathing in the warmth of the breeze,
We will journey through a land where,
Baboons lope alongside our taxi, in a hectic rush,
And warthogs dart helter-skelter,
Into the ever-thickening brush

Take pictures of wildebeests, a lone rhino, and buffalo,
And, while stalking a herd of impalas,
A female lion crouches low,
We will roam through hills, that are honeycombed with
Caves, some as large as the inner sanctuary to FAME,
With domed ceilings and floors,
Thickly caked with ash, from an ancient flame

We will be held in awe,
By the majesty of Victoria Falls,
As it plunges 350 feet,
Into the mile wide Zambezi below, and
Reaffirm our love in the misty glow,
Where Angels soar, somewhere over the arching rainbow,

As the river churns and foams,
Over the mouth of volcanic basalt,
It reaches the bottom, in a reverberating roar,
That seems to extol, in native lore,
Mosi-oa-tunya, or smoke that thunders,
Nature's symphonic overture in cascading wonders

Rendezvous with me to a realm of,
Sapphire-blue skies, balmy temperatures,
And emerald waters that are distinctly unique,
To the diversity of terrains
In Jamaica, Barbados, and Martinique,
From azure-blue seas, to a deserted beach,
From dense green rainforests, and vast arid deserts,
To an overlooking mountain retreat

We will watch scuba divers,
Off the Cayman Island rocks,
Sail in the easterly trade winds,
Which blow at a steady ten to fifteen knots,
Drop anchor, in a quiet, clear-water oasis,
Encircled by an unbroken beach, a coral reef,
And Crayola-colored fish,
Go shopping in duty-free St. Thomas,
And experience the excitement, and lure,
Of gambling in the Bahamas

Partake of sumptuous seafood,
In the resort towns of Aruba, and Curacao,
And enjoy the sounds of a culture,
Rooted in the rhythms of Reggae and Calypso
We will shop, tour, wine and dine, dance and romance,
And then, return to our private
World of intimate circumstance

Moored in a moonlit bay,
Under a dome of shimmering, glimmering stars,
Which seem to circumscribe the Milky Way,
I will gaze tenderly, into the Chaka Kahn heralded,
Eyes of my "Every Woman," with gratitude and love,
Eyes that rival the beauty, of the midnight skies above

And I'll promise her a lifetime,
Of joy, and happiness,
But, above all this, I'll explore with her,
Fathomless depths of uncharted tenderness,
As together, we'll celebrate our vows anew,
Serenaded by a tune first sung by Dolly Parton,
And later made even more popular by Whitney Houston
"I Will Always Love You."

If I Could

The herd of reddish-brown Arabians,
Tan-gold Palominos, Cocoa-and-white Pintos,
Black, and albino Stallions seemed to prance,
With pride in each stride
As captured in a choreographed stance,
The essence of the moment,
Accented by the unicorn's pointed lance

As radiating spectra of bright ceiling lights,
Reflected from mirrored panel walls,
The carousel gradually accelerated,
Into a revolving gyration,
Its circular platform whirling,
Against the earth's rotation

And a posse of wide-eyed, open-mouthed children,
First shouted, and then screamed, with gleeful laughter,
As their staggered mounts began
The ascent toward golden rafters,
Each horse moving in pace,
With the organ-chimed hip-hop rapture

The inviting aroma of buttered popcorn,
And salty roasted nuts,
The sweet scent of cotton candy,
And green grass, freshly cut,
Permeated the warmth of the expansive park's summer air,
As excited parents jockeyed for camcorder position,
In this ice cream, candy apple, and hot dog abundant affair

Alone, on a shaded redwood picnic bench,
Under pine tree-embraced gazebo tops,
I sipped cool liquid, from a frosty strawberry snow cone,
And watched you in blue Levi's, white T-shirt, and Reeboks

The snug waist harness, reinforced by five-year-old hands,
Holding tightly, to the Palomino's
Gingerly painted black reins,
The serious expression on your dark ebony countenance,
Revealing the depth, of your will to maintain

Tilted backward in your diamond-studded, bronzed saddle,
As if to defy, the rearing Mustang's efforts to un-straddle,
Ever persistent, in your quest to complete,
Destiny's imaginary sojourn, to victory or defeat

A journey which may someday, require you to negotiate,
The delicate balance, between career and future romance,
To traverse the warring borders separating,
Self-determinism, and random circumstance

271

To brave the blinding sandstorms of emotional chance,
Forebear against uncertainties,
Often veiled by a mirage's dance
And often obscuring from vision, crucial markers
Guiding you, toward true romance,
And away from wandering happenstance

And as I envisioned your future passage
Through place and time,
Precious lyrics from Regina Bell's
"If I Could," came to mind,
"If I could, I would teach you all the things I never learned,
And I'd help you cross the bridges that I burned,
Yes I would, if I could"

And someday when I should,
I will share vast treasures of wisdom's goods,
And tell you that a heart
First charmed by romance's perplexity,
Will never regain its original simplicity
That desired romance isn't just sent from above,
You must first have a vision of your future love

That you cannot direct the winds of offing romance,
But you can protect your heart from random perchance,
That in pursuit of new romance,
Do not fear life's unpredictable advance, instead,
Let the self-awareness gained, lift you to a higher plane

That it is difficult to enhance the brilliance of fiery passion,

And at the same time kindle,

The embers of a fading obsession,

That real romance soars like an eagle, in solo flight design,

You discover it one exhilarating experience at a time,

That if you accept the challenge of a blossoming romance,

You will at first be enraptured, and then joyfully captured,

By arms that embrace you tightly,

And intoxicating perfume, which engulfs you nightly

And that when you discover a sincere romance, you will

Realize, the enchanting powers of a warm, moist, kiss,

Which will first brush teasingly,

And then press tenderly, against your lips,

Leaving you hopelessly entwined in romantic bliss,

And generating breathtakingly dizzy,

Sensations of heat and desire,

That will swirl all around you,

Like a spectacular wildfire

In June 2013 I attended a Beverly Hills retirement party in Frank's honor. He transferred into the First Private College from Panama in 1968, my junior year. He exceled in the PC1 environment, and in 1969, we both completed our B.A. degrees in Psychology at PC1. Frank completed his Ph.D. studies in clinical psychology at the UCBP.

Frank joined the faculty at the UCBP in 1974, and after forty-three years of service, Frank achieved the status of professor emeritus (primary area: clinical psychology, secondary area: health psychology).

In the Los Angeles area, he has served as director at the Research Center on Ethnicity, Health Behavior at Daniel Hale Williams University of Medicine and Science, and professor of psychology and director of clinical training in the Department of Psychology, UCBP.

Frank's next career move was to serve as professor of medicine, health and society and psychology at a southern university. He has published more than 180 journal articles and book chapters. Frank's publications have been featured in countless peer-reviewed journals, abstracts and presentations. Throughout his journey, he conducted numerous empirical research studies and authored or coauthored countless funded grant proposals.

At some point during the retirement celebration, I asked Frank how he felt about his lifetime of outstanding accomplishments. He said, "Gee, that went fast!"

My scholarly track record pales in comparison to Frank's. However, the path I chose has allowed me to experience several noteworthy job positions, obtain funding for quite a few grant proposals, and teach numerous courses in multiple college settings. So far, I have not published a journal article. However, I completed an education-related pilot study in 2012. My goal was to replicate the pilot in the form of a follow up study and publish the results in a peer-reviewed journal.

In reference to the First Private College, I regret allowing the academic advisor to persuade me into taking physiological psychology in combination with vertebrate embryology during my final semester at PC1. In part, owing to multiple labs, stress-related symptoms, distractions such as the Fourth Private College and Second Private College bombing incidents, and other activities linked to my interactions with the Black Student's Union, my last semester at PC1 almost ended in disaster. In retrospect, the resulting domino-style fiasco partially succeeded in derailing years of forward progress toward my graduation and medical school goals.

At no point during my two years of interactions with the deans at the UCBP Medical School did I disclose the fact that my BSU involvement may have had some impact on the final semester grades received at PC1. In addition, at no point did I reference my BSU involvement to my mentors. Out of an abundance of caution, it appears that I was operating under a self-imposed don't ask, don't tell policy.

Once I had arrived at the medical school, my primary focus was on making forward progress toward my goal. In addition, there simply was no easy way to explain what I experienced during my final semester at PC1. I am referring to bombs, which I had no control over, and packing up my belongings, as part of a BSU orchestrated protest, to depart the Clareville Colleges.

My reentry attempts were confounded by the fact that the alternative medical colleges had an abundance of first-time applicants who simply did not require a detailed rationalization for mixed undergraduate and graduate academic performance.

The PC1 academic advisor might say, "Serves you right." In his opinion, I should have been pursuing a career in creative writing and not medicine. However, in the late 1960s, I simply did not believe I could make a living as a creative writer.

I was, however, aware of numerous individuals who had mounted creative efforts such as oil painting and writing in their spare time, after their careers, or in retirement. John Grisham was a lawyer before he authored approximately forty novels. I published a collection of romance poetry titled *Wine Me, Dine Me, Dance Me, Romance Me* (2002, 2012, and 2022), and a novel will be added to my list of publications.

In reference to my premed coursework, I clearly performed better in the summer session math/science courses taken at First City College and the UCBP Extension than I did in the PC1 regular semester courses. The First City College, the UCBP Extension, and even the First Cal State University math/science courses seemed to lend themselves to a more level playing field in comparison to the Clareville college courses.

However, the combined summer session plus regular semester premed courses were intended to lay the foundation for the anticipated medical school studies. In many ways, those premed efforts were a lot like skiing in an Olympic downhill slalom race. That downhill race is comprised of a winding course marked by gates. If I was to succeed in medical school by taking the minimum number of courses required for admission, I needed a clean run.

Unfortunately, in the PC1 setting, I chose a few ill-advised courses in my junior and senior years. Some of those poor decisions fell too close to my graduation date. A few of those unwise choices were confounded by forced errors. And those errors were, in part, a result of recommendations and/or decisions from Clareville staff. Similar to the protagonist in *The Stranger* by Albert Camus, the resulting outcome was almost existential in nature. As the clock continued to move forward, I found it more and more difficult to undo what had already been set in motion.

Reverend Wayne C. Cooper, lead pastor of Lincoln Avenue Christian Church in Pasadena said, "It's always good to have a plan. Some of the most successful people in the world had a plan, but sometimes God says, 'Well, your plan isn't the plan I had for you,' and he decides to tweak it a little."

Perhaps it's only fitting that the youngest member of the ill-fated 1969 UCBP Medical School's special five-year program for disadvantaged students be the one to provide his version of the saga. After all, I was informed by two assistant deans during a UCBP Medical School Entry interview that out of the four students in the special program, I was the one they felt would have the least difficulty navigating the medical school curriculum—and the dean's office had even given serious consideration to enrolling me as a first-year regular admit.

I had already been admitted as a first-year regular student to an East Coast HBCU medical school and the First Southern Medical School. Out of an abundance of caution, I chose the UCBP special five-year program for disadvantaged students.

In regard to the special five-year program, poorly assessing and managing scientific ability were detrimental to a career in medicine. In voluntarily agreeing to be labeled as a member of a special five-year program for disadvantaged students, I inadvertently fell prey to what Rosenthal and Jacobson in 1968 termed the Pygmalion effect.

The Pygmalion effect study was one of the required readings for the PC1 B.A. degree program in psychology. Essentially, Rosenthal and Jacobson (1968) showed that teacher expectations influenced student performance. In the study, positive expectations influenced performance positively, and negative expectations influenced performance negatively.

I turned forty-five years old in November 1992. Earlier that milestone year the first race riots in decades erupted in Willowbrook, California. The riots occurred after a jury acquitted four White police officers of the videotaped beating of African-American Rodney King.

Two years later, in November 1994, I turned forty-seven years old. Earlier that milestone year the magnitude 6.7 *Northridge Earthquake* struck the San Fernando Valley region of Los Angeles. The earthquake killed more than 60, injured at least 9,000, and caused widespread damage. Included among the damaged structures were two of the Harris family's leased residences. Both properties experienced damage to their foundation and were later red-tagged.

As devastating as the 1994 earthquake was, it paled in comparison to the loss of Florence Harris to cancer at age seventy. In addition to being the family matriarch, her academic accomplishments included a B.A. degree from the *First Cal State University*, and an M.A. degree from a California-based private nonprofit university.

Prior to her retirement at age sixty-nine, my mother spent several years teaching arts and crafts to the developmentally disabled. She taught at an L.A. County Unified School District elementary school in Redondo Beach, California. *My mother was loving, caring, nurturing, and kind. And rarely a day goes by when I don't give thanks to God for having been blessed with her presence.*

I have been a Season Ticket Member with a Los Angeles basketball franchise since 1982. My affiliation with the franchise has provided various levels of exposure to past and present players. Included among these interactions were opportunities to experience fleeting moments in history with Kobe Bryant. I was a seat holder when Kobe first dawned the #8 (1996) and later #24 (2006) jerseys. Throughout his storied 20-year career, I was either present or viewed telecasts of the back-to-back championships in 2009 and 2010 as well as the 2000 – 2002 three-peat championships.

Owing to my seniority as a franchise Season Ticket Member I, along with other account holders, was invited to travel to Las Vegas, Nevada with the team. Activities scheduled during the period October 18, 2012 through October 21, 2012 included, an evening pool party, a poker tournament, and a pre-season game. Interwoven throughout these three days were signature gathering moments, photo-opts, as well as an opportunity to purchase official franchise memorabilia.

Ten years later I, along with several account holders, was again invited to travel to Las Vegas, Nevada with the team. The latter trip occurred during the period October 4, 2022 through October 7, 2022.

On October 31, 2019, I was given a copy of Koby's publication *The Mamba Mentality* (MCD x FSG publishers, October 23, 2018). The hardbound edition was provided to me by the franchise. A former franchise great autographed the edition during a small group luncheon at the team practice facility.

On January 26, 2020 Kobe, his daughter Gianna, along with seven other souls, lost their lives in a tragic helicopter crash. Ticket Master's Verified Fan took appropriate steps to ensure that seats to the proposed memorial service were made available to the public. Franchise Seasons Ticket Members were placed into a separate on sale for tickets. Proceeds from the sale of tickets to the memorial were ear marked for the *Mamba and Mambacita Sports Foundation.*

A primary goal of the *Foundation* is to provide access, opportunity, and to teach life skills to young girls and boys through the vehicle of sports. The franchise decided that the most equitable way to distribute tickets was to conduct a random draw among Season Ticket Members. Fortunately I was one of the grateful recipients of the selection process. On February 24, 2020, I attended the service at the Staples Center in downtown Los Angeles, California. The emotionally charged and yet truly inspirational gathering was titled, *A Celebration of Life Kobe and Gianna Bryant.*

From a self-confidence perspective, Kobe Bryant was the creative inspiration for the character portrayed in the poem titled "Shy Guy," (Gene Hewett, Ph.D., Wine Me, Dine Me, Dance Me, Romance Me, Author House, (2002, 2012, 2022)

The language in the deed for the (name of city), Texas property reads as follows: "The same containing 56 acres of land and being the same land as described in a deed dated August 2, 1898, from Sallie Simpson to Rosa Edwards recorded of record in Vol. 1, Page 10 et seq. Deed Records of [Name of County], Texas." In a 1986 Interlocutory Judgment, the court awarded a neighbor, accused of trespassing, 25 of the 56 acres of land. The property transferred to all the heirs of Rosie (my great-great-grandmother) and therefore lacked a clean title. The property is landlocked, and the family does not have easement rights. The Pittman line of Rosie's eight children has been paying the taxes. As recently as 2022, the property appears in the (name of county) records as 56-aces of undivided interest.

In 2013, a first cousin required assistance paying Geraldine Pittman Wooten's (Aunt Geri) taxes. I agreed to make the payment. In 2013 a (name of city), Texas-based attorney sued all the heirs of Rosie. His goal was to force the family to sell the remaining 30.8 acres to him for $400 an acre. The first cousin then asked me to locate an attorney for assistance with the lawsuit. The attorney I selected was licensed to practice real estate law in Florida, Oklahoma and, Texas. He provided the family with a plan to purchase the 25 acres we lost in 1986. The cost of the proposed purchase would be $400 an acre. Unfortunately, the family decision-makers were not in favor of the attorney I selected. The decision-makers were opposed to the fact that he resided in Florida. Instead, they chose to retain the services of a local attorney in (name of city), Texas. The latter attorney failed to perform to their satisfaction. In addition, the decision-makers released me from participating in the process because I did not reside in Texas.

In 2018, the first cousin requested additional assistance in paying Aunt Geri's back taxes. I agreed to pay the back taxes. However, this time I structured a general warranty deed. The general warranty deed allowed me to take the place of my 90-year old aunt on the county tax rolls.

Tasks I have completed since 2018 include:

(1) used e-mails to keep the family up to date

    (2) interacted with several title companies on behalf of
        the family

    (3) retained the services of a private detective

    (4) structured the Harris Family Tree on ancestry.com

    (5) filed 28 affidavits of heirship,

    (6) filed fifteen general warranty deeds,

    (7) participated in a site visit to the property

    (8) identified the easement rights pathway, and

    (9) retained the services of several law firms

    (10) contracted with a drone company – who provided
         1,450 images in 2D Orthomosaic, and

    (11) established a Pittman Family Fund Account – the voluntary
        contributions were to be used for future activities
        associated with the Texas property.

The marching orders from one of the law firms was to conduct discussions with the family, make sure everybody was on the same page, and use the general warranty deed and or waiver process to reduce the number of owners. The goal was to render the pending suit-to-partition more manageable. For example, if 20 individuals owned the property, then 20 subpoenas would have to be served. The charge for each service would be approximately $150.

All of the above activities assisted the family in re-establishing our claim to the (name of city) property. However, my last-minute decision to join two others on a site visit was noteworthy. I took an overnight flight from Los Angeles International Airport to Dallas Fort Worth. As a result, I only slept for about two hours before the visit. It was cold and showery that morning in February 2019. There was sleet on the ground and in the trees. I saw evidence where wild pigs had been forging for roots. We climbed over a barbed-wire fence to access the property. In addition, we broad jumped a 6-foot- wide creek. The creek separated one side of the property from the other. All 56 acres of undivided interest were being used for a deer hunting operation. The family was unaware that our portion of the land was being used for this purpose.

The (name of city) Texas journey has been both humbling and rewarding. There are still legal battles to be fought. However, I remain optimistic that someday the Heirs of Rosie will be able to hold a reunion on the grounds of property that has been in the family for the past 124 years. For the past few decades, the Heirs of Rosie have collectively mounted efforts on behalf of the property. In many ways, these efforts seem to mirror the struggles of the Bruce family to regain ownership of property stolen over 100 years ago. A summary of these historic events includes;

In 1912 Willa and Charles Bruce bought land in Manhattan Beach, a Los Angeles seaside suburb

Despite harassment and violence from White neighbors, the land evolved into a thriving resort operated by and for the Black community.

However, in the 1920s, the Manhattan Beach city council used eminent domain to take the land from the Bruce family.

The land allegedly was to be used as a park but remained unused until transferred to the state in 1948.

In 2021 the descendants of Willa and Charles Bruce, including the couple's great-great-grandson, witnessed California's governor, Gavin Newsom, sign legislation.

The signed law transferred ownership of the property known as Bruce's Beach back to the family.

The definition of *transition* is that it is a word or group of words that relate something that came before to what comes after. It is often said that, when we transition, we have passed from one form or stage to the next. Examples include the transitioning of the seasons, the rites of passage from adolescence to manhood, changes in academic goals, and changes in career plans.

In many ways, the changes can be illustrated by waterfalls. Many of us have witnessed panoramic vistas of misty white ribbons cascading over the sides of mountains. And we are often held in awe by the various shapes and forms the turbulent waters assume in their powerful descents.

With regard to the transitioning of the seasons, my mother gave birth to Lynette and me on the same day in November (three years apart). Bob was born in the spring, almost two years after me, and Rowena was born in the summer. My mother was born in the winter.

Transition milestones from adolescence to manhood and academic and career progressions have been highlighted throughout my life. However, I must admit experiencing several coulda, woulda, shoulda moments along the way. And these brief periods of time were captured by the words of Mark Twain. Among other illustrious works, he is credited with writing *The Adventures of Huckleberry Finn.*

In reference to ongoing decision tree of life choices, it is alleged that Mark Twain once wrote, "Twenty years from now, you will be more disappointed by the things that you didn't do than by the ones you did do. So, throw off the bowlines. Sail away from the safe harbor. Catch the trade winds in your sails. Explore. Dream. Discover." However, scholars have noted that the quote was first published in 1990 by H. Jackson Brown, Jr. Mr. Browne was the author of a book titled "P.S. I Love You." The latter text consisted of a collection of wise sayings from Brown's mother, Sarah Frances Brown.

Reflecting upon what at times appeared to be the hundred-yard dash of life, I realize I have stood on the shoulders of great visionaries. Many of them were aware of the promise of my potential and the pitfalls that lay before me. They had a sincere appreciation for my desire to persevere and my passion for medicine. These courageous individuals were transformational leaders by nature. They bestowed upon me wisdom and encouragement and shared the precious gift of time, which helped generate a surge when my quest toward the finish line occasionally faltered.

And here at the intersection between the promise of yesterday's past and the realities of tomorrow's future, I often wonder about the worst experiences of my high school, college, and postgraduate academic life.

At the beginning of my senior year of high school in 1964, I found myself alone in the late afternoon shadows of an alley, facing a felon with a knife, and all I had for my defense was a Purex bottle. Those ill-fated bombings on Tuesday, February 25, 1969, transpired during the last semester of my senior year at PC1. Later that evening, I received an urgent visit from one of my classmates, who emphatically stressed the need for us to depart the campus posthaste.

And so, owing to the perceived threat of vigilante retaliation, and under cover of darkness, I left my dorm room. In the middle of the night, I stood watch, along with another classmate, from a lookout position in front of a safe house. The next morning, two classmates and I patrolled one of the main walkways at the Third Private College, each of us hoping to not fall prey to a sniper's bullet.

Following the 1969 bombing incidents, I detected an unspoken code of silence among the Clareville college-based Black students. I have no idea whether anyone in the group had a hunch regarding the perpetrators of the violent explosions, but according to comments reported in the *Los Angeles Times* and the *Collegian*, students of all races and nationalities seemed to be equally perplexed by the bizarre occurrence of events.

Those events left us in a state of shock and dismay—and sent us scrambling for safety. The burning question in most of our minds was about who could have committed such horrific acts. Upon returning to campus, our primary objective was simply to reset and redouble our efforts toward completing the spring 1969 semester studies.

In 1971, at the end of my second year at the UCBP Medical School, I was summoned to attend an exit interview with the first assistant dean. The assistant dean seemed intent on extinguishing any remaining desire I might have had for a future career in medicine.

Shortly after departing the meeting with the first assistant dean, my thoughts drifted back to the almost prophetic greeting rendered by Ava, my 1965 Thomas Jefferson High School prom date. When I walked by, she occasionally shouted, "A raisin in the sun!" Perhaps she was referencing the play by Lorraine Hansberry or drawing a parallel to the poem by Langston Hughes. Ava shared the salutation with what seemed like the entire TJH student body, sometimes from distances as great as two hundred yards.

I reflected on the renowned literary expression of Langston Hughes in *Dream Deferred*.

> Maybe it just sags
>
> Like a heavy load
>
> Or does it explode?

I certainly wasn't blessed with the same natural running ability as the famed 1968 U.S. Olympians whose symbolic moment in history caused political controversy. These courageous young men gave the Black Power salute while standing on the podium in Mexico City. There have been times when—in lieu of the sharp crack from a starter pistol—it seemed like someone had created the incendiary bang of a Molotov cocktail or set off a resonating boom from a steel pipe bomb behind me. I was forced to achieve top-end sprint speed in life's hundred-yard dash just to keep from getting my ass singed.